THE WRITER'S TASK
FROM NIETZSCHE TO BRECHT

THE WRITER'S TASK
FROM NIETZSCHE
TO BRECHT

Hans Reiss

First published 1978 by
THE MACMILLAN PRESS LTD
London and Basingstoke
Associated companies in Delhi
Dublin Hong Kong Johannesburg Lagos
Melbourne New York Singapore Tokyo

Printed in Great Britain by
UNWIN BROTHERS LTD.,
Woking and London

British Library Cataloguing in Publication Data

Reiss, Hans
    The writer's task from Nietzsche to Brecht
    1. Criticism – Germany – History
    I. Title
    801   PN99.G42

ISBN 0–333–15840–7
      100190690 4

For
Elizabeth M. Wilkinson

Πολλὰ ψεύδονται ἀοιδοί

Greek proverb

*Das Gedichtete behauptet sein Recht,
wie das Geschehene.*

Goethe

Art is one of the powers that makes 'life' life.

Saul Bellow

Contents

Preface

This book deals with only one aspect of German literature between 1870 and 1956, but, I trust, an important one. Inevitably, the space at my disposal allowed for an analysis of only a few writers. However, what these writers had to say about the writer's task is of great significance for any understanding of German literature and thought during that period. It is also intellectually challenging. I greatly regret that I had to exclude other authors, particularly Robert Musil, the Austrian novelist, a writer of remarkable intellectual vigour. I do however hope to return to him at a later stage. Fortunately, there is a good recent study by Marie-Louise Roth (*Robert Musil: Ethik und Ästhetik. Zum theoretischen Werk des Dichters*, Munich, 1972) which deals with Musil's conception of the writer's task.

Space has also made it necessary to restrict the bibliography to a few important works for further reading. To have produced a comprehensive bibliography of all the books, essays and articles which I have read would have required a volume of its own. To read all the secondary literature on any one, let alone all, of the seven authors discussed in this study, is virtually impossible; for instance, a recent bibliography on Thomas Mann (Harry Matter, *Die Literatur über Thomas Mann 1898–1969*, 2 vols, Berlin/Weimar, 1972) alone contains some 15,000 items.

The chapters on Nietzsche and Kafka are based on material found in three articles of mine ('Nietzsches Geburt der Tragödie. Eine kritische Würdigung', *Zeitschrift für Deutsche Philologie*, XCVIII, 1973, pp. 481–511; 'Nietzsche's Birth of Tragedy. After a Century', *Journal of the Faculty of Arts. Royal University of Malta*, VI, 1975; 'Kafka on the Writer's Task', *The Modern Language Review*, LXVI, 1971, pp. 113–24). The translations of German quotations are my own unless there is a reference to another translator. References are cited in the text itself whenever the citation did not seem to interrupt the flow of the argument.

My acknowledgements for advice and help are, inevitably, many. My thanks are due to the Staff Travel Fund of the University of Bristol, to the Deutsche Akademische Austauschdienst and the Deutsche Forschungsgemeinschaft for grants which allowed me to visit libraries and archives in Germany and Switzerland. I should like to thank the staff of the following libraries: the University of Bristol library; the British Library; the London University Institute of Germanic Studies; the Universitätsbibliothek and the Germanistische Seminar of the University of Heidelberg, the Seminar für Deutsche Philologie, University of Munich; the Deutsche Literatur Archiv, Marbach, a.N.; the Freie Deutsche

Hochstift, Frankfurt/Main; the Stefan George Archiv, Württembergische Landesbibliothek, Stuttgart; Thomas Mann-Archiv, Zurich; and the Rare Book Room, Redpath Library, McGill University, Montreal. I have also to thank the University of Bristol for granting me a term's leave of absence in the autumn of 1973.

Mrs Edith Laidlaw, Mrs Elizabeth Jays and Mrs Rosemary White performed a near miracle in turning a very untidy manuscript into a neat typescript.

I owe much to the many friends and colleagues with whom I have talked about my work over the years. It would take far too much space to list them all. But I should like especially to thank T. J. Reed for helping me to track down some quotations, and J. Leighton, A. Wierzejewski and Hans Wysling who were good enough to read individual chapters. Above all, I want to thank John Hibberd, H. B. Nisbet and Michael Morgan for their careful scrutiny of my manuscript. Without their suggestions and advice this book would have been very much the poorer. For all errors and shortcomings that remain I am solely responsible:

February 1977   H. S. REISS
Bristol

Abbreviations

N	*Werke*, 3 vols, ed. Karl Schlechta, 2nd ed., Munich, 1960
N.Gr.	*Werke* (*Großoktavausgabe*), 20 vols, 2nd ed., Leipzig, 1901–26.
N.Br.	*Historisch-Kritische Gesamtausgabe der Werke und Briefe. Abteilung Briefe*, 4 vols to date, Munich, 1933– .
N. Ges. Br.	*Gessammelte Briefe*, 2nd ed., 4 vols, Leipzig, 1903– .
Gründer	Gründer, Karlfried (ed.), *Der Streit um Nietzsches Geburt der Tragödie*, Hildesheim, 1969.

HUGO VON HOFMANNSTHAL

H – G	*Gedichte und lyrische Dramen*, 2nd ed., Frankfurt/Main, 1952.
H – Pr.	*Prosa*, 4 vols, Frankfurt/Main, 1950–5.
H – A	*Aufzeichnungen*, Frankfurt/Main, 1959.

STEFAN GEORGE

G	*Werke* (ed. Robert Böhringer), 2 vols, Munich/Düsseldorf, 1958.
Bl.	*Blätter für die Kunst*, founded by Stefan George and ed. Carl August Klein, I-XII, Berlin, 1892–1919.
Br. SG–H	*Briefwechsel zwischen Stefan George und Hofmannsthal*, (ed. Robert Böhringer), 2nd ed., Munich/Düsseldorf, 1953.
Br. SG – FG	*Briefwechsel Stefan George – Friedrich Gundolf* (ed. Robert Böhringer and G. P. Landmann), Munich/Düsseldorf, 1962.

H – Br.	*Briefe*, 2 vols: I, 1890–1901 (Berlin, 1935); II, 1900–1909 (Vienna, 1937).
Br. H – CJB	*Hugo von Hofmannsthal – Carl J. Burckhardt Brief-wechsel*, (ed. Carl J. Burckhardt), Frankfurt/Main, 1958.
Br. H – EKG	*Hugo von Hofmannsthal – Edgar Karg von Bebenburg Briefwechsel* (ed. Mary Gilbert), Frankfurt/Main, 1966.
Br. H – EB	*Hugo von Hofmannsthal – Eberhard von Bodenhausen. Briefe der Freundschaft* (ed. Dora von Bodenhausen), Düsseldorf, 1953.

RAINER MARIA RILKE

R	*Sämtliche Werke*, 6 vols (ed. Ernst Zinn), Wiesbaden, 1955–66.
R – Br. 1899–1902	*Briefe und Tagebücher aus den Jahren 1899–1902* (ed. Ruth Sieber-Rilke and Carl Sieber), Leipzig, 1931.
R – Br. 1902–06	*Briefe aus den Jahren 1902–06* (ed. Ruth Sieber-Rilke and Carl Sieber), Leipzig, 1930.
R – Br. 1907–14	*Briefe aus den Jahren 1907–14* (ed. Ruth Sieber-Rilke and Carl Sieber), Leipzig, 1933.
R – Br. 1914–21	*Briefe aus den Jahren 1914–21* (ed. Ruth Sieber-Rilke and Carl Sieber), Leipzig, 1938.
R – Br. 1921–26	*Briefe aus Muzot 1921–26* (ed. Ruth Sieber-Rilke and Carl Sieber), Leipzig, 1937.
R – Tb.	*Tagebücher aus der Frühzeit* (ed. Ruth Sieber-Rilke and Carl Sieber), 2nd ed., Frankfurt/Main, 1973.
R – Br.	*Gesammelte Briefe 1897–1926*, 2 vols: I, 1897–1914; II, 1914–26 ed. Karl Altheim (Wiesbaden, 1950).
R – Br.j.D.	*Briefe an einen jungen Dichter* [F. X. Kappus], Leipzig, n. d. [1929].
Br. R – LAS	*Rilke – Lou Andreas-Salomé Briefwechsel* (ed. Erich Pfeif-fer), Zurich, 1952.
Br. R – Gr.S.	*Briefe an die Gräfin Sizzo*, Wiesbaden, 1950.
Br. R – TT	*Briefwechsel Rainer Maria Rilke – Maria von Thurn und Taxis-Hohenlohe* (ed. Ernst Zinn), 2 vols, Wiesbaden, 1958.

Br. R – B   *Briefwechsel mit Benvenuta* [Magda von Graedener-Hattingberg], (ed. Kurt Leonhard), Esslingen, 1954.

THOMAS MANN

TM   *Gesammelte Werke*, 2nd ed., 13 vols, Frankfurt/Main, 1974.
TM – Br   *Briefe*, 3 vols: I, *1889–1936*; II, *1937–47*; III, *1948–55 und Nachlese* (ed. Erika Mann), Frankfurt/Main, 1961–5.
TM – HM Br.   *Thomas Mann – Heinrich Mann Briefwechsel 1900–1949*, (ed. Hans Wysling), Frankfurt/Main, 1968.
TM – KK   *Thomas Mann – Karl Kerényi. Gespräch in Briefen*, Zurich, 1960.

FRANZ KAFKA

K – Tb.   *Tagebücher 1900–23* (ed. Max Brod), Frankfurt/Main, 1951.
K – Br. M.   *Briefe an Milena* (ed. W. Haas), New York and Frankfurt/Main, 1951.
K – Erz.   *Erzählungen* (ed. Max Brod), New York and Frankfurt/Main, 1952.
K – H.   *Hochzeitsvorbereitungen auf dem Lande und andere Prosa aus dem Nachlass* (ed. Max Brod) New York and Frankfurt/Main, 1953.
K – Beschr.   *Beschreibung eines Kampfes. Novellen. Skizzen. Aphorismen aus dem Nachlass* (ed. Max Brod), New York and Frankfurt/Main, 1954.
K – Br.   *Briefe 1902–1924* (ed. Max Brod), New York and Frankfurt/Main, 1958.
K – Br.F.   *Briefe an Felice* (ed. Erich Heller and J. Born), New York and Frankfurt/Main, 1967.
J   Janouch, Gustav, *Gespräche mit Kafka*, Frankfurt/Main, 1951.

BERTOLT BRECHT

B   *Werke (Werkausgabe)*, 20 vols Frankfurt/Main, 1967.
B.A.   *Arbeitsjournal 1938–55*, 3 vols (ed. Werner Hecht), Frankfurt/Main, 1973.

OTHERS

Dt.Vjs.	*Deutsche Vierteljahrsschrift für Literaturwissenschaft und Geistesgeschichte.*
GLL	*German Life and Letters*, New Series.
JDSG	*Jahrbuch der Deutschen Schiller-Gesellschaft.*
MLR	*Modern Language Review.*
PEGS	*Publications of the English Goethe Society*, New Series.
W.A.	Goethe, *Werke* (*Sophien – oder Weimarer Ausgabe*), 134 vols (in 144), Weimar, 1887–1919.

Acknowledgements

The author and publishers wish to thank the following who have kindly given permission for the use of copyright material:

Eyre Methuen Ltd for the poem 'Beim Lesen des Horaz' from *Bertolt Brecht: Poems 1913–1956* edited by John Willett and Ralph Marheim, from the German 'Buckower Elegien' Copyright by Stefan S. Brecht, 1964.

S. Fischer Verlag for the extracts from *Gesammelte Werke In Einzelausgaben* by Hugo von Hofmannsthal. Prosa II. Copyright 1951 by S. Fischer Verlag GmbH, Frankfurt am Main: 'Ein Brief', 'Der Dichter und diese Zeit'; Prosa III. Copyright 1952 by S. Fischer Verlag GmbH, Frankfurt am Main: 'Augenblicke in Griechenland'; Prosa IV. Copyright 1955 by S. Fischer Verlag GmbH, Frankfurt am Main: 'Das Schrifttum als geistiger Raum der Nation'; Gedichte und Lyrische Dramen. Copyright 1946 by Bermann-Fischer Verlag AB, Stockholm: 'Gedankenspuk'.

Insel Verlag Frankfurt am Main for the extracts from the German edition of *Der Tod des Tizian* by Hugo von Hofmannsthal.

The Hogarth Press Ltd for an extract from 'Book of Hours' in Rainer Maria Rilke's *Selected Works* 11, translated by J. B. Leishman; and the poems 'Magic' from Rainer Maria Rilke's *Poems 1906–1926* 'Blue Hydrangea' and 'Archaic Torso of Apollo' from Rainer Maria Rilke's *New Poems*, translated by J. B. Leishman;

The University of North Carolina Press for extracts from *The Works of Stefan George*, translated by Olga Marz and Ernst Morwitz, 2nd revised and enlarged edn., UNC Studies in the Germanic Languages and Literatures, No. 78, 1974, and Georg Peter Landmann, Chairman of the Stefan George Trust, for the poems 'Die Spange', 'Vogelschau' and 'Komm in den Totgesagten Park und Schau'.

We have made every effort to trace all the copyright-holders but if any have inadvertently been overlooked, we will be pleased to make the necessary arrangements at the first opportunity.

1 Introduction

Man is an animal that delights in telling stories to his fellows, and some (a few only – alas! – in any age) have, by dint of their great power over words, been far better at this than all the others. Quite rightly, they have received much attention; for not only did they have a story to tell but they also had the gift of telling it well. While it is impossible neatly to separate what they have said from their manner of saying it, the interest of man over the ages has been captured not only by the magic of their mode of speaking, but also by the conviction that they had knowledge to convey. At least their work has created the illusion that they were communicating truth, and their very ability to generate this illusion has appeared to widen the horizon of the human mind and thus convey some knowledge hitherto not perceived.

This illusion should not be easily dismissed; for it contains at least a kernel of truth. Imaginative writers tell us something about the world which we cannot get from any other source. Admittedly, their picture of the world is personal and subjective, but it is none the weaker for that. For the greater the writer the more intensely his vision will have been disciplined by the necessity of giving it form, the form of a literary work of art. And the writer deals also with those aspects of reality which are out of bounds to other modes of knowledge. His work also tells us something about ourselves as well as about others or, at least, about human potentialities; for imaginative literature provides a picture of reality created by men of ideas with a gift for language. And the writer's ability to convey concentrated thought compels us to think and to feel ourselves.

Of course, anyone telling a story does not do so in a vacuum. He must be aware of his culture – the past and present – and, unless he is totally insensitive, he must be alive to his audience. The poets of distant, almost prehistoric ages, had sung merely to those who were actually listening to them. But this simple state of oral communication ceased long ago, centuries before the art of printing was invented; though of course that particular technological innovation has more than anything else widened the writer's scope and changed the nature of his audience. Inevitably, while great writers have always stood out from the common fold their status has always varied from age to age. It would be foolish to expect that, for instance, an ancient Greek dramatist, a medieval court poet or a Renaissance or Baroque author played an identical role in society. Moreover, while in our age practitioners of all the arts are ranked together as creative artists this common nomenclature was not used before the eighteenth century. Indeed, in the Germany of the Holy Roman Empire poets belonged to different social strata from painters or musicians. These conditions changed towards the end of the eighteenth century,[1] though of course some of the developments involved can be traced to earlier times. But the principal source of patronage for writers until that age was still the court, although they found it useful, indeed necessary, to supplement their income from the proceeds of publication.

very loosely argued

The more independent from patronage writers became the more they became concerned with their own status, precisely because their status was so insecure on account of their fluid place in society. Also, they were not happy to be classed according to their material success. Concern with status is, of course, not a prerogative of writers, but a writer is almost necessarily very sensitive to such problems since he has to come to terms not only with the external world, but even more with himself, with what he has experienced and what he can do as a writer. He has to discover his own perspective which enables him to put his imprint on what he says about the world. To do that he needs self-awareness. The growth of self-awareness has been an increasingly important process. It has generated concern with the author's own mode of writing and brought about the desire to integrate this concern into his imaginative work. This preoccupation with one's own way of writing and one's position as a writer is, in the first instance, subjective, but, for writers, subjective opinions become, through embodiment in their work, objective facts.

Modern German writers were more directly affected by German Classicism and its aftermath; for, in the eighteenth century, the foundations of modern German thought and writings were laid. To look at the ideas of some of the great modern German imaginative writers is thus worth while, for the history since the eighteenth century of imaginative writers' concern with their own task has, to some extent at least, been recorded in literary works. The story is inevitably complex and cannot be related in detail. The seeds of modern opinion are found in the great period of German literature, in eighteenth-century Weimar Classicism, in the work of Goethe and Schiller, and many of their ideas were taken up again and again by twentieth-century writers, even though they were, on occasion, developed in a radically different way. The German eighteenth-century poet Friedrich Klopstock had first propounded the view of the divine mission of the poet,[2] but a much more profound and subtle analysis of the purpose and possibility of aesthetic experience was made by Schiller, who matched his understanding of literature to the analysis of culture and even society. For him the artist had a central role to fulfil in culture and society since the aesthetic experience is capable of profoundly moulding human behaviour. But Schiller developed his theory because he saw the growing gulf between the intellect and the emotions, between moral and sensory experience, as the central flaw in modern civilisation. Schiller, and Goethe too, had many misgivings about the contemporary cultural scene, and they had harsh comments to make on their contemporaries, who, in

their view, failed to appreciate their own idealist purposes. But such
criticism never made them waver in their conviction of the importance of
the artist's task, of his ability to make men understand nature, society,
indeed, the whole of life itself. But this task was not an easy one; for the
poet's very awareness and sensitivity might alienate him from the demands
of practical life. Goethe recognised his problem and, in his drama *Torquato
Tasso* (1789), he portrayed 'the tragedy of the creative artist'[3] in an alien
world. *Torquato Tasso*, a complex and most subtle work, provides the
portrait of a sensitive poet who claims to have rights equal to those of the
man of affairs. Goethe was not depicting his own experience but rather, as
poets often do, a potential experience, and such was his genius that Tasso
became accepted as the representative, not as some will even have it, of the
whole age itself, but of men of feeling and imagination. The tragedy of the
artist became the tragedy of subjectivity. Goethe's view is, as almost
always, balanced. He sides neither with the poet nor with his counterpart,
Antonio Montecatini, the Duke of Ferrara's Secretary of State and man of
affairs; for he criticises excessive subjectivity as he had already done in his
first novel *Die Leiden des jungen Werthers* [*The Sorrows of Young Werther*]
(1774), but he also reveals his sympathy with sensitivity.[4]

The consequences of *Torquato Tasso* were not those which Goethe
intended and did not correspond to his own attitude to poetry. His concern
was always to attain, and to further, an approach leading to objectivity.
That entailed awareness of practical affairs and an ability to respond to the
challenge of the day. It is therefore false to read *Torquato Tasso* as if Goethe
had merely meant to attack philistinism and defend subjectivity and
emotion. It is not that at all, any more than *Die Leiden des jungen Werthers* is a
plea for unrestrained feeling. What was, however, new about *Torquato
Tasso* was the choice of the poet as hero. The poet was given equal weight
with the leading statesmen at the court of Ferrara. To see him as the peer of
men of power was a distinct departure from tradition. The Romantics
seized upon this high evaluation of the poet ignoring Goethe's criticism of
excessive sensibility. Thus, Goethe's drama proved to be the starting point
or model for many poets in their enquiry into the poet's life and task.
Grillparzer, the Austrian dramatist, took it up in *Sappho* (1818), echoing
Goethe's conception though taking a more extreme view of the discrepancy between the poet and ordinary mortals. This gulf had also been
emphasised by the Romantics, for whom the creative artist became the
seer, the high priest capable of knowing and revealing, sometimes to the
initiated only, the secret of the universe, the essential mystery at the heart
of the world. As Novalis put it: 'Poetry is that which alone is truly real. . . .
The more poetic the truer'.[5] The poet is thus placed above normal men. He
endows reality with a higher meaning, thus giving it a romantic aura.

With the waning of the Romantic movement the Romantic view of the
poet was assailed, most scathingly by Heine, yet it was never totally
obliterated – and Heine himself certainly took over many Romantic ideas,

however much he modified them. In general, doubts about the poet's function continued to develop side by side with the belief in the greatness of his task. The artist was, in the years following Goethe's death, not portrayed in the main as an exceptional figure, but seen in a much more mundane way, as some one who had to learn to fit into the pattern of ordinary life without sacrificing his artistic integrity and individuality.[6] But there was no consensus of opinion. The Romantic view of poetry also left its legacy. To some extent, it reflected the artists' aspiration with regard to what they might wish to achieve if their creativity, their most precious gift, were duly recognised. It also represented an attempt to establish the value of art and the artist in a changing society. Indeed, the poet wanted to be at the very pinnacle of the new social order. *Torquato Tasso* is still set at a court, and though Tasso claims to be the equal of the statesman he does not claim to be the equal of the prince. The decline and final disappearance of court patronage changed the writer's position in society. Doubtless there had always been writers who felt uneasy about their place in the world, for after all discontent is a human lot, and sensitive men, such as artists, are not spared that experience. But the question of the writer's place in society was now becoming a public issue. The writers felt isolated, like all artists; they did not seem to belong to any clearly definable stratum of society. This experience became a central theme in their work: the ambiguity of their position, of being both high and exalted representatives of human endeavour yet outsiders in and even exiles from society, pre-empted their own attention. The artist was seen as a prince and an outcast, and so forced to play an uncomfortable role. Goethe had apprehended the problem, but in practice he had coped with it successfully: for the modern writer it became a major, if not the major, question. This is not at all surprising, for writers, understandably, felt the need to discover their place in society. They also, in an age of growing self-awareness, felt the need to communicate their own self-exploration to others, not only so that their readers could share the results of their awareness, but so that they could also vindicate their own activity in a world where the artist might no longer feel at home. At the same time, on a more mundane, but equally important level, they had to woo, win and keep their public. Yet more often than not, they wanted to be more than mere entertainers: they also wished to educate their public, thus following the tradition prevailing in the age of eighteenth-century enlightenment. They were facing, in a changing world, the same cultural problems which had faced German classical writers and which had engaged so much of their cultural efforts. The classical writers had, in the very first instance, been concerned with developing their personal culture, though it was rarely a question of a merely narcissistic enterprise – the very fact of writing about it indicates their attempt to reach a wider public. Yet it was not a popularising, but in essence an aristocratic attempt to reach like-minded men. The ideal of self-cultivation [*Bildung*] although evolved by liberal-minded men, belonged to a thin layer of society – to a group of cultivated men. Although Weimar classicism was an innovation in the realm of culture, its social foundations were formed in a pre-industrial society. The aristocrats of the mind had adapted themselves to a society whose way of living was set by the court and nobility, although they neither abandoned their bourgeois literary taste nor lived entirely on court patronage. Many eighteenth-century writers ignored the practical side of life, though Goethe did not, for he had always emphasised the need to marry thought and action and he had always been alive to the importance of science, to which he was led by his understanding of man's development in nature. Nor did Schiller think little of the demands of practical life. But both Goethe and Schiller, though they were fully aware, indeed apprehensive, of the development which industrialisation would produce, still belonged to a pre-industrial world, a world alien to the democracy appropriate to a developed industrial society. Hence their lack of concern with politics and their acceptance of the poet's place in society. The Romantics were different. They rebelled against the Enlightenment, against reliance on reason, against science and any kind of empiricism. However, although they harked back to a hierarchical social order and espoused a dangerous irrationalism in politics they did not wish to sacrifice the claims of their individuality. Indeed, their highly intellectual attitude did not allow for much attention to practical questions and they still wrote for a highbrow minority of readers and were, in the main, quite content to do so.

The Romantic view of the artist remained strong throughout the nineteenth century. Nor did it disappear in the early twentieth century, but many writers found it difficult to reconcile the Romantic tradition of art with the necessities and expectations arising from a changed social, economic and political reality, a task which bewildered them; and few could tackle it with adequate weapons. For Germany had become a different country on account of rapid economic change characterised by industrialisation, urbanisation following an explosive growth of population and political change resulting from unification as well as from liberal, socialist and democratic aspirations. Austria and Switzerland, too, had changed, less dramatically at first, though still markedly so – and of course in Austria in 1918 a whole world came to an end as the Hapsburg Monarchy disappeared and the nations held together by it formed independent states. The creative writer in all German-speaking countries faced at least from the eighteen-seventies onward a different audience – the educational and social background was different and became more so as time went on. Germany was rapidly changing from a socially and economically backward country to one of the most advanced societies in the world. That change brought gains and losses. Germany grew in wealth; that wealth was however unequally distributed, even if the worst excesses that had marred the British industrial scene were avoided. Still, Germany was no longer the country of small courts and stagnant cities. The increasing speed with which society was changing, leading eventually to political upheaval and violence, made it more and more difficult for the writer to find his public. He was writing no longer for an easily identifiable circle of friends assembled at court or for a limited social elite. His public became more and more amorphous. The gulf between high- and low-brow literature which has existed before was vastly accentuated as more and more people learnt to read and the first cheap paperbacks were published – a gulf which few works by great authors of the period were able to bridge. Thomas Mann's *Buddenbrooks* (1901), Hofmannsthal's *Der Rosenkavalier* (1910) made famous only since it was the libretto for Richard Strauss's most popular opera – and Rilke's *Cornet* (1906)[7] – a prose poem not all that far from *Kitsch* – are the most striking exceptions. Most important writers felt that they had something to say, a story to tell, but they were not always sure what audience they were able to reach. Thus, they felt that they had to create their own reading public. To do this they had to scrutinise their own mode of writing and define their conception of art and the artist. Of course, the need to understand their creative possibilities and scope of communication was not the only reason for the need for self-discovery; the necessity to reappraise tradition was another. The achievement of German classicism and the aspirations of Romanticism made the German literary tradition a heavy burden for any writer to bear, and it was not made any easier by the nationalist cultural campaign of many German nineteenth-century educationists, a campaign which thus produced a watered-down, if not distorted, public image of Weimar classicism. A genuine writer wishes to have a voice of his own; revolt against, and reappraisal and assimilation of, the tradition were the necessary responses. Yet language, the writer's tool, inevitably presupposes some continuity that can never be entirely eschewed, even when a deliberate attempt to break with tradition is made.

But it was not merely a question of surviving by comparison with writers of the past. The demands of the market-economy required success among contemporaries and inevitably for most men this success mattered greatly. Of course, recognition for a highbrow writer is not merely a matter of the sales of his books. However, the (perverse) idea that only those works which were read by the few are of high calibre is equally mistaken. After all, if carried to its logical conclusion, it would imply that the best book is the one that has never found any reader.

Almost any enquiry into modern literature has to start with Nietzsche, who suffered greatly from lack of appreciation during his lifetime. He challenged established assumptions and conventions wherever he could, in the field of scholarship, in religion, in ethics and in politics. He thought that a turning point in the history of ideas had been reached and that he was diagnosing, and ushering in, a new age. He proclaimed that a transvaluation of all values was taking place. In the wake of Schopenhauer he questioned the purpose of art. For Schopenhauer, art was the only, though temporary, escape from the will that ceaselessly brought suffering to man – a pessimistic view, popularised, in some ways, by Richard Wagner. Nietzsche too, like Schopenhauer, was convinced of the cardinal significance of art. But since he affirmed rather than negated life he sought to find a positive role for art. It was to be an aid to living but he also, at the same time, continuously questioned its value. Still, his endeavour set the scene for the creative efforts of other writers.

The history of their ideas cannot be properly assessed unless seen in the context of the rise of science and technology, as well as of the resulting secularisation and urbanisation of life. Of these factors secularisation has been the most important; nothing so decisively altered the temper of life. However, urbanisation speeded up the process of secularisation that had been afoot at least since the Renaissance and Reformation. The decline of a Christian conception of society brought about a pluralism of values and a fundamentally different climate of opinion. Man lost the shelter of a hierarchical society; at the same time he was confronted more and more with mass culture.

The unification of Germany in 1871, its rise to political and economic power, gave the Germans the feeling of belonging to the largest nation in Europe. It also raised the hopes of a bright cultural future, and cultural superiority over others, a view savagely and rightly attacked by Nietzsche. In fact, in those first two decades of German power German culture did not flourish: the poets who dominated the scene, men like Emanuel Geibel (1815–84) and Paul Heyse (1830–1914), were not innovators, but wrote in a conventional manner. There was Nietzsche, of course, but his poetry, and even *Also sprach Zarathustra* [*Thus spake Zarathustra*] (1883–91) was unknown. Detlev von Liliencron's (1844–1909) impressionistic lyric poetry was original in tone, but at best his is a minor talent – and apart from these men there were only writers who claimed to be innovators, but did not have the genius to support their claims by action, the action of great work. There was of course Richard Wagner (1813–83) – a man of genius undoubtedly, and many saw in him, as Nietzsche did at first, the herald of the future. The Wagnerites certainly took comfort from his work. But sensitive minds – and Nietzsche was again in the forefront – saw the dangerous, vulgarising impact which he had on the German mind. He was – and remained – an ambiguous phenomenon. It was not until 1889 that the situation changed and new modes of writing began. Naturalist writers came to the fore, among them Gerhard Hauptmann (1862–1946), who, however, soon abandoned the extreme realism of that movement. Stefan George was another writer who struck out on new paths and they were soon followed by other men of genius, of whom Hugo von Hofmannsthal and Rainer Maria Rilke are the most outstanding. The whole climate of writing changed, and these new writers, all influenced by Nietzsche, wrote in opposition to official Wilhelminian culture.

The quest for a genuine new German culture was of course an important issue, given the new feeling of national unity, the new fashions in nationalism and the rise of a mass urban reading public. Authors who felt isolated were looking, as artists had presumably always done, for kindred souls in cities other than their own. (For various reasons this feeling did not become so accentuated in Vienna.) The more sensitive the individual, the more prone he was to feel isolated. The more complex science became and the more powerfully technological advance and economic growth affected social life, the more alien the external urban world appeared to the writer. Goethe had still been able to bridge the gulf between art and science, though he had inveighed against the quantifying methods of Newton that appeared inimical to genuine perception. Of course, Goethe did not do justice to Newtonian science; yet the threat which a world seen merely in terms of quantification presented to the artist can be readily appreciated. It is not science that is dangerous, but the mistaken application of science to realms which are beyond its ken. A false view of science and scientism was propagated[8] and, in contrast, the artist set himself up as *the* antagonist of the scientist. He was to speak for those whose culture seemed excluded from a world dominated by science and technology as well as by a materialism that was exacerbated by Bismarck's political triumphs. His was to be the voice of protest against a facile optimism derived from ideas of the Enlightenment whose force had by now been much attenuated. It was believed by many that the mission of German culture was to carry forward the torch of that progress. But, ironically enough, the naive, uncritical belief in progress had an equally extreme counterpart in a pessimistic view of the decline of European culture, doubtless a reaction to the disappointed hopes of the Enlightenment and the growth of mass culture. Nietzsche, following Schopenhauer, had attacked the educational foundations and popular presuppositions of this facile optimism. He singled out David Friedrich Strauss (1808–74), a well-known rationalist critic of religious orthodoxy, as the prime example of an optimistic rationalist whose views and attitudes he abhorred.[9] Others echoed Nietzsche's strictness. In fact, the voices of protest were neither still nor small. The verdict was unambiguous. There was no cause at all for self-satisfaction. Culture was in peril; for what really mattered to humanity was threatened. Artists perceived the threat and knew that art itself was threatened. This threat could not be ignored. Indeed, it had become a central question; for art sprang from the very core of man's nature, from his imagination and sensibility, from man's basic irrationality. Artists suffered because the national intellect and its products were overvalued. Culture had lost its unity and direction. It was bereft of its purpose. False values were cherished. The decline of religious belief, the process of secularisation had deeply affected spiritual values – as the traditional consensus about which values truly mattered had been shattered. The quality of spiritual life itself seemed in jeopardy. Nietzsche stated the problem dramatically, as he was always prone to, by proclaiming the death of God. It is not necessary to accept his analysis or to agree to his cultural critique, however persuasive and even bewitching it appears at times, in order to recognise the widespread loss of confidence and certainty which religion had given to the faithful, and which had even been shared by the non-believer since it supplied him with a tradition of thought to rely on. Nietzsche had castigated the decadence of modern culture and thus promoted a belief that won much acclaim. Max Nordau's popular book *Entartung* [*Decadence*] (1893) (which exhausted seventeen editions by 1899 and four in the first few weeks) focused attention on a theme held to be highly significant at the time, although Nordau himself, unlike Nietzsche, wrote in the manner of an optimistic rationalist like David Friedrich Strauss. Yet both Nietzsche and Nordau, proceeding from different premises, detected decadence; though they singled out different symptoms, they both chided their contemporaries sharply.

Here is the crux of the matter. Imaginative writers seek to expose, correct or change the cultural pattern which they find. Theirs is more often than not the voice of protest, or at least of dissent; even when they approve they express reservations. But to protest or even to assent the writer needs first to understand. To understand the culture in which one lives is a way of understanding oneself. To explore the nature, potentialities and limits of art – and of the artist, too – is necessary in an age in which accepted models of art or conduct no longer suffice. To study great German writers, to examine their attitudes to their craft and their activity is to understand German, indeed, European culture better. It can also tell us something about the preoccupations, problems, issues and responses of their age. It is always a moot point how much an individual artist, however great his achievement, can speak for an age or even only for many of his fellow-writers, but the greater his achievement the wider the scope of his work is likely to be and the more of the traditions of the past and the tendencies of his age he is likely to have gathered into his net. Of course, some writers are iconoclasts whose work is idiosyncratic, but even they will have formulated some of the ideas cherished by those who cannot speak so well. The greater the reception which an author has, the more some of his attitudes and ideas are likely to be accepted, though the nature of this acceptance is of course not capable of being exactly assessed in quantitative terms. For one of the gifts of an artist is that he can give form to feelings obscurely sensed by common men; moreover, the impact of a great artist's work calls forth emotional responses from his readers which had beforehand been only latent. In either case a study of his work may allow us to gauge features of the sensibility of the age.

The most important and the most compelling way in which a creative writer can formulate his ideas is through his imaginative work. But to understand that work properly the ideas that formed the background of his creative activity have to be analysed. Hence the views expressed by writers in their essays, diaries and letters, i.e. in their non-imaginative writings, are worth studying, but since imaginative works can reveal depths not charted by discursive prose the views culled from a study of the latter have always to be corrected by an interpretation of the former.

In this study the views on the function of art and the artist of seven authors are examined. Of them Nietzsche is mainly known as a thinker, and not as a poet, though his lyrical poetry is impressive. Among the others, two, Stefan George and Rainer Maria Rilke, are famous for their lyrical poetry – although Rilke also wrote an important, though highly idiosyncratic novel, *Die Aufzeichnungen der Malte Laurid Brigge* [*The Notebooks of Malte Laurid Brigge*] (1910). Two others, Hugo von Hofmannsthal and Bertolt Brecht, are probably best known as dramatists although both of them are also lyric poets of the first rank; since Thomas Mann and Franz Kafka are narrative prose-writers at least all the important traditional genres are represented, and the spread may give this selection at least a certain balance. Yet another selection including some other writers – Carl Sternheim (1878 – 1942), Hermann Hesse (1877 – 1962), Heinrich Mann (1871 – 1950), Karl Kraus (1874 – 1936), Robert Musil (1880 – 1942), Gottfried Benn (1886 – 1956) and Hermann Broch (1886 – 1957), for instance – would also make sense; still, while a good case could be made for these or other writers, not to analyse the conception of art of the seven writers discussed here would assuredly also appear to leave out something that mattered. Moreover, their work has had the greatest impact in the English-speaking world (Hesse has, admittedly, gained many English-speaking readers of late, but in range and nature his views appear less interesting and compelling than those of any of the seven).

To sum up, the work of great artists tells us of phenomena not usually accessible to historians: it reveals the emotional undergrowth of history. Indeed, apart from works of art, there is very little other evidence which allows us to appraise the temper of an age by helping us to grasp its emotional quality and its sensibility. Of course, what a highly individual writer says is not likely to be universally true, but it may imply some general truth or at least some wider segment of the truth. And however limited this segment is it is virtually all we have, and by the artistic skill and power of a writer's voice it becomes more or less qualitatively representative. At the very least it is a significant sector of life that a student of the period should not ignore. But it tells us more; for an artist's response to the world in general and to new circumstances in particular can always exemplify the nature and scope of human responses themselves.

2 *Friedrich Nietzsche* (1844—1900)

In the past hundred years no other writer's impact on German literature has been as great as that of Nietzsche. Why was this so? The reasons are not far to seek. He challenged orthodoxy, and he did so more inventively and impressively than any other nineteenth-century writer of his generation. Other German nineteenth-century thinkers, too, had been radical in their attack on conventional wisdom – Schopenhauer and Marx come first and foremost to mind, but they were of an earlier generation. And the reputation of Freud (who certainly also challenged accepted views) belongs, in the main, to the twentieth century. Also, Nietzsche is far more ingenious and unpredictable in his onslaught; his range of interest seems wider and the style of his challenge, if not bolder and more radical, is more unusual and scintillating. Nietzsche's work is rich and varied so that writers of very different temperament and outlook could be attracted by it. He seemed profound and original, although it is a matter of controversy whether his thought is as deep and novel as many of the leading interpreters of his work have claimed. But his stylistic brilliance cast its spell – for he is one of the most skilful and impressive German prose writers, capable, at his best, like Plato, of adding a poet's touch to his prose without making it lose edge. Yet Nietzsche, on closer scrutiny, frequently appears to be a slippery writer.[1] Wittingly or unwittingly, he moves with great agility from one aspect of an argument to another, often remaining elusive and refusing to allow himself to be pinned down, frequently appealing by suggestion rather than by logic. He is even contradictory, and wilfully so. He adopts a stance only to abandon it. A polemic might carry him away so that Byron's indictment of Friedrich Schlegel might, at times at least, justly be applied to him: 'he always seems upon the verge of meaning and, lo, he goes down like the sunset, or melts like the rainbow, leaving a rather rich confusion.'[2] And this is so precisely because he took up different positions and because he could appeal to a wider range of authors than a more consistent and more logical thinker might have done. Also, the intoxicating nature of his writing was bound to move imaginative writers who are more easily kindled by appeals to the imagination than by exhortations to common sense. Nietzsche became widely known only in the eighteen-nineties. Georg Brandes, a Danish literary critic of stature had, so to speak, discovered Nietzsche in 1888 and by means of his considerable influence, standing and skill as a publicist, succeeded in making him fashionable within a few years. Of course, Nietzsche's solitariness and his later madness which broke out in January 1889 also helped by making him appear a Romantic of the most fascinating kind.

What is more important, German literature, as we have seen, had been in the doldrums for a generation. There was a general feeling abroad that a change was needed. Young writers once again felt that a new era of writing ought be inaugurated. Almost inevitably, they paid heed to any radical criticism of the prevailing culture, more especially to a clarion-call for a new way of looking at the world trumpeted forth so stridently and skilfully by Nietzsche.

It was not the first time that German imaginative literature had been stimulated by a thinker or scholar: German Reformation literature arose in the shadow of Luther; 'Storm and Stress' was inspired by Hamann and Herder; German classicism owed much to Shaftesbury and Winckelmann; Fichte, and, to a lesser extent, Schelling had charted much of the thought of the German Romantics. Nietzsche was to become the lodestar for a generation of German writers who could boast a galaxy of talent such as few periods of German literature have known. Writers as different in style and outlook as Gerhart Hauptmann, Arno Holz, Stefan George, Rainer Maria Rilke, Hugo von Hofmannsthal, the brothers Heinrich and Thomas Mann, Herman Hesse and Gottfried Benn, to mention only some of the most outstanding figures – all, at some time or other, fell under Nietzsche's spell.[3] So did most Expressionist writers.[4] He also greatly influenced German and French, though not English and American,[5] literary criticism.

However, neither the brilliance and range of his writing, nor the Romanticism associated with his solitude and later madness, nor the outrageous and perverse claims advanced by him, and later by others on his behalf, would have sufficed to guarantee the imprint of his thought on the work of many writers. He struck the right note at the right time by questioning the role of the artist in European culture. European culture, he claimed, was doomed unless its whole orientation was profoundly changed. How could this be brought about? Only by great art and the great artist. Art alone, Nietzsche contended, could deal with the basic problem of life – the need to live life without succumbing to despair, to nihilism – and it alone could give men the resources to vindicate experience. The artist is the essential outsider, yet he is placed at the very centre of life. Art is the pivot of culture. It gives meaning to an otherwise meaningless existence.

I

All these ideas can be culled from Nietzsche's work, to a great extent a concealed *apologia pro vita sua*. They are seductive in manner, complex in detail but, like so many of his ideas, never fully elaborated. Nor are they consistently and rigorously argued. Indeed, the impression cannot be entirely gainsaid that Nietzsche himself never entirely made up his mind, but hesitated to commit himself fully to one line of thought. However bold his stance, he derived much pleasure from the play of ideas and often shirked commitment; indeed, at times he does not even seem to have been fully aware of all the implications of his thought. Or, in other words, his mode of thought it best described as moving around a problem rather than getting to its core in order to solve it. His style of thinking is multiperspectival,[6] for he delighted in seeing a problem or in looking at an idea from many different angles without committing himself or even without defining it unambiguously. This is frequently the case, although the audacity of his formulations give the impression of his having settled once and for all some of the most complex philosophical questions. However, precisely because he does not always, or indeed often, come down clearly on one side or the other, his work stimulates an imaginative response peculiarly suited to imaginative writers and poets who found in the range of his ideas enough material on which to base their work.

Nietzsche's attitude to art and the artist has proved most potent in the field of German literature. To understand it properly we have to appreciate the impact of Nietzsche's academic career on his conception of art. Nietzsche started as a classical scholar and classical education moulded much of his thinking. His first important analysis of the nature of art and the function of the artist purported to be, in the first place, a treatise in classical scholarship. In that work, *Die Geburt der Tragödie aus dem Geiste der Musik* [*The Birth of Tragedy from the Spirit of Music*] (1871/72) he mapped out his ideas on art and the artist, ideas from which he never departed fundamentally, though from time to time he changed the angle from which he surveyed the terrain.

How did this marriage of classical scholarship and art in Nietzsche's mind come about? He had been brought up in the tradition of German scholarship, then the best in the world. German classical scholars felt unbelievably self-important. They saw themselves as *praeceptores Germaniae* and the mantle of theology had – or so it would appear from their conduct – fallen on their shoulders. They held classical philology to be the queen of the sciences, a pretension nowadays usurped by economists. They felt that they set the pace for culture throughout the country and it is not surprising that a sensitive and highly gifted young man like Nietzsche would have absorbed and later rebelled against many of their attitudes.

In the *Geburt der Tragödie* Nietzsche wanted to settle accounts with scholars of that mould. He criticised them as much as himself; for he had started life as a conventional scholar, albeit of high promise and unusual early success; on the strength of his first publications he was invited to the chair of Classics at Basle when still an undergraduate at Leipzig. A surprised, but appreciative university awarded him a doctorate without examining him after he had accepted the appointment. (He was also awarded the higher doctorate [*Habilitation*] which gave him the right to lecture.)

Nietzsche who had already – like many gifted students – understandably entertained doubts about the value of his academic study, quenched them for the time being on his election to the chair. When the first flush of enjoyment of his high academic office had vanished these doubts returned.[7] He felt that the whole tendency of classical education as carried on in German-speaking countries of the period was sadly and dangerously mistaken; for it was fundamentally and philosophically unsound. It served its own ends and not life; it was an obstacle to genuine philosophy and true living.

Nietzsche became convinced that in adopting this stance scholars were failing in their task which should be much more comprehensive: a new scholarship had to be born, and Nietzsche was to give birth to it. What manner of thought was to shape it?

His aim was to foster philosophical scholarship, i.e. scholarship that questioned values and raised profound questions as to the nature of scholarship and of the literature under discussion. He confided his hopes in a letter of 11 April 1869 to Carl von Gersdorff, a close friend, soon after his election to the chair at Basle:

> To permeate my scholarship [*Wissenschaft*] with this new blood, to impart to my listeners that Schopenhauerian seriousness which is imprinted on the brow of this sublime man – this is my desire, my bold hope. – I want to be more than a master who trains capable scholars. (N-Br, II, p. 310.)

Nietzsche desired to bring about this new kind of scholarship since he was convinced of the poverty of historical scholarship, the dominant mode of investigation in nineteenth-century Germany which had become for him a merely conventional, and thus, unfruitful, exercise. It was above all sterile because it could not be justified at the bar of life itself (whatever that vague term might mean). Nietzsche's aim is to relate scholarship to life, to cure the disease of modern life which he diagnosed and which was caused by an excessive intellectualism that was unrelated, indeed, hostile to life. Yet, a typical scholar himself, he wanted to save the world – and that meant for him, in the last resort, culture which had to be saved by the knowledge which he had gained in his academic studies. In other words, he went to Greek culture to find the medicine for the ills of the day, certainly an unusual road to travel on.

But the term 'philosophical' had, for Nietzsche, a particular slant. His conception of philosophy was unusual, and understandably, philosophers of distinction, though by no means all philosophers, have refused to accept him as one of their peers. For his conception of philosophy, at least in the days of the *Geburt der Tragödie* had, though influenced by Schopenhauer, a poetic flavour; not only was his grasp of a problem intuitive, but he often displayed his argument, if argument it can be called, in a poetic rather than in a ratiocinative manner. He himself later realised that the genre of poetry would have been more appropriate to this early work than that of a learned treatise – 'it should have *sung*, not spoken, that "new soul"'',[8] as he put it in his characteristic poetic manner.

Nietzsche's temper of mind was too poetic for classical scholarship to be the only source of his inspiration for the *Geburt der Tragödie*. There was another almost equally powerful motive at work: the impact of Richard Wagner.[9] This is not entirely surprising. Nietzsche had a great love and aptitude for music, and Wagner was the most striking figure in the German theatre of the day; indeed, he was more than that, he was (whatever reservations may have to be entertained about his work and there are many) *the* contemporary German artist whose work showed most power and flamboyance. Also, he had, for good or ill, a magnetic personality. He was a man of genius. Moreover, he enjoyed being in the company of those who worshipped him and served his turn, consciously or unconsciously, casting a spell over them.

Nietzsche, when still a student, had been introduced to Wagner, at the soirée of a Leipzig professor. They took to each other immediately. Nietzsche was flattered by the interest which Wagner, already a famous composer, showed in him, and Wagner perceptively recognised that there was a bright young admirer of promise who might be useful to him and whose conversation did not bore him. Nietzsche was clearly attracted by Wagner's magic charm; in turn, Wagner was willing to receive him at his house in Triebschen near Lucerne where he was living when Nietzsche arrived in Basle to take up his professorial duties. Nietzsche greatly enjoyed his days in Triebschen; he found Wagner's company stimulating and he took even more to Cosima von Bülow, Franz Liszt's daughter who was openly living with Wagner before her divorce from Hans von Bülow, the celebrated conductor, and her subsequent marriage to Wagner. The idyll of Triebschen was reflected in the *Geburt der Tragödie* on which he was working at the time. The exchange of thought between the most exciting, though by no means the soundest, German minds of the day was fruitful. Nietzsche combined his radical reappraisal of Greek drama with an account of Wagnerian music. At the same time he forecast and prescribed the future course of German culture, thus combining a scholarly treatise with a piece of cultural propaganda, a most unusual combination. Nietzsche not only wanted to change the course of scholarship, but also to bring about a revolution in culture, both remarkably high aims. In short, Nietzsche had recourse to his two main fields of interest – classical studies and music – where he hoped to find the medicine to cure the disease of modern civilisation.

The championship of Wagnerian music was as always with Nietzsche not without self-interest; for he cherished musical ambitions and the *Geburt der Tragödie* contains an element of concealed autobiography. Nietzsche was a gifted poet; his lyric poetry and *Also sprach Zarathustra* prove it beyond doubt. But he was not only a poet, but also a composer (even if of rather limited talent), a composer who perhaps even dreamt of becoming Wagner's successor. Indeed, he may have even gone as far as to think of Wagner merely as a harbinger of his own great music drama to come – the new tragedy in which as in Greek tragedy poetry and music would combine to produce the most powerful effect on the mind and emotions. These dreams came to nothing; for when he sent a composition to Hans von Bülow[10] soon after he had completed the *Geburt der Tragödie*, he received a devastating reply in which this composition was linked to hangover music.[11] Nietzsche never forgot that particular disappointment, but seems to have continued to harbour vain expectations for his music's success.[12]

II

Nietzsche thus set himself the task to reform classical scholarship and thereby to initiate a revolution in contemporary culture. To do this he set out to analyse the nature of tragedy – in his view, the most distinctive achievement of Greek culture – and to vindicate Wagnerian opera, the art-form of the future.

The *Geburt der Tragödie* is a classic. But like many classics it is little read. This is not surprising; for it is not a readable book. Although it contains some most impressive passages and touches on many interesting ideas, it is confusing and at times even confused. A most perceptive contemporary critic recognised these features when, less than fifteen years after its first publication, he called it:

> an impossible book . . . badly written, awkward, embarrassing, frantic and confused in its imagery, sentimental, in parts sugary to the point of effeminacy, uneven in its tempo, not revealing any intention of logical neatness, and it is so self-confident that it feels no need to supply proof for its argument, even worse, it suspects the very notion of proof . . . an arrogant and enthusiastic book. . .[13]

Who was this critic who condemned it so radically? None other than Nietzsche himself – for who else could have written so brilliantly at that time? But however just some of these strictures may be, the book still repays reading. Not because Nietzsche had solved any problem or developed a new, consistent approach to scholarship or art, but because it is the prelude to a new period of German writing and because it raises central problems for our understanding of the nature of art and scholarship. He claimed that he had been 'the first to tackle the task of seeing scholarship from the point of view of art and art from the point of scholarship'[14] – which was, in his view, a new problem indeed. Was he right in this claim?

Greek culture for Nietzsche was the prototype of a great culture; for it reflected the wholeness of a nation's life where unity was revealed in all its particular manifestations. He never questioned, let alone examined, this assumption which struck him as self-evident. Thus, he never offers any proof, but seeks to discover the nature of Greek tragedy, its origins and the reasons for its decline and disappearance in order to prescribe the conditions for its rebirth. So his investigation runs, from the very beginning, counter to the spirit of historical scholarship; for it is meant to be a guide to action as much as an intellectual enquiry. It is also wedded to a suggestive, but controversial theory – a theory as dubious and unprovable as it has been influential – a theory that all genuine art embodies an opposition of the Apolline and Dionysian elements which make up all genuine art.[15] For Nietzsche, great Greek tragedy – and that is for him essentially the tragedy of Aeschylus and, to a lesser extent, of Sophocles, combines these elements or forces to which the Greeks had given the names of two Gods, Apollo and Dionysus. Apollo, the God of measure and harmony, symbolises the principle of individuation, while Dionysus, the God of ecstacy, stands for the dissolution of individuality in the original unity of all life. In other words, Apollo is the power that gives form to the inchoate, primordial, irrational forces that Dionysus represents, and art will only be great when both elements completely coalesce. In Greek tragedy, this fusion took place. The Apolline element conquered the Dionysian forces; reason triumphed over the irrational, the word was united with music, music which preceded the word in Greek tragedy and which was based on the irrational, primordial experience of the death of Dionysus. It told the tale of his suffering and end; it sprang from a basic disgust with life which was however turned into art, Apollo conquering Dionysus or at least becoming reconciled with him. Only then could art arise. Without the Dionysian fundament there could be no Apolline harmony; for knowledge of the irrational basis of life and the inevitable destruction of individuality was necessary for the creation of great art. Yet if Apollo seems apparently triumphant, the real hero is Dionysus; for Apollo is only the God of semblance, while Dionysus is the God of life, of Being, to which the individual must return. Art is semblance, not reality, but since life is not reality either, but semblance, art is, so to speak, at one further remove from reality; it is the semblance of a semblance. The influence of Schopenhauer is noticeable here, but Nietzsche develops his ideas in his own peculiar way. For him, art is necessary for life; for without it life would be unbearable. Music is essentially the Dionysian art; poetry is by nature Apolline; for to use words is to attempt individualisation. It is, though, like all Apolline art, however beautiful, a form of semblance, inadequate in its very nature and hence, in principle, mendacious and misleading. Nietzsche's scepticism as to the use of language is extreme. He does not believe that words can precisely correspond to the things which they denote. It is absurd to demand an adequate form of linguistic expression; for language can do no more than denote relations. It does not reflect reality, nor does it deal with the causes of events (N, II, p. 751), but only with the effects. Indeed, language relies on convention (N, I, p. 202) and conceals prejudices (N, I, p. 109f.). It is seductive (N, II, p. 789) and, like all modes of knowledge, it can prove an obstacle to our recognising our true inner processess and drives (N, I, p. 1090). Language is but another fallacy of reason. It pretends to convey that which, in principle, is incommensurable. Our thought is in fact limited by the boundaries of language. Words can never catch up with, or match, experience. Nietzsche here attacks the very foundations on which writing had been based in Germany since the classical period; for Goethe, although convinced of the inadequacy of language none the less believed that words have symbolic meaning, denoting universal truths.

Nietzsche goes even further: in the *Geburt der Tragödie*, he seeks to reverse a whole movement of ideas which had been dominant in German thinking about Greek art and culture since the middle of the eighteenth century. For he fundamentally attacked the German classicist conception of the Greeks, first initiated by Winckelmann, summed up in his famous phrase of 'noble simplicity and calm greatness',[16] and then securely established by Goethe and Schiller. These writers had, he thought, misunderstood the Greeks, and their inferior successors had promulgated a doctrine of Greek optimism dangerous to art and hostile to life. Nietzsche's was a full-scale attack on Greek serenity,[17] an attack mounted in the spirit of Schopenhauerian pessimism, but he was a Schopenhauerian with a difference. Although life was semblance, he affirmed it instead of rejecting it.

In Nietzsche's view, Greek tragedy is the highest form of art so far known; for it portrays starkly the inevitable process of life, the tendency to individuation and the dissolution of the individual by bringing about the return to the primordial unity. It is of course the old problem of the one and the many which Nietzsche here adumbrated, but with his own peculiar sense of drama he depicts it as a series of dramatic scenes which tell us about the rise and fall, i.e. the tragedy, of the individual, for which among the Greeks the life and death of Dionysus was the appropriate symbol.

What Nietzsche wanted to point out was the irrational basis of Greek culture.[18] The Greeks were not serene. He had no truck with the portrait of the Greeks as apostles and practitioners of harmony. Of course, Winckelmann and the other German classicists knew of the storms in the hidden – and not always hidden – depths of Greek experience, but they had stressed the poise and balance, the calm and serenity which they nevertheless achieved. But in their wake many nineteenth-century interpreters, particularly German schoolmasters, had ignored any irrational elements. Greek serenity had been overemphasised and trivialised; for the Greeks were made out to be harmless optimists presenting an ingenuous and cosy picture of life. Nietzsche protested against this view as false and pernicious. For if men believed that they did not understand the Greeks at all. His own view, after a time-lag, gained general currency. The Dionysian and Apolline elements were widely accepted as true bi-polar manifestations of reality. Neither the term nor the conception was Nietzsche's own however. Earlier scholars, such as F. G. Welcker and Friedrich Wilhelm Ritschl, his own teacher, had used them, but Nietzsche put them into the very centre of his argument and dramatised them with great skill. As a result, many German writers from 1890 onward accepted them. Yet Nietzsche never made it clear whether they were psychological elements, historical forces or aesthetic criteria. Indeed, his argument for the superiority of Greek tragedy on the ground of the (alleged recon-ciliation of the Apolline and the Dionysian is circular. Classical scholars certainly did not, in the main, accept Nietzsche's theory of the origins and nature of Greek tragedy. Indeed, his disdainful refusal to produce any evidence, since he mistakenly believed his argument to be self-evident, only made his colleagues more distrustful. However, whether it was a consequence of his writing or not, Winckelmann's conception of Greek culture has been superseded in the public mind by Nietzsche's and even classical scholars paid attention to the Greeks' awareness of the irrational.

Nietzsche, thus, equated culture and art; a great culture was possible only if there was a great art which was accepted by the whole nation and permeated its life. But Nietzsche's assertion remains dogmatic. So does his account of the relationship between art and life. Not only is it the task of art to make life endurable; it and it alone gives it meaning. It is 'the enchantress that saves and cures, for it allows us to turn our disgust with the terrible or absurd nature of life into ideas with which man can live' (N, 1, p. 48f.). Indeed, 'only as an *aesthetic* phenomenon *is* life and existence *for ever justified*' (N, 1, p. 40). This sentence is at the root of Nietzsche's philosophy as expounded in the *Geburt der Tragödie*. It has usually been taken to mean that art vindicates life or that Nietzsche is advocating an aesthetic philosophy, judging life by aesthetic criteria only, though, in fact, it is not entirely clearly whether this is its meaning.

We are left with a number of questions, the most important of which concerns the relationship between fiction and truth.[19] The problem is this: if art is fiction and thus a lie why should we prefer it to truth?[20] But what is truth? Are scholarship and science more likely to lead to it? Nietzsche, at this stage of his development, suggests that they are not, for reason has its limits. Indeed, the belief that the whole world can be known is profoundly mistaken. It reveals a shallow optimism; for the intellectual pursuit of truth soon meets boundaries and the scholar or scientist must discover that he has succumbed to another illusion, that of believing that it is possible to discover truth; whereas in fact, what we call truth is but a convention formed by habit and common usage, disguising another form of error or fiction.

What then is truth? A mobile sea of metaphors, metonyms, anthropo-morphisms, in short, the sum of human relations which were poetically and theoretically intensifed, translated, adorned and which appear, after long usage, firm, canonical and binding; the truths are illusions, metaphors which have become used and are without sensuous strength, coins which have lost their face and are of use only as metal, but no longer as coins.[21]

Consequently, Nietzsche in the *Geburt der Tragödie* rejects the scholarly or scientific search for truth as inadequate. Indeed, it is dangerous. Existence as we perceive it, the phenomena of the natural and social world which we inhabit are all semblance, a part of the process of individualisation which disguises the primordial unity of being. Yet once individuality is destroyed chaos results – hardly a condition to be desired. The intellect is powerless to arrest this inevitable process. So is art, but great art gives us a sense of heroism. It tells us that great ages have been and can therefore come again.

Why did the great age of Greek culture, the only one which history had ever known, not last? How and why did it decline and come to an end? Or – what brought about the death of Greek tragedy, the greatest form of art that ever existed? To answer this question is part of Nietzsche's investigation. He tells his tale in a series of striking dramatic scenes. To the question of how Greek tragedy came to an end he gives a most provocative answer: 'it died by suicide' (N, I, p. 69). How was it possible for it to take its life? It happened because the last powerful tragic dramatist, Euripides, willed it. He was dissatisfied with the tradition which he had inherited. He sat discontented in the theatre because he did not understand the work of his great predecessors. Unable to create spontaneously and naively, he wrote not for the public at large, but for two spectators only, and in doing so made it impossible for traditional tragedy to continue. One of these two spectators was Euripides himself, not the poet, but the thinker, who reflected on his poetic work, thus sapping his own creative power. (N, I, p. 69) But he alone would not have been able to put tragedy to death. Who was the ally with whose help he wrote the new tragedy that spelt the end of all great tragedy? It was none other but Socrates. 'In league with him Euripides dared to be the herald of a new art' (N, I, p. 69), but in fact he destroyed tragedy and thus Greek culture.[22] Aesthetic Socratism invaded the drama of Euripides and brought about the end of Greek tragedy; for Socrates was the arch-rationalist who pursued intellectual knowledge to the detriment of the poetic spirit; proudly, defiantly and foolishly he proclaimed the primacy of the intellect and the possibility of rational knowledge. Euripides and Socrates, the two arch-villains, drove Dionysus, the all-powerful God, to flight and robbed tragedy of its necessary basis (N, I, p. 75f.); it became impoverished, emasculated, and died; it was no longer the suffering and death of Dionysus but the fate of Socrates which was enacted and Socrates was a trivial substitute for Dionysus. Tragedy, with that subject, could not last. Intellectualism is not the ground on which genuine tragedy can flourish; the scientific spirit is inimical to poetic creation; for it fails to understand reality properly since it is shallow, mistaken and misleading. It pretends that absolute knowledge exists when it has no justification for doing so.

Scholarship and science cannot therefore provide the basis for a renaissance of culture. Nietzsche here implicitly attacks German education in general and prevailing classical scholarship in particular; he finds it arid. Classical scholars lacked the true lust for literature and culture. Their concern was for learning and not for life, and they followed false and even dangerous paths.

III

The *Geburt der Tragödie* was unfortunately not a success. Only some of Nietzsche's friends, above all Wagner himself and Erwin Rohde, a fellow Leipzig student who later on became a very distinguished Hellenist, were enthusiastic; the overwhelming majority of scholars were hostile. Even Ritschl's response was cool. As a scholar whose approach to classical studies was historical he refused to reject scholarship in favour of art or to look for a philosophical method that was to save the world.[23] Privately he went further: in his diary[24] he accused Nietzsche of 'megalomania' and called the work 'a piece of clever charlatanism'. Nietzsche was disappointed by Ritschl's reaction and by the silence of his fellow-scholars in the first months after publication; for he had believed his work to be a manifesto that required an enthusiastic response.[25] Rohde broke the silence with a panegyric in the *Norddeutsche Allgemeine* (26 May 1872),[26] a daily newspaper since he was unable to find a learned journal to sponsor his views. That only roused the anger of classical scholars even more, and a young man of twenty-three, Ulrich von Wilamowitz-Möllendorff, later one of the greatest classical scholars of all time, published early in June a violently polemical pamphlet *Zukunftsphilologie* [*Scholarship of the Future*] (Berlin, 1872)[27] – the title is an allusion to Wagner's tract *Das Kunstwerk der Zukunft* [*The Future Work of Art*] (1849). Despite an open letter by Wagner himself in the *Norddeutsche Allgemeine* (23 June 1872),[28] which, since it came from an outsider of course cut no ice with the scholars, and a highly polemical reply by Rohde published in October and entitled *Afterphilologie* [*Bastard Scholarship*] (Leipzig, 1872),[29] Wilamowitz won the day.[30] Nietzsche was ostracised by his colleagues. As a result, he became completely disillusioned with classical scholarship and content to view art in a different context, in the context of philosophy.

But though Nietzsche was critical of scholarship and, in his writings of his middle period, cruelly lambasted the scholars he did not rate the artist higher than the man of intellect, the true philosopher. The reason for not doing so was undoubtedly his break with Wagner. After that event he deemed it necessary to revise his view of modern art in general. For in attacking the modern artist he attacked Wagner himself. More than that, he criticised his own ambitions. Had he not hoped to be not only the cultural leader of Europe, but also the artist who was by his own work, to create the new tragedy? Clearly tragedy had not been reborn, either in Germany or elsewhere. Nietzsche's forecasts of future cultural events were as wide of the mark as his predictions of the future course of scholarship. When Nietzsche became aware that he had not realized his ambitions he blamed the age for it on account of its decadence and nihilism. It had not lived up to the goals which he had set for it. Wagner, Nietzsche had come to think, was the prototype of the artist and the embodiment of decadence. How had this change of mind that led to his break with Wagner come about?

Undoubtedly he was repelled by Wagner's condoning of Wagner idolatry. Also, he abhorred Wagner's espousal of Christianity in *Parzifal* (1882), but mutual psychological incompatibility may well have played its part, too; two egomaniacs rarely live long in harmony. Nietzsche had to emancipate himself from Wagner who had always been the dominant partner during their period of friendship. Moreover, he appears to have felt that he had been mistaken about the philosophical basis of Wagner's work. Each of them had thought of Schopenhauer as their philosopher, but Nietzsche had discovered that Wagner's interest in Schopenhauer was superficial. Wagner's music on which after all his achievement rests did not save him from Nietzsche's wrath. Nietzsche had greatly liked *Tristan und Isolde*, but whether he knew the later works well is not clear. It is unlikely that he ever saw the whole of *Der Ring der Nibelungen*. As usual, Nietzsche exaggerated his criticism, and he now found in Wagner all that he detested in his own age. Yet he shrewdly appraised the nature of the impact of Wagner and the Wagnerites on German society and culture. Not that he ceased to take Wagner seriously; on the contrary, by singling him out as *the* artist of decadence, he turned him into a central figure who merited the most serious attention and criticism. The case against Wagner proved how far modern culture had deviated from real culture which he had perceived in pre-Socratic Greece and which he associated with health, strength and spontaneity untainted by reflection. Wagner, he had mistakenly thought, would be able to save German culture from decadence. But the very epitome of decadence himself, he was naturally unable to do that. Why had Nietzsche himself succumbed to the disease of German culture that he had wished to cure with the help of tragedy? His error sprang from the very essence of Wagner's character and work, which were bogus, not genuine. Wagner was an actor at heart and played the part of a genuine artist instead of being one. He was an usurper who failed to create art on account of his character but also because cultural life had become so impoverished that genuine achievement was no longer possible. Only pretence could prevail. Wagner was a mere entertainer (*Komödiant*), not a true artist; his art was sick—he was a neurosis;[31] his work constitutes a real danger[32]—with dire results for art. True artistic values were debased. Wagner's life and work were in fact the symptoms of decadence;[33] for decadence meant that culture no longer constituted a whole, that men no longer conveyed the unity or wholeness of life in works of art or felt it in their own personal experience. Culture was dissipated; personal experience fragmented: life itself was helpless and cultural life in ruins. And Wagner's cultural nationalism was appalling. With his usual verve Nietzsche summed up his own experience to attack Wagner in Bayreuth. (It is an ironic comment on his earlier hopes and later disappointment that *Richard Wagner in Bayreuth* (1876) was the title of the last of his *Unzeitgemäße Betrachtungen* [*Untimely Reflections*], an essay that contained a fulsome panegyric of Wagner.) He wrote:

> One day I woke up in Bayreuth, I felt I was dreaming . . . Where was I? I did not recognise anything, I did not recognise Wagner again. In vain did I turn the leaves of my recollection: Tribschen—a distant island of the happy: not a shadow of similarity . . . *What had happened?*—Wagner had been turned into a German. The Wagnerite had vanquished Wagner! *German* art. The *German* master . . . *German* beer! . . .[34]

Nietzsche's condemnation, indeed hatred, of Wagner born of disappointed love was, then, blended with his hostility to and contempt for contemporary German culture and European political life. But however much he was for ever ready to develop a sustained and coherent criticism of culture and however much the artist mattered to Nietzsche he was not prepared to ascribe to him a political function. Not that politics were of no consequence for him; indeed, his attitude is well known.[35] As always it was extreme, radical in conception and formulation. He detested liberalism, democracy and socialism since they were, in his view, the products of the slave-morality nurtured by Christianity to which he was vehemently opposed. But nationalism and militarism were for him—at least in his mature years—equally abhorrent. They, too, were symptoms of decadence. Yet his nefarious elitist view of a ruling class composed of the strong, an aristocracy of 'masters' (*Herren*) which could not emerge from a democracy of slaves, was rooted in the same belief in the primacy of life as was his conception of art. Although he himself was not a racialist it is easy to see how his ideas carried the seeds of perversion within them,[36] though we should beware of assuming that an admiration of cultural achievement, such as Nietzsche cherished for the Greeks, is necessarily linked to elitism in politics; for that would mean falling into the trap of a false analogy; an artist's excellence (or indeed achievement of any kind) does not necessarily rule out the pursuit of political freedom or equality. To embrace this view would entail committing Nietzsche's own error in reverse; for, once Wagner had become for him a fallen idol, a symptom of decadent German, indeed, European culture he believed that liberalism, democracy and socialism were hostile to artistic and cultural achievement since they sapped the strength of all heroic effort. In the last resort, here as elsewhere, these ideas reflected the vision which he had of his place in the age – he saw himself a giant among pygmies; there was no one to rival his genius, and only a few kindred souls were willing to understand him (although, understandably, all-too-human himself, he appears to have none the less hoped for a wide response to his teaching). Once Wagner had failed him and had become the apostle of German philistinism the burden of saving not only German, but European culture itself, fell on Nietzsche. At least so he appears to have thought. But Nietzsche was never a narrow nationalist, but a cosmopolitan who wanted to be a good European and who found his precursors not only in Goethe and Heine, but also in the French philosophers, above all in Voltaire and in the pre-Socratic Greeks.

IV

In the first shock of disappointment and anger with Wagner and his fellow-scholars Nietzsche attacked art as such and emphasised the quest for truth, ranking intellectual endeavour above artistic creation, though even at that stage it is never entirely clear whether he is merely down-grading 'decadent' art, or is indeed assailing all art which, as a mode of lying, must be inferior to truth.

But Nietzsche's revision of his view of art was not an accident contingent on the reception of the *Geburt der Tragödie* or his relations with Wagner; it arose organically from his earlier view of art. For Nietzsche had not solved the problem of the position which art was to occupy in his philosophical scheme of the world. As semblance, art is a lie, even if it might be a lie born of metaphysical necessity. There was no intrinsic reason why the illusion of art should be preferred to the illusion of scholarship, except for the claim that art reconciled man to life and the inevitable destruction of individuality. Yet this claim was of limited validity since the intellect[37] appeared to be able to see through the smoke-screen put up by art over life, thus weakening the impact of art, rendering it nugatory. Also, why was he writing a treatise in discursive prose, such as the *Geburt der Tragödie*, to prove the intrinsic and patent superiority of art? He was using philosophical argument, and was appealing to the sanction of philosophical reflection which, by definition, he held to be unable to establish truth and which, in his view, fell short of the power of art to convey meaning. When writing the *Geburt der Tragödie* Nietzsche, although, in fact, subordinating scholarship to art, was still intent on proving himself in the field of scholarship – by being a philosophically-minded scholar. His disappointment at its reception made him turn against scholarship and welcome the opportunity of resigning from his chair when his health made it difficult, if not impossible, for him to carry on his academic duties. The work of a professor had become uncongenial, but not the task of a philosopher. He sought to salvage the philosopher (as he understood the term) from the ruins of scholarship which he saw scattered across the academies and universities of Europe.

In his first collection of short philosophical pieces *Menschliches Allzu-menschliches* [*Human – All too Human*] (1876–80), art is taken to task for using deceit (N, I, p. 545), for looking backward (N, II, p. 546), for providing a palliative only (N, I, p. 546), for admittedly making life bearable but only at a high cost; for it does so only 'by casting a veil of impure thought over life' (N, I, p. 548). The question is still the same. What is the true nature of life? Can art tell us something about it? Can the artist be a guide? For Nietzsche it appears beyond doubt that modern artists cannot do so – they live too closely to latrines, they are too superficial; they pretend to possess knowledge where they have none. They also claim to communicate higher truths when in fact they are merely telling lies. The artists use all kinds of tricks to create the impression that their works reveal inspiration (N, I, p. 549f.) without which they do not have any power. The artist, too, never leaves the stage of childhood or youth and thus remains essentially immature; for he believes in an imaginary world. The philosopher's task rests on a mature conception of life. Consequently, he has to uncover this deceit so as to prevent the artist from casting his spell on others; for the artist has a weaker morality than the thinker (N, I, p. 545); he pretends to fight for a higher dignity and significance of man, but has no use for the sober and simple (N, I, p. 545): he is interested in imaginative extravagance and the effect which his work creates, not in its intrinsic substance. Motivated by self-interest, he sacrifices truth to being able to continue creative work (N, I, p. 545f.). The artist values his personality and activity far too highly, he believes that what he does is more important than any scientific truth. Art is, then, a substitute for religion; it renders reflection difficult by obstructing thought.

Nietzsche thus seeks to understand the psychological reasons for artistic creation; he sees it as a form of escapism from the unpalatable truth of the meaninglessness of life. The artist is weak. Strong minds do not like the images created by the artist because art undoes the work of the philosopher, since it does not grasp the essence of life which only the understanding can do (N – Gr, x, p. 72). It also preserves outmoded ideas.

These are harsh words. This phase, however, is but another chapter in Nietzsche's own autobiography when he was discovering his own role as a thinker and was moving away from his early philosophical position and from his adulation of Wagner. It did not last. Indeed, Nietzsche never abandoned his basic belief that it was life above all that mattered and that art, like any other mode of experience, had to be justified at the bar of life. But as so often, even in that phase, Nietzsche is not consistent.[38] He does seem to make exceptions. He speaks of great figures in art. He admits that past periods of great art give us the feeling of powerful reminiscences of a better age which, though it may never have existed, inspires us with the valuable feeling of magnificence. He harks back to the times when great men lived who were strong since they exercised self-mastery. Great art – the art of Homer, Aeschylus, Sophocles, Theocritus, Calderon and Racine (all of them strong men) – reveals a harmonious conduct of life. It can succeed in making life more beautiful and more tolerable and hence more agreeable. It can even make the ugly pleasant. All pain and suffering, as a result, appears significant. As he stated elsewhere, what is harmful to weak minds is innocuous for the strong (by which he presumably meant heroic figures, such as he hoped or claimed to be himself).

Nietzsche did not, however, cling for long to the extremely critical views expressed in *Menschliches – Allzumenschliches*. In *Morgenröte* [*Dawn*] he believed that art was able to equip men for the adventure of living (N, I, 117if.). Yet again his attitude is ambivalent. Art has to be rejected since it is hostile to intellectual integrity, and yet it is the only effective weapon with which to fight the principle of integrity that destroys life; for the quest for objectivity is a mistake. It is impossible to attain objectivity, and the belief that we can do so is but another delusion. Moreover, man cannot always be logical and rational; he needs continuously to return to nature, and this means to illogicality.

Nor did Nietzsche at that time always clearly distinguish between modern art and Wagnerian art which he detested and great art (pre-Socratic art) which he admired. At times it seems as if he consigned all art to a place below philosophy, at others he appears to differentiate. But consistency was never one of his virtues. However, by the time he wrote *Also sprach Zarathustra* he had – again for obvious autobiographical reasons – shifted his ground; for after all, he saw himself as a poet when writing that work.

Art – so he thinks at this stage – is still dangerous. He says: 'The poets lie too much' (N, II, p. 382). They do not know enough – they are not scholars, hence they have to tell lies, and, indeed, much of what they say is suspect, poisonous or at best superficial. Yet Zarathustra, Nietzsche's spokesman, is a poet himself, as he admits in a moment of self-indictment (N, II, p. 383).

V

Nietzsche oscillates continuously between despair at the artist's essential mendacity, on the one hand, and praise of the potential value of poetry, on the other. This uncertainty is rooted in his fundamental conviction that art is semblance and cannot do justice to life. And it is needed to vindicate life and make it bearable. In the last year of his sanity he attempted to resolve the problem by emphasising the indispensable character of real art and by distinguishing it sharply from modern art as practised by Wagner and other decadent artists.

The sense of truth and the love of life itself are in conflict and the practice of art is one way of attempting to solve this conflict. So Nietzsche returns to his early belief that art exists for the purpose of making life bearable. Art is then a metaphysical activity. But Nietzsche is not consistent in equating the importance of art with the intellectual search for truth; for the will to semblance strikes him as deeper than the impulse for truth. For truth is ugly and thus frightening; we have art so that we may not perish through truth. Art is necessary, not only because it serves life, but because it is inevitably interwined with the search for truth. And thus the ambiguity of Nietzsche's position is revealed. Suspicious of art, he still feels himself to be an artist – the artist's role is complex. On the one hand, he appears given to vanity and superficiality and is inferior to those who know what is true, but, on the other, he is superior to the latter since their knowledge is, in the last resort, mistaken, too, and the artist at least has the freedom of play. The rivalry between art and knowledge then dominates Nietzsche's work and is never finally resolved;[39] again and again he returns to the expectations glorified in the *Geburt der Tragödie*. He looks forward to the future when the right kind of artist will arise. But however ambiguous his view of art and the artist, in one respect he never wavers; he is adamant and persistent in his conviction of the primacy of life over all manifestations of mind. In the last resort, art, and thus also the artist, derive value from life. It is worth while only if it affirms life, inspires it with strength and makes existence heroic. Only then has it fulfilled its task.

Nietzsche thus returns to an early position held before he completed the *Geburt der Tragödie*; for in his inaugural lecture *Homer und die Klassische Philologie* [*Homer and Classical Scholarship*] (1869) he had already given art and scholarship equal weight, but his inability to persist in this view points to a basic unease. He was never content with any of the positions which he adopted. Of course, he never realised that these vacillations arose from his basic approach to the whole problem, from his denigrating scientific thought when arguing in a manner that belonged to a scientific tradition. He did not apprehend that this way of looking at art, truth and the world were just as little likely to solve the problems under discussion as when he wrote poetry in order to advance philosophical arguments. He was never content with the house which he had built; this discontent was as fruitful as it was frustrating and irksome.

Art then is necessary. It is no longer opposed to truth, but complementary to it. Nietzsche thus continuously seeks to reconcile art and truth and reconcile either or both of them with life. He denies the possibility of truth, but acknowledges its necessity. He doubts the truthfulness of art, but he asserts its value. He denies that intellectual enquiry can yield truth and yet he engages in intellectual enquiry. He is dissatisfied with his intellectual argumentation, and turns to poetry for assistance, only to turn away again from poetry to discursive prose. Nietzsche never entirely escapes from the dilemma in which his original view of art and the artist placed him. His very inconsistency provided a challenge and that is why he is so seminal a writer.

3 Stefan George (1868–1933)

Stefan George was a great poet. Through friendship and precept he directly influenced a number of gifted writers, academics and intellectuals who formed that loose, influential conglomeration usually called the *George-Kreis*,[1] and so played an important role in German social and intellectual history. He attacked the prevailing tendencies of his time. Inevitably, like all those who oppose established or fashionable values and currents of thought he was much criticised. Of late, he also been accused of lack of social and political commitment.[2] Much of the criticism, and some of the adulation, has been undiscerning and insensitive. Still, his ideal of a chosen elite has, however much it attracted some, understandably repelled many.

George's reputation has, to some extent, become the victim of his own way of life, of his belief in his own superiority, not only as a poet, but as a man, whose unusual style of living, coupled with an imperious manner, set him apart from the common multitude and attracted an entourage which claimed to be a spiritual and intellectual aristocracy and which protected him against the world at large. George himself, somewhat ironically, called the circle that gathered around him 'the state'. Its membership changed, the connections between its members were loose; as time passed, some were expelled, or rather banished from the sight of the master, others in turn were admitted or co-opted after his approval had been given. No explicit code of conduct prevailed, but unwritten rules which it was hazardous to break, for to do so might earn reproof, if not total exclusion from the circle, a fate not to be courted by its members.

The intellectual stature of this group, inevitably, varied. The first members were, in the main, poets and writers, including even one gifted foreign poet, Albert Verwey (1865–1937), a Dutchman.[3] Later on scholars were admitted and, as time went on, gifted and sensitive younger men, not necessarily poets or scholars took the place of some of the older ones. The story of the *George-Kreis* is fascinating, though strange. Some of its members, like Karl Wolfskehl (1869–1948), the poet, and Friedrich Gundolf (1880–1931), the Heidelberg professor of German literature, were well known; others far less so. Nazism divided them, as it did many

Germans. Some were sympathisers, while others, especially the many Jewish members, emigrated, and some joined the resistance. One of the youngest members, and a close disciple at that, was Claus Schenk Count Stauffenberg, who on 20 July 1944 planted the bomb which unfortunately failed to kill Hitler.

George did not succeed in winning over any other great poet to join him in his literary enterprise. Hugo von Hofmannsthal, the Austrian poet, rejected his overtures in 1892 after which an uneasy relationship continued for almost a decade and a half;[4] Hofmannsthal contributed poems to *Blätter für die Kunst*,[5] the journal founded by George and edited by his disciple Carl August Klein (1867–1952), until in 1906, George finally broke with him. Once their relationship had grown cool, George criticised Hofmannsthal's later work severely. To criticise was not unusual for him, for he had no use at all for most contemporary German writing. He condemned the work of Thomas Mann, as, indeed, he deprecated all novel writing. In Rilke he saw no more than a poet of promise and did not appreciate his genius when it flowered.[6] His conception of poetry was so idiosyncratic that he was unable to approve any contemporary German work that was not moulded by him or did not at least tally with his preconceptions.

I

But what was George's view of art? His reflections on poetry and on the poet's task are, in fact, intermittent. None the less both his own signed remarks and the reflections published in the *Blätter für die Kunst* (which, since he virtually controlled the journal, closely reflect his own ideas) consistently champion an unmistakable position, even if they neither precisely define it nor amount to a cogently reasoned argument.

From his early days onward, George wanted to be a poet, and as such felt apart from and superior to the world. The poet's task was heroic; he had to write poetry that transformed life by way of art. To do so entailed selfless devotion, but it was also a source of pride; for the true poet served beauty with a genuine passion.[7] Of course, George was fortunate that first the generosity of his father, a well-to-do vineyard owner, and later the help of wealthy friends enabled him to devote all his life to the pursuit of poetry.

George never wavered in his belief that poetry was paramount. Without it nothing else was of value. His cosmopolitanism fostered by travels in his youth to London and to Italy confirmed his conviction. For he had found intellectual life at Berlin University, then at the height of its academic renown, disappointing; he had a Nietzschean contempt for German bourgeois life and culture.[8] The Germany of his day did not provide him with any intellectual and artistic stimulus at all. It was dull by comparison with the society of Mallarmé and other French poets with whom he had become acquainted in Paris and felt a spiritual kinship. But French symbolist poetry was not the only influence. Earlier poets – Homer, Dante,

Petrarch, Shakespeare, Goethe, Jean Paul, Novalis, Platen and, at a later stage, Hölderlin – also affected his thought and poetic practice.

To say, however, that poetry mattered to George is not enough. George and his friends claimed far more for poetry than is usual. The poet had to be at the pinnacle of culture, indeed, of society itself. Nothing less would do. Poetry like George's was a momentous event whose consequences were far-reaching; for it could transform a whole culture. A poet like George was seen as a touchstone by which a whole civilisation was to be judged. Only if his values were accepted and his warnings and precepts heeded, only if he was seen as the great spiritual leader, could German culture be saved.

The task facing George was, like his achievement, unique. Earlier poets had been able to draw sustenance from an untilled and unexhausted soil, but a modern poet had to dig much deeper, to draw forth the strength for the creation of great art.

George's own self-appraisal was shared by his disciples. They revered him. This reverence was apparently fostered by George himself, who seems to have needed and enjoyed primacy of attention. Their respect for him knew no bounds: they believed him to be not only a great poet, but the greatest German poet since Goethe and Hölderlin who, alone in German literature, could, so they thought, be ranked as his peers. They went even further: George had achieved more than any poet before him; he had not only continued Goethe's work, but reached depths uncharted by him. Likewise, however intense Hölderlin's vision had been, George's achievement surpassed his. He was indeed the culmination of the great heroes of European culture, literature and life. His true predecessors were Homer, Alexander the Great, Caesar, Dante, Shakespeare, Goethe and Napoleon. Thus, cult of genius was necessary, they thought, since all liberating ideas, like all great art, have always emerged from the initiated who, by way of habit and tradition, form secret associations. Therefore, George was always intent on initiating a few chosen disciples who alone were capable of acquiring knowledge and whose commitment to art and the life of the spirit had to be fostered. To foster an elite did not mean, so George thought, that an artist lost touch with the people. On the contrary, in later ages, those who know what matters would recognise that he alone spoke for the culture of the whole nation and ensured its cultural greatness; for poets are the true leaders and the conscience of any age. A poet is no less than Caesar, indeed, he may be the Caesar of the age. To appreciate great poetry, such as George hoped to write – and later on thought he wrote – is more important than commitment to the ephemeral issues of the day, for it makes men aware of the right values. Indeed, a true European culture can prevail only if the right values are recognised and heeded and if a tradition embodying these values has been fostered for generations (cf. Bl., III, p. 35). Poetry is, then, the key to successful living and political and cultural prosperity.

These views are, to say the least, extreme. Some disciples went even further. The historian Friedrich Wolters claimed in his monumental, hagiographical book *Stefan George und die Blätter für die Kunst: Deutsche Geistesgeschichte seit 1890* (Berlin, 1930) that the story of George's work and of the *Blätter für die Kunst* constitutes the real German intellectual and literary history of their period. This contention is so mistaken as not to merit discussion.

George was, then, a poet with a mission, a conviction that moulded his life and to which he subordinated all other concerns. Whence did this belief in his mission arise? And what were the values for which he stood and which he wished to impart? The belief sprang from George's faith in his own spiritual and intellectual powers and poetic genius, as well as from the conviction that since the age was corrupt, decadent and hence doomed, it needed to be redeemed by a great poet. Like Nietzsche, he rebelled against his age and castigated it severely. False voices, so George maintained, were being heeded. Spiritual values had been undermined, though he hardly specified precisely what particular values he had in mind. His assertions and demands alike remained vague. All writing was in need of reform, public opinion was hopelessly confused, blind to true worth and esteeming poor poetry. Above all, the prevailing belief in progress was mistaken. Progress is indeed often no more than destruction of the environment (*Raubbau*) (Bl. IX, p. 4), an insight likely to please the environmentalists, even if George's main concern was always the spiritual realm rather than the world of nature or society. Sustenance and strength have to be taken from other worlds. We must ensure that the products of this world are not being abused in the here and now. The fundamental laws of life have to be respected. In George's view, enlightenment and applied technology ignore these basic laws. Anglo-American commonsense and utilitarian assumptions are particularly naive and oversimplify complex issues, a view echoing Romantic ideas. Men steeped in these wrong preconceptions mistakenly believe that scientific discovery is more important than art. They also believe that men can live without real values. Those however who are able to understand these basic laws of life realise that George and his school are not decadent or alienated from life, but are aware of what really matters – Indeed, the use of the term 'decadence' implies the existence of higher values that have to be rescued (Bl. II, p. 33) from the prevailing vulgarity and base condition of contemporary writing (Bl. I, p. 130). Of this George's art conveys symbolic information. But what the laws of life are we are never told. Presumably we have to turn to poetry to grasp these truths intuitively.

The age, then, needed George, but it did not seem ready for him. Nor was it certain that it would respond fully, whole-heartedly and responsibly to the clarion-call if it came. Still, it is doubtful whether George ever envisaged that the age or the German nation would do so. Of course, George did want to reform, indeed, to revolutionise German poetry, but, at first at least, not necessarily German society.

To write poetry meant to master language.[9] George had always wanted to do that. Yet language was something else as well: it was a means of mastering others – indeed the world, as he encountered it. To do this the German language had to be cleansed – by exercising and establishing the right use of the word. These two features – cleansing and mastering the world – are of course different, but they were, for George, different aspects of the same endeavour. After an early attempt at drama, soon to be seen as an uncongenial and untimely mode of literary expression, poetry and literature came to mean for him lyric poetry alone. But existing lyric poetry – and with it all literature in German in 1890 – seemed inadequate.

George's criticism was not unfounded. The greatest German prose-writer of the previous twenty years, Nietzsche, was virtually unknown when George began to write in the late eighteen-eighties. Conrad Ferdinand Meyer (1825–98), the major Swiss symbolist poet, was still alive, but he lived outside the mainstream of literary events and his work was not appreciated then as it is now. The prominent school of poetry of the day was the Munich school. Under the leadership of Emanuel Geibel, the Lübeck poet who had for some years been a resident in Munich, this school is now known for pleasing, but not truly great poetry; for these poets were content to preserve literary traditions and did not strike out on new paths of their own. Thus, their poetry appears sterile. For George, however, poor poetry was pernicious. It destroyed spiritual life. Hence the need for a poetic revolution. This demand had also been made by the Naturalists, and for a while, as a young man, George sympathised with their aims, though not with their methods. He had established contact with some of them and was present at the performance of Gerhard Hauptmann's *Vor Sonnenaufgang* [*Before Sunrise*] in 1889 at Otto Brahm's *Freie Bühne* when the battle for Naturalism broke out into the open. But he soon dissociated himself from the movement and from that time onward had only scorn for its activities. The loud fanfares of Naturalism, so he then thought, failed to achieve what its advocates and practitioners had set out to do. He admitted, with some hauteur, that even Naturalism had some good qualities. But by concentrating on details, the Naturalists gave them undue importance. They mistook a part of reality for the whole, thus making it impossible to create great works of art which must, by implication, concern themselves with that which is essential. To believe, as the Naturalists did, that everyday reality comprised the whole of experience was fundamentally mistaken. In contrast, George demanded: 'Spiritual art based on a new mode of feeling and novel manner of writing' (Bl. 1, p. 1).[10]

The desire to rescue culture by reviving poetry recalls Nietzsche's argument in the *Geburt der Tragödie*, a book which George may not have known at the time, but which he later on claimed to be Nietzsche's greatest work.[11] But Nietzsche and George differed in strategy, and not only because Nietzsche, in his early period, believed that the cultural revival would be brought about by Wagnerian opera or its successor while George put his faith in the power of lyric poetry. Their approach, too, was different. Nietzsche assaulted his age first as a scholar, then as an essayist, and finally as an aphorist, but never, even in *Also sprach Zarathustra*, primarily as a poet. His lyrical poetry remained incidental. George did not believe that success in public affairs could be achieved by bombarding the age with pamphlets. To speak in prose was to descend to a lower level of argument, not appropriate to a poet. Thus, he criticised Nietzsche precisely for his philosophising in prose, and later ended his poem 'Nietzsche' with those own words of self-criticism which Nietzsche had, in retrospect, applied to the *Geburt der Tragödie* (N I, p. 2) 'It should have sung, not spoken, that new soul' (G, I, p. 232). Poetry, thus, provided the sole criterion of judgement on life (cf., for instance, Bl. III, p. 33).

What matters is song. For song survives, not views or deeds. People change their views, their deeds are forgotten, but songs are perennial. However, only the good poem lasts. It is not easily written. George therefore counselled fastidiousness and warned against premature publication. For if the poet does not find the form adequate to his ideas he will betray them; indeed, it may be impossible to find the right form later (Bl. III, p. 34). It is not merely a matter of finding the truth, but of excluding everything unnecessary from language and giving a poem the right splendour, through polishing, purifying and cleansing its language. It was also imperative to bring out the plasticity of language and to teach poets the need for linguistic craftsmanship.[12] To make was to select. Although the basis of poetic inspiration was intuitive and unconscious the material of each poem had to be thoroughly turned into form so that this formal power becomes apparent even in the least important part of the work. The poem had thus to be seen as a well-organised, indeed, as an organic, whole. It had also to be symbolic.[13] Under the influence of Mallarmé and his school, George believed that art does not represent the general by means of the particular as it did for Goethe, but it sets out to evoke a deeper meaning. This symbolism was the necessary consequence of 'spiritual maturity and depth'. (Bl. II, p. 33)

Symbolism requires poetry which is not sectarian, but exists for the sake of the highest spiritual satisfaction. It may portray personal experience, but it does so indirectly. Thus Vogelschau [Augury]; the last poem of *Algabal*, a cycle of poetry published in 1892, sums up the poet's experiences depicted in the whole of the cycle, but also intimates how his achievement in recording these experiences in his poetry has resulted in spiritual change and the renewal of his poetic power.

VOGELSCHAU

Weisse schwalben sah ich fliegen
Schwalben schnee – und silberweiss
Sah sie sich im winde wiegen
In dem winde hell und heiss.

Bunte häher sah ich hüpfen
Papagei und kolibri
Durch die wunder-bäume schlüpfen
In dem wald der Tusferi.

Grosse raben sah ich flattern
Dohlen schwarz und dunkelgrau
Nah am grunde über nattern
Im verzauberten gehau.

Schwalben seh ich wieder fliegen
Schnee- und silberweisse schar
Wie sie sich im winde wiegen
In dem winde kalt und klar![14]

In this poem little is said explicitly. The reader is given only an image, or a set of images, reflecting spiritual change and renewal – and much else is evoked as well.[15] The poet relies entirely on the power of language to capture attention and to make the reader ponder all the implications. As always with George, the poetry is immeasurably more powerful and convincing than his theoretical statements, as he knew himself; for he was extremely economical in promulgating his theories.

Sibylline writing, he was convinced, is better than clear statement. Poetic language needs to be different (Bl. II, p. 34) from normal speech. It needs to be selective and to satisfy the canons of sonorousness, proportion and the demands of rhyme (Bl. II, p. 34). Free rhythm is rejected. A rhyme once used becomes rapidly worthless by repetition; hence rhymes have to be used sparingly (Bl. II, p. 35). Only thus can the abuse of language be avoided. George, then rejected prosaic language and carelessness of style, such as he found in the work of Richard Dehmel (1863–1920), a popular poet of the period.[16] For him, poetry was to be different from ordinary speech, as different, indeed, as language permitted.

This could not be otherwise, George maintained, for few German poets had so far had an ear for assonance and rhythm, necessary for great poetry. These qualities had usually been associated with poetry in Latin and Romance languages, and not with German poetry. In keeping with his own views and talent George valued the chiselled poetry of August Count Platen (1796–1835) much more than poets or critics had done before him. And of later nineteenth-century poets he esteemed only Conrad Ferdinand Meyer, whose fastidious pursuit of formal perfection he respected. For George's taste, although informed by wide reading and a remarkable knowledge of language (he translated from French, English, Italian, Spanish, Norwegian, Danish, Dutch, Polish and, in his early youth, from Ancient Greek, and he also knew Latin, of course) was by no means catholic. He rejected much poetry usually highly (and justly) esteemed by literary historians of repute. His choice for the three volumes of German literature he edited reveals his peculiar point of view. He totally rejected many poets, including Schiller and Heine – he thought the former too rhetorical and the latter too easy-going and journalistic. Against this he included Jean Paul [Friedrich Richter] (1763–1825), an idiosyncratic poetic prose-writer, a highly unusual choice for that time. Goethe indeed he accepted, but gave short shrift to the *Sturm und Drang* poems, usually so popular with anthologists, and had no room for Goethe's Rococo poetry, for his recreations of folk-song, or for most of his ballads. George concentrated – and this too was highly unorthodox at the time – on Goethe's mature and later poetry.

George's regard for form was rooted in his life and personality. In his youth he developed a private language, known only to himself, into which he translated the first cantos of the *Odyssey* (the notebook containing the first translation was destroyed by his literary executors after his death). This language, to judge by the two lines preserved in the late poem *Ursprünge* [*Origins*] (G, I, p. 295), was very sonorous, calling up associations with Romance languages and Ancient Greek. Presumably his practising this secret tongue helped him to develop his mastery of the art of translation and his own style of poetry. Similarly, he created a 'lingua romana' based, in the main, though by no means exclusively, on Spanish. He wrote poetry in that esoteric language just as he did in French, and some of his early German poems are translations from his own private language or from French. Indeed, he may well have written poetry in other languages before he wrote in German.

George was born a Roman Catholic, and he first profoundly experienced sound and poetry in a majestic setting, that of of the liturgy of the Church, an experience to which the short prose piece of *Der Kindliche Kalender* [*the Child's Calendar*] bears witness (G, I, pp. 479–81). Of course, this upbringing did not differ materially from that of many others poets, but on George the impact was deep and lasting. The atmosphere of Divine Service became for him an example which he expected his own poetry to follow. The strength and sonorousness came to express for him something sacred.[17] Indeed, more than that, as religious faith waned, poetry took the place of religion and became sacredness itself. Thus, George fostered a myth which he needed and which accounted for his astounding sense of superiority and his disdain for the views of others.

For George, poetry (provided it is good poetry) needs formal perfection and majesty resembling liturgy. It therefore has to be different from everyday life and language. Like religion, it dwells at higher altitudes. George invoked this conviction to justify his own style, a style that presumably suited his natural inclinations.

Although George took over the motto 'Art for Art's sake' from the Parnassian movement in France he interpreted it in a different way from the Parnassians. He knew of their limitations: their poetry did not reveal the

the sense of mission which inspired his work. But he was prepared to learn from the Parnassians' method, from their attempts to achieve 'plasticity of language'.[18]

George's belief in great poetry expressing absolute truths and values reveals his debt to the Platonic tradition.[19] But George is never precise in stating what specific truth his poetry is to reveal, nor does he argue the case for the autonomy of art in any detail; rather he explicitly rejects all art that has rules or follows a programme as not genuine at all.

George's manner of writing is to be radically different. The injuction 'Poems are not the reproduction of an idea, but of a mood' [*Stimmung*] (Bl. II, p. 34) heralds this new approach. It is neither contemplation, nor does it offer entertainment, nor does it report fact, but it conveys impressions which the poet experienced. Yet the aim of George's poetry is not to show feeling, and he wishes to turn his back on moral issues since they have lost all value. He is concerned with events only as a means for artistic stimulus. Of course, we must not necessarily accept this belief at face-value. George certainly did not seek to avoid value-judgements and his values were by no means only aesthetic ones, as is revealed by his condemnation of his age. But poetry was not to enter directly into the political arena. Nor was it to raise moral issues openly. Form had, as Schiller had enjoined, to consume the material. And hence symbolism was necessary. Forceful and direct expression of feeling is no proof of genuineness or depth or truth or importance. To shout loudly is a sign of immaturity or of an attempt to persuade the reader to accept falsehoods. The smooth and chiselled form of his own poems was deceptive. For it concealed his rebellion against society, his protest and deep feelings which were more powerful than polemics could ever hope to be.

Genuine poetic power is achieved only by control and sublimation of feeling. Art is neither pain, nor sensuous delight, but triumph of form (G, I, p. 537). Nietzsche's injunction, 'write with blood', has to be understood in this way, for otherwise he would have exhorted poets to write with 'red ink' (G, I, p. 532).

Art, then, exists for its own sake. Beauty is neither the beginning nor the end of art, but the climax.[20] Beauty means selection, not merely of theme, but also of words. George sought to avoid emptiness of speech, he sought to banish not only jargon or slogans, but also foreign loan words. If they were excluded nothing was lost to the language. To purify and improve language George wished to use words in their original German meaning. Equally, he was quite willing to coin new words or to use words in an unusual manner. Moreover, the outward appearance of a poem mattered.[21] Following the injunction and example of the brothers Jacob and Wilhelm Grimm, the great philologists, George disdained using capitals for nouns, save at the beginning of a sentence or in proper names, thus departing from customary German usage. He had also an idiosyncratic use of punctuation. For instance, he did not use commas. His spelling, too, was

different from common usage. Moreover, the typographical appearance of *« preint !*
the poem mattered. The external appearance of a work of art as such is not
to be a matter of no consequence.

All such stratagems were deployed to prepare the ground for the rise of a
future culture. But quick results were not to be expected; indeed, the
reactions of many of the contemporary men of letters, critics and scholars
almost proved, in George's view, the worth of the movement set in train by
him (Bl. III, p. 132); for they did not, in contrast to George, understand
what was afoot in society and art. Unlike George and his disciples, these
men were unrealistic and escapist. For to strive to write good poetry, to
write inspired by 'the delight of working at words, by ecstasy and sound
and sun' (Bl. III, p. 2) was the only way in which a poet could carry out his
task in the world. It was by far the most meaningful way to answer the
challenge of the day.

George's insistence on form earned him the reproach that he turned his
back on German culture and courted foreign culture. But his reply was
confident; he took the view that the German spirit cannot take from the
Nordic spirit (he here implicitly accepted this nebulous terminology) what
it does not already possess. It can learn from the Romance world, however.
For there it can find qualities, such as clarity, broadness of mind and
genuineness. In responding to the stimulus offered by the Romance world,
George and the poets accepting his lead were, so they believed, following a
historical tradition established by the Holy Roman Emperors (whom he
considered cultural and political heroes) and were thus acting in a manner
which was natural to the German mind. George was never backward in
staking high claims.

II

Such were the views of the early George, formulated in the first decade of
his creative writing. He did not come to them as easily as his self-asured
manner may suggest. His first volumes of poetry of quality, in particular
Algabal and *Das Jahr der Seele* [*The Year of the Soul*] (1897), tell of the inner
strain occasioned by his endeavour to blaze a trail as a poet. Indeed, most
of his poems and cycles of poetry deal, in some measure, with his struggle to
understand and come to terms with his poetic task.

It is not easy to cull ideas from this early poetry. Interpretation of all
poetry, like all interpretation, is hypothetical, but symbolist poetry has
additional hazards. The evidence it affords is most elusive and calls for
added circumspection. George's poetry alludes frequently and obviously
to the problems arising from the poet's task, but it is difficult to pin the
utterances down to an exact meaning.

Hymnen [*Hymns*] (1890), the volume published first (a volume of early
verse, *Die Fibel*, was published only in 1901 when George had become a
well-established literary figure), shows the poet detached from his world.[22]

The last lines of the poem 'Im Park' ['In the Park'] sum up this stance:

> Der dichter auch der töne lockung lauscht.
> Doch heut darf ihre weise nicht ihn rühren
> Weil er mit seinen geistern rede tauscht:
>
> Er hat den griffel der sich sträubt zu führen.[23]

It is as if he regards the world as a spectacle. It is not poetry describing an experience, but rhetorical poetry. His task is stated: as a solitary man he is not moved by nature, by the here and now, but he has to concentrate on the task of poetry. He has to wield the recalcitrant pen.

In the next volume, *Pilgerfahrten* [*Pilgrimages*] (1891), the search for poetry is described. The poet does not doubt the value of his ideal, but he wonders whether he will have the strength to realise it in practice. To carry out his purpose he needs to be an ascetic, for poetry requires the concentration of all his faculties.[24] But it is more than that: art is a religion; his poetic vocation is a moral task, and the poet adopts the guise of a religious figure. Still, the poet must accept that the medium which he wishes to fashion may prove recalcitrant and may, as the poem 'Die Spange' ['The Clasp'] indicates, be of a different nature from what the poet had wished.

> Ich wollte sie aus kühlem eisen
> Und wie ein glatter fester streif
> Doch war im schacht auf allen gleisen
> So kein metall zum gusse reif.
>
> Nun aber soll sie also sein:
> Wie eine grosse fremde dolde
> Geformt aus feuerrotem golde
> Und reichem blitzendem gestein.[25]

Thus, the poet also has to rely on the material available and on the medium which he uses. He has to adapt the form to what he finds both within and outside himself. Again and again George evokes in his poetry the poet's feeling of isolation from the world, and he describes his response, the refuge found in the poet's power to create an autonomous realm separated from the world around him. Yet this stance is full of problems which fill the poet with terror. He scrutinises them in his poetry, but above all he examines the use of language itself. The pitfalls threatening the poet are emphasised, particularly that of self-indulgence. Likewise, in *Das Jahr der Seele* the poet's emotional strain and stress and his victory over circumstances form the story of the cycle. Art is seen as a personal matter far removed from any utilitarian purpose, but nothing explicit is stated about art or the artist.

III

In the following period the apparently impossible happened. George grew even more self-assertive, even more certain of the vital importance of his mission. He increasingly felt the need to oppose the prevailing quantitative evaluation by a qualitative appraisal of life. This approach is closely bound up with George's indifference, indeed his hostility, to science. In this respect, he differed fundamentally from Goethe whose greatness is marked by his ability to bring poetry and science together. Furthermore, George rejected – and so did his followers – the standards of objective scholarship championed by Max Weber, the eminent sociologist, whom he met, but whose greatness as a thinker he seems not to have appreciated at all.[26] Following Nietzsche, he repudiated orthodox nineteenth-century scholarship since, in his view, it was incapable of differentiating between appearance and substantiality. In a lapidary sentence he summed up his attitude in a conversation with Kurt Hildebrandt, one of his disciples: 'From me no road leads to science [*Wissenschaft*].'[27] Very much like Nietzsche, too, he demanded synthesis and rejected analysis of details. Indeed, the scholars of the *George-Kreis* wanted to concentrate on the 'whole' – a very vague concept – a grasp of which alone could, so they claimed, guarantee the right approach to culture and history.[28] Not surprisingly their works of monumental biography are idiosyncratic, even though the best among them – Friedrich Gundolf's *Goethe* (Berlin, 1915)[29] and Ernst Kantorowicz's biography of the Hohenstaufen Emperor, *Friedrich II* (Berlin, 1927)[30] – made a powerful impact on the German reading public and are still worth reading.

George's views on politics were similarly idiosyncratic. In his youth he had been indifferent to politics; in later life he observed political events from a distance and had some, but only some, judicious comments to make: in principle, he held almost all politics and politicians in contempt since he did not think that they dealt with what appeared to him the fundamental problems of life which, in his view, were spiritual ones. In this respect he echoes Romantic ideas.

Whether this view of politics is sound is another matter. It certainly led to some curious and mistaken political judgements; for instance, he naively admired Hindenburg and believed him, when President of the Weimar Republic, to be the only man of any calibre in Germany,[31] a mistaken, though widespread and – as events proved – pernicious assumption. At one time during the First World War, he is said to have made the astounding remark to one of his followers, the historian Kurt Breysig, that if events deteriorated further he might eventually have to assume the office of Chancellor of the Reich himself.[32] Apparently there were no bounds to his self-esteem and self-deception. George was certainly not cast in the role of a political leader. Romantic, too, was his belief that to create or appreciate art is a more powerful political weapon than to pursue political polemics (Bl. III, p. 98), or his conviction that political power prevents the regeneration of the spirit, inevitably bringing about unsound politics and an unstable society.[33] More realistic was his refusal in the pre-1914 period to sign an open letter designed to avert an Anglo-German war,[34] as was urged upon him by Hofmannsthal,[35] for experience has shown such appeals to be of no avail; and he was not far off the mark in perceiving that many of the political postures of well-known writers often touched the surface of politics only.

George never promulgated a social or political programme. He appears to have thought that if the right attitude of mind prevailed among the intellectual and spiritual elite the rest would take care of itself. In any case, a political programme would have had to be based on a coherent rational argument. But that was not George's way of championing attitudes of mind or poetry. For he, in the main, relied on poetry and on his personal impact on his disciples.

One particular change of emphasis in his later period stands out, however. The relationship between art and life is differently evaluated. In the early years art was to be kept strictly apart from life. Any concern with the everyday world was ruled out. But from 1896 onward George gradually assumed a different stance, and, in the end, donned the mantle of a prophet, and, perhaps even more strikingly, that of an advocate of action; for it seems as if he wished art to have an impact on life. This impact was to go beyond his circle and be felt by the world at large.

IV

In his later years, George did not so much change his point of view as develop tendencies which were already latent in his mind and thought. While not ceding any of the territory claimed for art, he mapped out a new area where art leaves its imprint on life. If great art is not produced, even the treasures of the past will soon be lost and traditional beauty will no longer be able to speak to us. These dangers are not merely the concern of a few creative individuals, but of a society of like-minded men which will supply the basis of a new literature, in particular a new drama.

George and his followers therefore claimed to be the true educators of the nation. They hoped to continue the campaign abandoned by Nietzsche after his disappointment with Wagner. Germany had failed to attain the cultural level reached by other civilised countries. The Germans had ceased to be good Europeans. Genuine changes had to be brought about so that spiritual barrenness and cultural superficiality would no longer threaten the nation. George now felt himself to be a champion of the future as well as an heir to a great tradition; for he was changing German culture for the better and he was harking back to great figures in German cultural history, such as Goethe and Nietzsche, who had chastised the nation to arouse it to better and stronger efforts. Where others, such as the post-classical poets, had failed in their quest to preserve tradition George hoped to succeed; indeed, he believed he had done so. The proof was there in the *Blätter für die Kunst* for all to see. As early as the preface to the title number of the third volume (October 1898) it is maintained that valuable work had already been achieved amidst the arid and cruel waste of contemporary writing (Bl. III, pp. 129–32). The craftmanship necessary to foster the right spiritual climate for good poetry had been nursed, and there was the great poetry of George for all to see.

George also claimed the sanction of tradition by emphasising the specific characteristics of German culture.[36] He appealed to a tradition, that of Weimar classicism, which he interpreted in his own idiosyncratic way. His conception of the beautiful life, i.e. a life full of measure and harmony, a high-minded cosmopolitanism which brings out the best national virtues and which is steeped in humanism and indebted to Ancient Greece (cf. Bl. IV, p. 4; IX, p. 2), recalls Schiller's conception of aesthetic education,[37] though the argument and general strategy of thought is very different both in intention and in detail. Moreover, his notion of a school of poetry is an attempt to revitalise a Renaissance idea. The message of a beautiful life calls for a new world which does not exist in the present, but which has existed in the past and will exist again in the future.[38] However, this picture of the beautiful life as revealed in the cycle *Der Teppich des Lebens* [*The Tapestry of Life*] (1900) is also an ideal in the tradition of Platonism, an ideal of which human empirical existence is always only a distorted reflection.[39] But this ideal, as the cycle also suggests, allows the poet to acquire new confidence in his art and the ability to accept the insight that his life must be one of toil and renunciation.[40] He wishes to create a new style which is, in the last resort, much more important than political or military victories, more important than conquered provinces.

George here inveighs against political and cultural nationalism, he criticises existing political and social systems and condemns Prussianism (Bl. V, p. 2). He defends the artist against the bourgeois who, on account of their lack of taste, had a perverse sense of aesthetic values (Bl. V, p. 2). But he has no use for naturalism either (Bl. VII, p. 1). The common multitude bases its optimism on the out-of-date views of yesterday (Bl. V, p. 3). It is incapable of appreciating the higher forms of art which are 'neither for hungry bodies nor fat souls' (Bl. VII, p. 5). To believe in political revolution is to embrace yet another outmoded concept. The wrong means cannot create a better world. What is needed is a higher and nobler conception of life, and a more intimate sense of beauty. Poetry alone can create a society whose members are linked together by a common spiritual bond and temper of mind. The foremost task then remains what it was before: the poetic revival, the driving out of sugary and formless bourgeois literature by the renaissance of beauty (Bl. VII, pp. 3ff) and this can be achieved only by poetic perfection. All effort has to be concentrated on attaining this goal. Because the writing of the accomplished 'perfect' poem is a self-sufficient activity (Bl. VII, p. 5), the poet should ignore other considerations.

George, like Nietzsche and the eighteenth-century classical writers from Winckelmann to Goethe, harked back to Ancient Greece. It set the goal for later generations. In Greece not only was perfection found, but truly profound ideas on culture were formulated. The body, that symbol of the ephemeral, became deified. This idea is, for George, the most creative and boldest ever expressed. It alone is worthy of man, much more striking and formidable than any Christian idea. It is right to call it nothing less than the 'Hellenic miracle'. What was manifested in Greece as the creation of the Hellenic spirit is, like Roman Catholicism, a primordial form of being [*urseinsform*] which does not belong to a particular period of history, but is perennial (Bl. IX, p. 3), a view which is attributed to Goethe. For George the Greek belief that the body symbolises God appears the most creative, boldest and greatest idea of history, the one most appropriate to man and more sublime than that of Christianity (Bl. IX, p. 2).

The poetic renaissance was to have Greek culture as its model. Yet antiquity was not superior in all respects. However troubled the present age may be, at least it permits freedom of movement and the ability to live apart from others and free from constraint (Bl. VII, p. 4). Yet George always seeks to look beyond the moment; though he may again and again deplore the prevalence of mass rule, he always sees the artist as standing above 'international, political and social changes as the guardian of eternal fire' (Bl. VII, P. 11); for he is the keeper of spiritual truth and power.

Poets, indeed, have a higher task. True, they are only the guardians, not the creators of the Divine. Yet George may at least implicitly have claimed more, for the conception of the poet creating values and myths, even gods, underlies his poetry and is recounted in the preface to the book *Maximin* (1907). It also informs the thought of *Der siebente Ring* [*The Seventh Ring*] (1907), another cycle of poetry. *Maximin' becomes the central part of*

The Maximin episode is strange in the extreme. George had, in 1902, befriended a poetically gifted young boy of fourteen, Maximilian Kronberger. Maximin, as he called him, died suddenly in 1904 of meningitis at the age of only sixteen. Whatever George may have thought of him when he was alive – and the exact nature of their relationship is not clear – once he had recovered from the first shock of his death, his response was unexpected, indeed, astounding: he decided to celebrate him as a God. As he explained in his preface to *Maximin, Ein Gedenkbuch* (*A Book of Commemoration*) (1907) he had, alluding to Dante, also crossed the midday zenith of his life and was viewing the future with apprehension:

We had just crossed the midday zenith of our life and were afraid at the sight of our immediate future. We were walking towards a mankind that had been disfigured and had grown cold, which boasted of its

multifarious achievements and subtle feelings while the great deed and
great love were disappearing. . . .

A sickness appeared to rage against which no medicine could be found
and which would end with the whole race losing its soul. Already some
were turning away to the dark regions and praised madness as a source
of bliss — others retreated into their dwellings full of sadness or hatred:
when the sudden arrival of one single man amidst the general confusion
gave us back our confidence and filled us with the light of new promises.

(G, I, p. 522)

Neither George nor his friends had the strength necessary to combat the
evils besetting the world. They had been, so he claimed, saved by
Maximin's appearance, for he appeared to represent the ideal which they
had fashioned in their mind. His sudden death cast the poet and his circle,
we learn, into deep sorrow, but the voice of the dead boy spoke to George,
and through poetry Maximin's life and death were given public currency
as a myth. The poet has now a new task: to create a new myth which gives
meaning to the poet's experience. It seems that this myth of Maximin's life
and death mattered more to George than the youth when he was alive.[41]
Be that as it may, George used this experience to give new life and a new
goal to his poetry which, as always, supremely mattered to him. He had
also recourse to ideas which he had gathered from his encounter with the
cosmic movement, a group of men mostly living in Munich of whom some,
but by no means all, were disciples of George. Among them Karl
Wolfskehl, Alfred Schuler (1863–1923) and Ludwig Derleth
(1870–1948) were the main figures. A curious mixture of spiritual longing
and high-flown ideas, on the one hand, and sensuality, on the other,
proliferated.[42] George, as always, turned the ideas to his own use, claiming
wide implications for the myth which he was creating. For, through
poetry, it could be shared by others. Even more, it was the symbol of the
nation's inner soul.

V

All these ideas underlie *Der siebente Ring*, George's most ambitious cycle
of poetry. In the section *Zeitgedichte* [*Poems of Our Times*] he speaks to a few
friends and attacks Prussia, Germany, and the whole of Western
civilisation. He forecasts disaster, but he sees it as a necessity, perhaps even
as a salutary event.[43] He expressly rejects mere aesthetics and stresses that
the poet's concern with wider issues is necessary. Yet without art the poet
would be unable to enter the arena and attack the corruption of society.
Indeed, he can do so only by pointing to and praising the right values and
the right kind of personality which embodies these values. The present age
is at fault; firstly the powers that be are guilty, but so, too, are the masses
who are incapable of understanding and living in accordance with higher

ideas. Poetry matters because it tells the truth to an age unaccustomed to hear it. It alone can sit in judgement.

In the 'Maximin' poems George sets out to deify the body and 'bodify' the god – cf. 'Der Templer' ['The Templar'] (G, I, p. 256) – an ambiguous statement, and deliberately so; for these two attitudes are impossible to reconcile.[44] What George celebrates here is a religion of innocence, of respect for the body. At the same time he makes the body subservient to higher powers, to art. The poet creates a god, i.e. a myth, in order, in the end, to be left with the consciousness of his own solitary state.[45] His own dream or belief is made real in his poetry and through his poetry the divinity of man is asserted.

> Nun geschieht das höchste wunder:
> Fliessen traum und traum zusammen.[46]

The next cycle of poems, *Der Stern des Bundes* [*The Star of the Covenant*] (1913) conveys similar ideas. It speaks of the importance of the birth of the god and the fulfilment which his coming about, reflecting ideas which originated in Oriental mysticism.

> Da kamst du spross aus unsrem eignem stamm
> Schön wie kein bild und greifbar wie kein traum
> Im nackten glanz des gottes uns entgegen:
> Da troff erfüllung aus geweihten händen
> Da ward es licht und alles sehnen schwieg.[47]

The poet's task is however to condemn the age because of its inability to appreciate the spirit implicit in the birth of the god: this lack of awareness tells of a sick age: 'Siech ist der geist tot ist die tat' ['Sick is the spirit, dead is the deed'] (G, I, p. 360). It reveals that quality is not esteemed and that scientific knowledge is preferred to genuine wisdon.

In this cycle the poet tells of what he sees; he seeks to awaken men to awareness. He rejects the world and replaces its preconceptions by the myth created through his poetry. Spirit and matter are divided in the modern world, but poetry is to state the need for ending this unhappy division and achieving unity. Poetry does not merely evoke and even create a realm of the spirit; it also fosters in the elect to whom the poet speaks the readiness imperative in times of disaster. War is seen as a scourge necessary to rouse men from their spiritual corruption. Indeed, civilisation has to be destroyed before a new culture can, Phoenix-like, arise from the ashes, an event which poetry, as we have been abundantly told before, alone can bring about.

After the end of the First World War, in 1919, the last two issues of the *Blätter für die Kunst* were published in a single volume. Success was claimed;

a tradition of poetry and thought, of myth and belief, had been created in
the twenty-seven years since the publication of the first number, a tradition
which was still productive and guarded the nation's true character (Bl.
XI – XII, pp. 5f). Three generations, so it was maintained, had spoken aloud
in its pages. This work stood in striking contrast to the chaos prevailing in
the world – a chaos that arose because the warnings of men like Nietzsche
had been ignored (Bl. XI/XII, p. 6). But in the age of confusion the truth is
not listened to and the whole enterprise of the *Blätter für die Kunst* had not
been heeded by the many.

Similar ideas inform George's last volume of poetry *Das neue Reich* [*The New
Realm*] (1928). George here sums up his ideas. He sees himself as successor
of Goethe and Hölderlin. Gifted with a deeper insight than Goethe and a
more realistic sense than Hölderlin he can establish a new myth like
Hölderlin and give it universal currency, such as Goethe gave to his ideas;
for like Hölderlin, he has succeeded in breaking up language and
concentrating it anew. The poet's task is to praise and to condemn, to pray
and to atone. He is to forecast the future where one a day a new culture will
arise, the image of which the poet guards. The poet alone is the seer who
perceives what is really happening, but as he is not listened to there will not
be an order that gives meaning to life. As he states in the poem 'Der Dichter
in Zeiten der Wirren' ('The Poet in Times of Confusion').

> Wenn alle blindheit schlug er einzig seher
> Enthüllt umsonst die nahe not. . dann mag
> Kassandra-warnen heulen durch das haus
> Die tollgewordne menge sieht nur eins:
> Das pferd das pferd! und rast in ihren tod . . .[48]

George feels the whole misery and shame, but he alone is able to keep
values alive by making sure that the true symbol is proclaimed, the symbol
which will plant the seed of the new realm.

> Und wenn im schlimmsten jammer lezte hoffnung
> Zu löschen droht: so sichtet schon sein aug
> Die lichtere zukunft.[49]

VI

Stefan George did not reach the goal which he had set himself early in life
when, as a youth, he rebelled against the world as he found it and which he
never abandoned – that is, not surprisingly, he failed to attain the aim of
regenerating or saving the world through poetry; indeed we may even
consider it a mistaken aim, though we may do well to remember the faun's
warning in one of George's last poems 'Der Mensch und der Drud' ['Man
and Faun'], viz. that 'nur durch den zauber bleibt das leben wach' ['it is

only through magic that life stays awake'] (G, I, p. 432) – a teaching that
implicitly informs the work of Max Weber, his great contemporary.[50]
George himself however was convinced that the poet alone could dispense
magic; for he was the sole custodian of values and real knowledge in a
world that had lost its magic and power to enchant.

Whatever view we may take of George's claims – and they are unusual,
to say the least – his great poetry reminds us, through the fog of his ideas, of
the need to pay attention to imaginative insights, of the human need for
beauty and for aesthetic experience and, above all, of the power which
poetry can exert on spiritual life even in an apparently disenchanted
world. He himself gave expression to that magic power in most of his
poems, in none perhaps more memorably than in the opening poem of *Das
Jahr der Seele*:

> Komm in den totgesagten park und schau:
> Der schimmer ferner lächelnder gestade
> Der reinen wolken unverhofftes blau
> Erhellt die weiher und die bunten pfade.
>
> Dort nimm das tiefe gelb das weiche grau
> Von birken und von buchs der wind ist lau
> Die späten rosen welken noch nicht ganz
> Erlese küsse sie und flicht den kranz
>
> Vergiss auch diese lezten astern nicht.
> Den purpur um die ranken wilder reben
> Und auch was übrig blieb von grünem leben
> Verwinde leicht im herbstlichen gesicht.[51]

4 Hugo Von Hofmannsthal (1874–1929)

Hugo von Hofmannsthal is probably best known to the world at large as the librettist of *Der Rosenkavalier* (1909), in which the brilliance and power of Richard Strauss's music is so felicitously matched to an enchanting text. Indeed, few twentieth-century dramatic works have been so widely acclaimed as that delightful, bewitching masterpiece; and, of course, for opera lovers, Hofmannsthal exists as Strauss's librettist since their fruitful cooperation extended over more than two decades until Hofmannsthal's untimely death at the age of fifty-five. During that period they produced together a number of well-known operas, including *Ariadne auf Naxos* (1911), *Die Frau ohne Schatten* (1913) and *Arabella* (1929). But Hofmannsthal was also a poet of the first rank. He sprang to fame when he published his first verse under the pseudonym of Loris. This early poetry seemed to reveal a rare maturity. The Austrian writer Hermann Bahr tells the story (doubtless duly stylised) that he expected a man in his fifties when he arranged to meet 'Loris' for the first time and, much to his surprise, he encountered a schoolboy of just seventeen. Stefan George believed the young Hofmannsthal to be his peer as a lyrical poet and hoped to revolutionise German poetry in league with him. However, his overtures frightened Hofmannsthal. They appeared too impassioned, tempestuous and imperious, demanding too much. Although capable, as his letters reveal, of intense friendship as well as of enjoying the stimulus and the company of others, Hofmannsthal always needed his own private sphere of independence into which he could retreat if he felt in the least imposed on. So soon, at their second meeting, in January 1892, he rebuffed George, which George took very badly. And Hofmannsthal's father had to intervene to compose the quarrel.

Nor did George's itinerant life appeal to Hofmannsthal who, at an early age (in 1901, after his marriage) was able to purchase an eighteenth-century baroque country house in Rodaun near Vienna, where he lived, in style, though not extravagantly, keeping up a flat in town as well. A doctorate in French literature had prepared him for a life of self-cultivation marked by wide, discerning reading and profound aesthetic sense. However, the post-1919 inflation made life very difficult for him, but he was still able to stay in Rodaun where he led an exemplary family life until the shock of his eldest son's suicide disturbed him so profoundly that it precipitated his death; he suffered a stroke at the very moment when he was setting out for the funeral. The manner of his death proved that his praise of sensitivity was not mere shallow rhetoric.

I

Hofmannsthal was, indeed, a man of extreme sensibility who, unlike George, was not content merely to write lyric poetry or even lyrical drama. He felt the need to speak to a wider public, to tackle problems relating to man's relations with others and with society, for which drama seemed the appropriate form. Although his early success as a lyric poet makes him, together with George and Rilke, one of the three great poets of that generation whose first writings appeared in the nineties, he was in fact for almost all of his creative life a dramatist rather than a lyric poet. He wrote virtually no lyric poetry or even lyrical drama after 1900 when he had become fully aware of the problematic nature of language and poetry summed up so powerfully in his *Ein Brief* [*A Letter* – by Lord Chandos] (1902). He created work that was less self-centred, more objective, and more securely anchored in life and in the social sphere; this meant for him adopting traditional forms and writing plays that could be staged successfully. Apart from writing librettos (an activity that gave his work a much wider currency than it might have otherwise enjoyed) he wrote many plays, in particular some superb comedies; *Der Schwierige* [*The Difficult Man*] (1921) is his masterpiece in that genre and one of the great comedies in the German language. He also wrote several festival dramas, among which his version of *Jedermann* [*Everyman*] (1911) became one of the mainstays of the Salzburg festival, and appealed to a very wide audience.

But Hofmannsthal was not only a lyric poet and dramatist. He was also an essayist of note. It is no accident that his most famous essay, the '*Chandos Letter*', is addressed to Francis Bacon, who, with Montaigne, is the progenitor of the essay as a genre in European literature. Hofmannsthal's essays are very different from those of Montaigne and Bacon,[1] however. He is not an original thinker like either of the two great Renaissance writers. His mind was too receptive to strike out new paths. He was too much of a poet in temperament and outlook ever to be an abstract thinker of note. He lacked the forthrightness and vigour of thought which characterise, for instance, Lessing or Schiller. Also, in his essays, he deliberately eschewed the discursive mode of writing, for it did not suit his mind. In the main, he preferred to be allusive. He distrusted abstract reasoning which – and we shall examine his reasons more closely later – in his view, (and here he is close to Nietzsche) was incapable of both penetrating to the core of a problem and conveying its essence. Instead, he often sought to convey his view, as poets are wont to, in an image. The argument of his essays is thus often elusive, at times even appearing vague; for Hofmannsthal is often attempting to suggest an attitude of mind or to capture a mood, to portray fictitious characters wrestling with problems rather than to provide a clear-cut, logically impregnable analysis. He is not a systematic thinker[2] nor does he wish to be one. His style is rarely terse. Nor do all of his *pièces d'occasion*, though often charming and delightful, always possess weight. But however occasional the essay, it always reveals a creative mind at work. For whatever he wrote he had to find a form appropriate to what he had to say – and he did not apparently mind publishing slight pieces if the occasions so required. In that case, the formulation and arrangement of the essay suggests that he is more or less improvising. But at his best – and it is by his best work that it is wisest to judge any artist – his ability to conjure up a character, a situation, a relationship, and through them to confront his reader with a problem, is memorable. And he does have important points to convey. However much the reader may cavil at vagueness of phrase or inconsistency of terminology (if terminology is the right word to describe his usage of words such as *Geist*, *Seele*, and *Leben*) he is likely to remember the '*Chandos Letter*' and in particular its most powerful passages where Hofmannsthal not infrequently coined memorable phrases, and, in the style of great poets, portrayed an individual and an unusual situation in a striking manner. The same is true of the imaginary conversation between Balzac and the celebrated Austrian orientalist Baron von Hammer-Purgstall about epic or dramatic poetry – *über Charaktere im Roman und Drama* [*On Characters in Drama and in the Novel*] (1902) – or of the fictitious *Unterhaltung über den Tasso von Goethe* [*Conversation about Goethe's (Torquato) Tasso*] (1906), because Hofmannsthal used an artist's power to clothe ideas in the form of speech – either in the form of a letter used with a skill reminiscent of Goethe's *Werther* or of a dialogue recalling the drama of ideas. Indeed, particularly in his middle period, he was fond of dialogue[3] which, if elegantly used, allowed him to avoid discursive reasoning but conveyed his views without limiting him to one-sidedness and sacrificing the full interplay of ideas. Also, it afforded him an opportunity to use the poet's licence to suggest his views rather than to state them un-ambiguously.

Hofmannsthal was always receptive to current ideas and to the intellectual tradition. He cast his net wide and assimilated much of the past and contemporary literature and ideas. And since he always knew that he could not stand still intellectually, however much he may have wished to, he had to be content with absorbing the past and, as a creative writer, attempt through his works to turn it as best he could into a living past. Yet he never wished to state all that he knew and had experienced. Rather he relied on suggestion and allusion, and this is perhaps why the impact of his conversation was so powerful. This reticence and receptiveness also characterise his letters. Generally, he here appears to have stimulated others with the minimum of effort rather than having to expend all his creative energy. His correspondents frequently took pains to be interesting.

Hofmannsthal did not always try to do so. The others often wrote wide-ranging, perceptive letters. Carl J. Burckhardt, the Swiss diplomat and historian, affords the most striking example of Hofmannsthal's ability to bring out the best in his correspondents without stretching himself to the full.[4] Hofmannsthal gave much less – on the whole he was happy to receive and acknowledge the ideas put to him by others and rely on a few well-chosen remarks, often about his own work, but he continuously inspired his friends by the integrity, warmth and strength of his personality[5] which, in Burckhardt's words gave them 'power, love and hope',[6] an experience which the encounter with George had given to Hofmannsthal, though George had also inspired him with a sense of the uncanny, an experience which Hofmannsthal did not impart. Only the correspondence with Richard Strauss presents a different picture.[7] Here he wrote freely about the work on hand, but even here, in the main, he kept silent about the ideas underlying his plays, discussing primarily how the right effect could be achieved in the theatre.

Thus, Hofmannsthal's letters,[8] unlike those of Rilke, yield relatively little information about his ideas in general and his conception of art and the artist in particular. Even only very few of his essays such as the '*Chandos Letter*' are informative on that score. We must discern his ideas by analysing not only what he said (and he did make some quite specific points), but also have to appreciate how he said it and in particular note the undertones and overtones of his writing.

II

Hofmannsthal's ideas are thus not easy of access. Above all, since he was not a systematic thinker any attempt to systematise his thinking is liable to go astray. Yet some distinct strands of thought can be discerned. His ideas about the status of the poet and poetry are related to his belief that European culture was threatened, that this threat was particularly dangerous in Germany, but that as an Austrian poet he belonged to a culture different from that of Germany; and, more alive to its heritage, he could accomplish something that would go some way at least to arresting, if not repelling, the forces of disintegration threatening the cultural life of Europe. He was not conscious that he lived in an age in which traditional values were being eroded. But he knew that traditions had to be re-created anew for every age. Thus, he did not merely emulate Greek models and themes in his creative work, but sought to modernise them by adapting them to the prevailing intellectual climate. Thus, he made them alive again for the contemporary world and also showed that the past could become alive in the present, revealing the unity of all cultural life.[9] In his earlier years, like many Austrian writers he had experienced a *fin-de-siècle* melancholy. It was widely known that the Hapsburg empire was in many ways an anachronism and that substantial changes were afoot. Moreover, without being a Nietzschean he was, from his early years, familiar with and impressed by Nietzsche,[10] and, like Nietzsche, he feared cultural decadence. So did George, but Hofmannsthal's response was different. He never had the self-assurance which George possessed in so extreme a form. Disarming in manner, he possessed a questioning mind, and preferred to rely on persuasion rather than on injunction or invocation. He did nevertheless have convictions too. He believed in the need to regenerate the poetic and cultural tradition, though he differed fundamentally from George in his view of tradition. This is not entirely surprising. His personal background (he had Austrian, Swabian, Jewish and Italian blood in his veins) was international,[11] and Viennese culture, by virtue of the heterogeneity of the Hapsburg empire, had a cosmopolitan as well as a metropolitan flavour. He was also aware that the appeal to tradition would not by itself regenerate poetry and culture; for the disease was present in the very medium of poetry, in language itself the cancer grew. The inadequacy of language was the curse under which the modern poet laboured:

> All that we say, all that we, on occasion, still say, appears dead . . . the genuine experience is always inexhaustible, its presentation is always inadequate, two-dimensional. . . .
> Whereas, in art as in life the three-dimensional is the miracle of the miracle, the real mystery by which creative nature comes to the fore.[12]

But how could these doubts as to the value of language be overcome when the poet was facing cultural change, if not the decline and dissolution of culture? This experience brought forth disturbing uncertainties; values, rules of conduct, even experience itself began to appear questionable.

Of course, this conviction that language was inadequate was not at all new; for instance, Goethe had experienced it a century earlier, but had never doubted the symbolic power of language. Nor had it prevented him from carrying out his task as a poet. He was content to accept that not all can be said and that there must remain a residue of silence.

For Hofmannsthal, the problem was different. It became the central issue.[13] He asked whether the poet can say anything meaningful if language is incapable of saying what he wishes to say. His own words, 'We can never say in words exactly how things are',[14] sum up his conviction. The inadequacy is, however, the more trying if poetry prevents the poet as a man from responding to the challenges with which life confronts him.

Hofmannsthal's scepticism as to the use of language is, thus, deeply rooted in his sense of the poet's isolation as an individual. The poet feels separated from his fellows not merely because, as a sensitive individual, he finds his social environment alien, but because, fundamentally, all men are alone.

In the wake of Nietzsche and Schopenhauer, the principle of in-

individuality, of which man is the supreme example and the poet the foremost spokesman, gives rise to anxiety because communication between men becomes increasingly difficult if not impossible. The meaning of what men say remains elusive because words cannot convey it adequately. In order to speak at all, in order to make judgements and to convey values, we have to rely on generalisations or refer to universally valid rules or principles, but these are meaningless in a world ruled by individuation. This experience grew stronger and stronger. Hofmannsthal wanted to get to the essence of things,[15] but felt unable to do so. For language seems to have lost the strength to endow statements with general significance or universal validity. Any theorising which he puts forward appears trivial in relation to experience; the words which he uses are worn and deteriorate into clichés. At best some half-truths, misleading and inadequate, can be conveyed. The original force which language once possessed has been sapped by its abuse. Thought itself seems impossible once we attempt to clothe it in language. Hofmannsthal here does not merely refer to the inability of language to do justice to immediate experience, but reveals a neo-Platonic view of the world. He was dissatisfied with the view of the world which he had gleaned from the writings of Henri Bergson (1859–1941) and from the teaching of Ernst Mach (1836–1916), whose lectures he had followed at the University of Vienna; particularly he felt he had to come terms with Mach's theory that the world is composed merely of fragmented sense impressions which, basically, do not cohere.[16] In contrast, Hofmannsthal came to postulate, in the neo-Platonist tradition, a body of general truth and spiritual values which language cannot convey on account of its decadent condition. There is some primordial unity not only of matter, but of mind. If words and ideas do not correspond, if language, a system of external signs, cannot match the experience and insight which the poet, or, indeed, every man, has within him, if whatever we express outwardly through words must falsify truth itself and corrode these perennial ideas and values of which our inward experience has caught a glimpse – then, indeed, the poet's task is virtually impossible.

Hofmannsthal, as he was wont to do, summed up his apprehension of a world in travail in an image that reveals his poetic mettle: in *Ein Brief* he tells the story of Philip Lord Chandos, a young English nobleman of the age of Elizabeth I and James I who writes to Francis Bacon, the great philosopher. This letter in essay form has been taken to refer to a particular crisis in Hofmannsthal's own life, but this is a mistaken view, an illegitimate conclusion resting on the biographical fallacy. What Hofmannsthal portrays is, as Rolf Tarot has convincingly argued,[17] the general situation of the modern artist. Hofmannsthal's choice of period, the late renaissance, and of the addressee of the letter, Bacon, is significant. The Renaissance is the age in which the medieval conception of the world gave way to the modern age, and Bacon is the first great philosopher of science and champion of the inductive method of reasoning. For Hofmannsthal, the philosophical problem of vindicating induction became a profound emotional experience: the impossibility of vindicating induction philosophically, of not seeming able to derive valid universal laws from particular events greatly disturbed him.[18] But that is not all. Eventually all experience of reality becomes suspect. Language itself seems incapable of depicting both feelings and intellectual judgements because they imply general propositions the truth of which cannot be proved.

> My case is, in a nutshell, as follows; I have completely lost the ability to think or speak about anything whatsoever in a coherent manner.
>
> At first it became gradually impossible for me to discuss a higher or general theme or to use those words which all men and women use fluently without compunction. I felt an inexplicable unease in uttering such words as 'mind', 'soul' or 'body'. Something within me made it impossible for me to pass a judgement on affairs of the courts, events in parliament or whatever and this is not from any fear of hurting people's feelings for, as you know, I am frank even to the point of frivolity, but the abstract words which the tongue must use in order to pronounce any judgement disintegrated, in my mouth, like rotting toadstools.
>
> Gradually this anxiety spread like corroding rust. All the judgements that are normally made lightly and with the assurance of a sleepwalker became for me even in the familiar situation and everyday conversation so doubtful that I had to cease taking part in such conversations. . . . I was no longer able to grasp them (men and their actions) with the simplifying view of habit. Everything disintegrated into parts, the parts again into parts, and nothing could any longer be subsumed under concepts. The individual words were swimming around me; they coagulated to eyes which stared at me, and whose stare I had to return – they were whirlpools. – It made me feel giddy to look into them as they were incessantly spinning and because, on the other side of them, one reaches a void. (H – Pr. ii, pp. 12ff.)

Sophisticated modern man thus finds himself in a position quite different from that which any one could have experienced in earlier times. His experience also differs from that of a child (or possibly an adolescent) whose reaction to life is intuitive or spontaneous. He is also far from the goal for which he should aim to round off his self-cultivation so that he can foster the right kind of culture.

It is mistaken to believe that Hofmannsthal's scepticism concerning language is grounded in social criticism. Nor is it right to assume that his scepticism about the poet's ability to use language arises from a desire to bring about social or even cultural change. Neither should we look for the origin of his view of language and poetry in his private life although inevitably the course of his own life and of the culture into which he was born forms the background against which he developed his ideas. Hofmannsthal became sceptical about the adequacy of language because of his experience as a poet. It was not, as some have thought, a sudden crisis which he depicted more or less immediately in the '*Chandos Letter*'; rather the '*Chandos Letter*' sums up ideas and experiences with which he had been wrestling from the beginning of his poetic career.[19] The conviction that all abstract thought is suspect is very much a poet's experience, for the poet turns naturally to images and allusions, and not to philosophical discourse and concepts, he may then consider discursive language to be inferior since it is inadequate. But, unlike Nietzsche, Hofmannsthal does not use scholarly or near-scholarly prose to complain about the inadequacy of scholarly discourse. The '*Chandos Letter*' is a work of art – and is, like many works of art, ambiguous. Admittedly, when Lord Chandos finds that he is incapable of writing at all he explicitly blames the mistaken view of the world produced by inductive reasoning and, implicitly, the scientific outlook itself. But Hofmannsthal does not deal with this problem in the form of a philosophical treatise, he sees it as a problem to be evoked and solved by poetic language. He creates images. Thus, he is able to communicate his experience and ideas in a manner not open to a discursive thinker; for he sees forms of experience where the thinker sees only principles and abstractions. The poet may well see the world as lacking in unity because he is divided within himself, but by conjuring up the image of this experience he is on the way to conquering it. So does, if not Lord Chandos himself, its author. At least so the '*Chandos Letter*' implies; for the very eloquence of the letter almost gives the lie direct to the contention that the noble lord is incapable of using words.[20] It would seem that he – or certainly the author – is on the way to overcoming this impediment.

III

For Hofmannsthal, language was, then, incapable of conveying the full experience of life. But this did not mean that language and life were not meaningful, for if he had believed that he could not have written at all. In his view, language formed a realm of its own which did not correspond to the world of countless things. Admittedly, language never penetrated to the meaning of things and experience. Yet a kind of mystical insight was possible, a view which also agreed with Hofmannsthal's Roman Catholicism. Children – and here Hofmannsthal is close to Rilke – possessed this insight. Adolescents, sometimes, too – and here he is generalising from his own experience as a precociously consummate lyric poet – have this intuitive power. Those who have it are aware of life, of its unity and meaning in which the various phenomena appear interconnected. Hofmannsthal called this experience 'pre-existence' [*Präexistenz*] (H – A, pp. 213ff.) But this insight is quickly lost as men grow older and become entangled with the demands of living. Men incur guilt if they do not grow mature. Man – and of course the poet, too – must learn to reach a new state, which Hofmannsthal called 'existence', where he is fully involved in life and capable of having a grasp of unity again, at a higher level, this time not naively, but supported by reflection and experience.

Much ink has been spilt – for the most part pointlessly – in analysing Hofmannsthal's often cryptic sayings recorded in his *Aufzeichnungen* [*Observations*], especially in *Ad me ipsum*, a collection of notes and aphoristic reflections. Nor has the attempt by critics to relate them to his imaginative work been any more felicitous. There is no need to refute such misinterpretations here, let alone attempt to produce another one. A poet's own terminology, particularly if esoteric, is in principle the wrong meta-language to use in literary criticism. Suffice it to say that while Hofmannsthal did not make his doctrine accessible, and while there is thus much room for argument, if not speculation, it can be agreed that one of his major concerns was the belief that man is no longer capable of experiencing the unity of life – that the more our education progresses the more we are prevented from having this spontaneous insight into the wholeness of life, but have to be content with contemplating fragments of experience. Likewise, the notion of wholeness in art had been lost.[21]

The artist must, then, have that sense of unity so that he can show others the way to regain this lost experience. But the return to childhood is barred for the adult. And life itself, in its wholeness, proves elusive. Hofmannsthal obviously feared not being able to regain this lost sense of wholeness. He also dreaded falling into a mere solipsistic aestheticism which would stunt his own poetic development, because to trivialise life necessarily means producing poor art.

Above all, Hofmannsthal, as he grew more mature, sought to write poetry that was not alienated from life; for poetry belonged to life and the poet ought to be placed in the midst of its stream. To be able to sustain that belief was imperative; for he must vindicate what he was doing as a poet if he wanted to answer his own indictment of language and overcome his scepticism. Otherwise it was pointless to write at all.

What kind of literature did Hofmannsthal then hope to create as an answer to these objections? What he envisaged was not particularly original, though he gave it a somewhat idiosyncratic slant. He realised that the poet's relationship with life is not a simple one since poets themselves are not simple people.[22] On the contrary, they are sensitive and restless souls, full of yearning for a different world. But the poet's deep insight into his material is the source which gives art the power to convey experience to others. Life is not however to be conveyed in an undifferentiated form by art.[23] It has to be tamed by the artist. A work of art is unsatisfactory if it is not distanced from life. Yet it has to be rooted in the tangible experience of things. At one time, though not for long, he even thought that there was no direct path from poetry to life, from life to poetry,[24] but he soon took a subtler view. Experience has to be purified by art. Beauty can be created only if the work of art succeeds in confronting the reader or beholder with an experience of the wholeness of life. In order to convey that experience an artist needs to possess inner stillness and harmony. A work of art, however, requires more than this; it must direct him who approaches it back to life itself (H – A, p. 128). In fact, art ought not to be apart from life; if it were so it would lose its purpose.

For the mature Hofmannsthal a balance between art and life had to be struck. Both posed the same challenge. To be a poet and to appreciate poetry both required the same response, viz. the response of the whole man. Hofmannsthal was fond of quoting Lichtenberg's use of Steele's dictum stated in the *Spectator*: 'The whole man must move together.'[25] The act of poetic creation demands this wholeness from the poet. He has to learn to harness all his faculties to the poetic task, to combine spontaneity and intellectuality. For language, if properly used, must be able to crystallise life. The poet must seek to achieve a sense of equilibrium within his work. He must create an organised world and he must find the appropriate image through which to focus his disparate experience. Likewise, art must move the whole man. Great art is form which ought to speak to man as a whole, and not merely to one part of his personality. (Here he is following Schiller's aesthetic theory.) Such an experience of a work of art is an epiphany, a revelation, that makes a deep impact on us and allows us to see how our own life fits into the whole cosmos of 'relations' (*Bezüge*), which the poet establishes through his work. These relations form a world of their own, thus giving the work autonomy. By creating this nexus of relations the poet makes the dead speak again; the past becomes alive and is linked with the present, and the future is anticipated. He is also able to subsume things and experiences, however fragmentary, under a conception of life as a coherent totality; he is able to relate them to other things and experiences with which they would otherwise not have appeared to be connected, thus greatly extending and refining our vision. As a result, our whole being is affected. The spiritual revolution which Hofmannsthal deemed necessary can be brought about.

The test of a great work of art is whether it can speak to us in that manner. Hofmannsthal uses an example in his *Briefe des Zurückgekehrten* [*Letters of the Returning Traveller*] (1907) when he describes how Van Gogh's paintings deeply moved an Austrian traveller returning to Europe from overseas. The experience of these paintings, the way in which Van Gogh colours the objects depicted, indeed, everything in each painting, spoke to him. Hofmannsthal shows how the traveller becomes completely absorbed in the paintings and how he regains his composure, how he knows that they had been born of doubt, of a fear of nothingness and how, by their very existence, they once and for all cover the abyss in which life would otherwise be engulfed. These paintings bring to life that which man can otherwise feel only darkly. They made clear the profound inter-relations of all things, the unity underlying all experience just as each work itself is organised to achieve a similar unity. Since a mysterious force is at work which defies analysis and description Hofmannsthal has to resort to imagery to intimate the nature of his experience.

In another prose piece, *Augenblicke in Griechenland* [*Moments in Greece*] (1908–12), a similar confrontation between art and man takes place.[26]. Time appears suspended, the past, present and future are merged, a timeless experience is grasped as all the Greek statues in the museum visited by the traveller suddenly speak directly to him so that he feels them to be directly present and alive.

> At this moment something happened to me, an unutterable fright; it did not come from without, but from somewhere within the unfathomable depths of an inner abyss, it was like a flash of lightning; in that moment, a light, much stronger than was actually present, filled a real room which was rectangular, with its whitewashed walls, and the statues that stood in it; the eyes of the statues were suddenly directed upon me and in their faces there shone an utterly inexpressible smile. The real content of the moment within me was however this: I understood this smile because I knew I was not seeing it for the first time, in some way, in some world I have stood in front of them before, I had consorted with them and since then everything within me had waited for a terror of that kind and so terribly had I had been obliged to agitate my inner self in order to become again him who I was. — I do say 'since that time' and 'at that time', but nothing of the conditionalities of time could strike a chord in the abandonment which I had lost myself; it was timeless and that which had filled it took place outside time. It was a state of being interwoven with them, of being swept on somewhere with it an inaudible rhythmic movement, stronger than, and different from music, proceeding towards a goal. . . . (H – Pr., iii, pp. 36f.)

Hofmannsthal here uses almost mystical language to depict the impact of art. He seeks, as he stated explicitly, to intimate that which can neither be described nor intellectually apprehended. In the last resort, it is a mystical or religious experience which he is conjuring up. Here again, he also gives expression to his deep-seated neo-Platonism. The poet has to evoke a spiritual response — even more than that, he has to move the whole man, his spirit mind and senses. The impact of poetry ought to be overwhelming. At the same time, though, the aesthetic experience doubtless justifies art. Poetry overcomes the scepticism as to the use of language of which the '*Chandos Letter*' speaks. Hofmannsthal writes of the impact of states, and not of poetry, but the very act of writing about that experience suggests his assuming that the medium of language can also succeed in a similar manner. His description of the use of words by the celebrated Viennese actor Friedrich Mitterwurzer confirms this interpretation. An epiphany of the kind which he describes is necessarily a rare occurrence. Though Hofmannsthal never says so explicitly, he does suggest that art, through this power, can make man whole; and that once a man has been wholly moved he will be able to play his part in culture and thus also in society.

The poet, like the child or adolescent, has to see life as a whole; but what comes to the child or adolescent naturally does not come in the same way to the poet; he has to mobilise his inner resources to have such an experience. In seeing life as a whole he also transcends temporal frontiers – and in doing so he endows a great work of art with eternity; for any genuine work of art, like the Greek statues depicted in *Augenblicke in Griechenland* and Van Gogh's paintings described in *Briefe des Zurückgekehrten* belongs both to the here-and-now and to the past. A true work of art preserves tradition. It is also alive to the present. Works that possess that degree of power, i.e. genuinely perfect works of art are, of course, very rare.

In a sense, then, Hofmannsthal saw the poet as a sorcerer. By the magic of his poetry he creates a spell that exorcises chaos. Poetry expresses meaning in a world where meaning seems lost. It points to order and law. It also strikes a moral, indeed, a religious stance where disorder and relativity of values threaten to prevail.[27]

Hofmannsthal's approach to the poet's task is thus based on a moral attitude; for he wishes to correct cultural and spiritual defects. Likewise, his commitment to poetry necessarily entails a moral decision. And aesthetics cannot be separated from morals. In order to live up to his poetic mission, the poet, too, ought to lead a life regulated by self-imposed rules, as if he were a member of an order. Indeed, anyone who loves language and who devotes his life to its service must exercise self-denial. In this respect, the dilettante or the adventurer differ from the poet who serves art.

IV

In an important essay, *Der Dichter und diese Zeit* [*The Poet and this Age*], delivered as a lecture in various cities (Munich, Frankfurt-am-Main, Göttingen, Berlin and Vienna) in January 1907, Hofmannsthal sums up some of these ideas and develops them further in his usual expressive, poetic manner, revealing some of the many impressions which the poetic imagination seizes and binds together. He here emphasises the importance of the poet for the age, although the contemporary situation appears anything but propitious. But he does not consider it hopeless. Admittedly many phenomena of the age are ambiguous but it is still a highly poetic age; for books are still part of life. He appeals to the time-honoured conception of the poet slumbering in all those who are alive to imaginative needs, a conception inherited from both Classicism and Romanticism. He sees the poetic force latent in all men, even if it comes to the fore only in a few. But science, scholarship and journalism interfere with man's yearning for poetry. Men have become victims of shallow theories; yet Hofmannsthal is convinced that, basically, they yearn for deeper experiences which the poet alone can provide. This yearning springs from an awareness, however obscured it may have become by the to-and-fro of daily life, of the poet's power. That power is great and real; for the poet is the secret ruler of the world, however much men may deny or ignore that truth. He rules because everything that is written, spoken or even merely thought of in any language (and there can be no thought without language) descends from poets and is, thus, although men may not be aware of it, conditioned by the poet's view of the world.

> It is by virtue of language that, from a position of obscurity, the poet governs the world whose individual members may disown him, may have forgotten his existence. And yet it is he who leads the thoughts to each other and away from each other, who rules and manipulates their imagination, even its arbitrary acts and its grotesque leaps live by his grace. This silent magic works inexorably like all real powers. All that is written in a language, and let us dare to use the word, all that is thought in it is descended from the product of the few who have ever creatively used this language. (H – Pr. II, pp. 276f.)

Poets create great poetry not primarily on account of their sensitivity, although this is great, but because, like Midas, who turned everything he touched into gold, they turn life into words, inner experience into images (H – Pr. II, p. 45). The yearning for poetry, too, even if it is hidden from those who have not experienced these feelings, is capable of moving men deeply. Hofmannsthal is not asserting the primacy of the poet in the manner of George, but he does emphasise that the poet as guardian, creator and innovator of language wields a latent, subterranean power greater than is admitted by those who look after the affairs and arrangements of the society in which we live. The poet may dwell unknown and unnoticed in the house in which every one of us lives; yet his presence can be felt everywhere, provided we have ears to hear and eyes to see; for through him we see how 'relations' (*Bezüge*) are established.

The poet's sensitivity enables him to be receptive to everything, to all experience, to all sufferings and joys, to all deeds, thoughts and even to the figments of the imagination, but he is, so Hofmannsthal claims, able to make a harmonious pattern out of these experiences by his gift of coordination and his imaginative power. His visions enable him to see the world as it is. He is the seismograph of the age, but his creative power makes sense of disparate fragments of life. He has to cast aside undue concern with the particular and to discover the common ground underlying many conflicting forces. He imposes an intelligible pattern on what would otherwise be inchoate. The age must appear to us ambiguous and uncertain in its features, incapable of an easy synthesis. Yet the poets who have, by some mystical power, access to deeper sources, do not create a conceptual synthesis, but, by an exercise of magic, their work tells of what really matters in the age. And they speak for the age as a whole, not for any particular opinion or movement.[28] For Hofmannsthal, as for Novalis, the poet is a magician, even though the poet's magic is for him no longer the spontaneous force of his early work, but a magic firmly rooted in life and in reflection.

All these ideas on the poet's function are, perhaps inevitably, rather general, and the claims are large. Hofmannsthal did not, however, prescribe solutions for the prevailing cultural malaise. It would have been surprising if he had. He dealt, as poets are wont to do, with the problem of writing poetry, which is after all a highly urgent personal problem for any poet, although it is one that can have practical consequences undreamt of by him. For if a poet creates genuine poetry he changes the cultural landscape and counteracts the dissociative and centrifugal forces that threaten social and cultural stability. Thus, a poet can heal wounds which spiritual disease has inflicted on culture and even on society.

V

Hofmannsthal's approach to art then is an attempt to cope with the problem of writing in the age in which he lived. Not only did he wish to overcome his doubts about the validity of linguistic utterance, but he also felt the need to cope with the disruptive forces threatening the tradition which he had so far nurtured in imaginative writing. He thought the age unpropitious for writing, and yet he was convinced that the poet was able to fulfil his task provided he tapped hidden resources.

In the pre-war period, Hofmannsthal was deeply concerned about the danger of war and felt, with other leading writers and scientists, such as George Meredith, Swinburne and Lord Kelvin, almost a decade before its outbreak in 1914 that public opinion should, by an open letter, be alerted to the danger of an Anglo-German war and warned of the impending catastrophe which was likely to impair, if not to destroy, civilisation.[29] As George predicted,[30] the attempt was futile.

Hofmannsthal had, before the war, gauged the strength of rising nationalism among Austria's non-German population and knew how fragile the stability of the Hapsburg empire was. Yet he clung to the Austrian tradition because emotionally it meant so much to him, for it provided the atmosphere in which he had learnt to breathe and try his wings.

Inevitably, the 1914–18 war confronted Hofmannsthal with the reality of these fears; still, he felt impelled to speak up for Austria – not because he wished to defend its foreign policy, but because he believed that its cultural tradition represented much of value;[31] it stood for European culture both of the past and of the present. He greatly valued this most precious heritage which alone made genuine, meaningful poetry possible. To emphasise the singularity of Austrian culture he contrasted it with German culture. Admittedly, Austrian culture was part of German culture, but it was a specific part of German culture in which some of its more humane aspects had become crystallised. It must be contrasted with German culture in the narrow sense as it had become exemplified by Prussianism, even by Berlin.[32] The comparison was favourable for Austria, which showed signs of spiritual strength noticeably lacking in Germany. For tradition was stronger here than in Germany, and Austria had not suffered from so extreme a nationalism which, in his view, was a corrosive force. Austrian tradition was, for him, exemplified in great Austrian figures of the past, in Prince Eugene, the great general, in the Empress Maria Theresa, in the statesman Count Stadion and in the dramatist and poet Grillparzer, all of whom, in his (rather controversial) view, rated culture above military conquest or politics. Their mental horizon was cosmopolitan, and yet their experience was rooted in the Austrian people. They had a sense of Austria's cultural mission and knew how to further culture. This ability showed that they were cultured; for only those who further culture are themselves truly cultured.

Yet even in Austria Hofmannsthal had long perceived the signs and symptoms of a great spiritual crisis. Admittedly, in his essays and lectures of the war years he emphasised the positive aspects, doubtless feeling that in moments of extreme cultural danger public attention should be focused on that which is worth preserving. Awareness of these values therefore might rally men to defend them. Yet the tone of his addresses and essays is never narrowly nationalistic. Indeed, in defending and fostering Austrian culture he was defending and fostering European civilisation itself (H – A, p. 363). His cultural nationalism is always orientated towards, and subordinate to, his conception of Europe as a whole. What he feared was the decline of European civilisation itself. For everywhere he had noticed the dissociation between feeling and intellect, between tradition and actual life. Values had become eroded and spiritual poverty ensued. Above all, the pursuit of technological success and material satisfaction proved to be insidious, sapping or wasting spiritual strength. As a result, men indulged in idle speculation or undisciplined enthusiasm. The desire for freedom led to abuse and degenerated into licence. As a poet, Hofmannsthal was appalled that words were used without care and thus devalued. Mere rhetoric had usurped the place occupied by language related to meaning and reflection. The poet had lost his rightful place and was considered a mere entertainer. Consequently, life appeared frightening.[33] This experience had a paralysing effect on sensitive minds, exercising a power similar to Medusa. What was the root of the evil that threatened to destroy culture? Like Nietzsche, Hofmannsthal felt that decadence meant the loss of the sense of unity of culture. Man is, as a result, no longer able to react to his surroundings as a whole man; he experiences disintegration within himself. He responds with, and thus is able to develop, only a part of his personality, stunting the growth of other parts and of his personality as a whole. And yet all is not lost: even in these very moments of confusion the seeds of future awareness and achievement may be found.

Hofmannsthal's analysis of the decadence of European life is neither detailed nor comprehensive, but this is not surprising. Unlike Nietzsche, he was not first and foremost a cultural critic. He was content to point to tendencies and situations rather than to produce detailed evidence. He distrusted those who spoke too much about the lack of values, about spiritual disintegration and the loss of quality, as is revealed by his criticism of Walther Rathenau, the industrialist and statesman. Nor is Hofmannsthal's lament about man's inability to achieve wholeness new. Many writers had lamented, including Schiller, who however put forward, in his philosophical masterpiece *Über die ästhetische Erziehung des Menschen*, an elaborate, comprehensive and profound theory of culture and society which showed how the problem might be solved.[34] Hofmannsthal is far too impressionistic a writer even to approximate to the intellectual rigour of Schiller's argument. There are many differences too between the models of the whole man conceived by them; none the less, the basic conception, despite all these important differences, is similar, and Hofmannsthal was groping for rather than precisely defining a solution similar to that developed by Schiller, even if his account fell far short of that of Schiller.

After the war, when the Hapsburg Empire had disintegrated and Austria had become a small, politically insecure state and the German Empire an unstable republic Hofmannsthal himself had suffered heavy financial losses during the inflationary aftermath of the war, losing most of his fortune. Yet he still saw it as the writer's task to look for stabilising forces; he thought that it was necessary to draw on the heritage of the past, but that past had to be adapted to the needs of the age. It had to be used creatively so that new attitudes of mind and modes of thought and conduct could develop.

In his lecture *Das Schrifttum als geistiger Raum der Nation* [*Writing as Spiritual Realm of the Nation*], delivered at the University of Munich in 1927, two years before his death, Hofmannsthal defends the poet once more; he again emphasises his conviction of the poet's central role; for a nation is held together by language, and language is not merely a means of communication, but also a vehicle of tradition. But Hofmannsthal perceptively discerns the cracks in the German nation's fabric; he notices that in Germany men were not conscious of German cultural unity and the German cultural heritage to the extent that the French were; he agreed with Nietzsche's strictures on the Germans for mistaking the military victory of 1871 for a cultural triumph,[35] and he traced many of the defects in contemporary culture back to this unstable premise. But he had not abandoned hope. The poet, if he overcomes his isolation, natural to his temperament, can establish links with the life of others, even with that of the whole community. But he has to wrestle with the word in silence and solitude to accomplish his work and grasp the power of poetry. Yet if he succeeds his magic allows him to transcend the limits of self and make an

impact on the community at large. He can in fact impart the idea of
Europe as a whole. Language belongs to a nation, but by selective,
fastidious and creative use of language the poet revitalises tradition and
necessarily brings the whole of European cultural tradition to life. Since a
genuine poet must speak with his own voice – for otherwise he would not be
genuine – he inevitably breaks new ground. Thus, any poet of stature is a
revolutionary, but he is a revolutionary who is absorbed in and is building
on tradition.

Hofmannsthal defined this process when he wrote:

> I am speaking of a process in the midst of which we find ourselves, of a
> synthesis, as slow and sublime – if we are able to see it from outside – as it
> is dark and trying if one is in the midst of it. We may call the process slow
> and sublime if we consider that even the slow sphere of development
> from the convulsions of the age of the enlightenment until our own
> present age is only a short period, that it really arose as a counter-
> movement against that spiritual revolution of the sixteenth century
> which, in its few aspects, we customarily call renaissance and refor-
> mation. The process of which I am speaking is nothing but a
> conservative revolution of a scope unknown to European history. Its
> goal is form, a new German reality in which the whole nation could
> participate. (H – Pr. IV, pp. 412f.)

It is in that sense of continuing a tradition that Hofmannsthal's much
maligned and much misused phrase 'conservative revolution' has, in the
first place, to be understood. It means more than this of course; it signifies
the attempt to bring out the European element in European culture, to use
tradition to establish new bonds in Europe, to make a stand for civilisation
by combining established values with a new, forward-looking outlook no
longer restricted by a narrow cultural or political nationalism. It should
not, however, be taken as a party political slogan or dogma. But it should of
course not be denied that this passage – and indeed the whole essay – is
imbued with the spirit of political Romanticism.[36] For Hofmannsthal's
desire to support 'a new ideal of form [*Bildung*] for the German nation, a
form imbued with a sense of community, of ancient traditions, of
rootedness'[37] recalls the organic conception of the state, just as his *not neces-*
welcoming 'a new German reality' unfortunately carries – for us with the *sarily so*
hindsight of Hitler's rise to power and in the context of German politics of
the time – a ring of Nazi terminology, though, in a different context, it
might be construed as a clarion-call for Christian Democracy, for a new
conservatism, an attitude of mind of course germane to Hofmannsthal's
thought as Nazism never was. Hofmannsthal was aware of some of the
dangers threatening the society of his time, but he was not a sufficiently
perceptive judge of prevailing political tendencies. His innate tradition-
alism blinded him to the pillaging of Romantic and even conservative

ideas by the precursors of fascism. Thus, he assuredly did not realise that, by coining the watchword 'conservative revolution', he might have fostered these dangerous but fashionable currents of thoughts and was in fact furthering an ideology which he would have detested. Yet although it would be wrong to blame a poet too much for lack of political understanding, his grievous error of judgement was perhaps inevitable once he had impaired his own cosmopolitanism by his urging the concept of the whole man, 'this golden rule of conduct, not upon anyone in the world, but upon the Germans in particular',[38] thus echoing earlier Romantic notions of the German mission.

Hofmannsthal appealed to future writers to prove their mettle by exercising their cultural leadership as well as by revealing their sense of tradition and their power of innovation. If they followed his call they could make a powerful impression on society. Hofmannsthal felt that the theatre offered most scope to the writer. It allows him to raise society to a qualitatively higher level. But if his conception of the writer's task undoubtedly has social implications, Hofmannsthal does not, as Brecht later did, prescribe dramas with a social or political message. The poet's task is still essentially to be a poet, and through his work, indirectly, to help the nation to find its centre – an injunction sufficiently imprecise to allow for many interpretations. But Hofmannsthal strongly resisted any submission to a programme or a creed. Just as, in his youth, he had rejected George's tempestuous wooing, so in his later years he never joined a literary movement or a political party. Even when he delivered some semi-official addresses in neutral Scandinavia during the 1914–18 war[39] he did not make propaganda, but emphasised the civilising tradition of Austrian culture. Hofmannsthal was far too sensitive a man not to see the need for balance and a sense of proportion. It was out of character for him to speak in a loud and apodictic manner. Even when he touched on politics tangentially he was always restrained; for his whole approach to poetry and life rested on a profound awareness of, and commitment, to civilisation, which for him precluded partisanship in day-to-day politics. But then it was his good fortune not to have to witness the rise of Nazism to power. In any case, it would be mistaken to blame a poet who put forward suggestions of a general and basically non-poetical nature for their perversion by political practitioners, particularly when they ruthlessly raided the history of ideas for their purposes.

VI

In Hofmannsthal's imaginative work the artist does not often appear as a major figure, nor is the question of art and the artist the dominating theme. Yet there are many poems that deal with art. Yet, only in one of the early verse plays, in *Der Tod des Tizian* [*The Death of Titian*] does an artist, the dying Titian, dominate the action – although he never appears in it. This play, like all the early verse plays of Hofmannsthal, conjures up an atmosphere; the action is minimal. It is more an extended lyrical poem than a conventional drama. Disciples of Titian, together with his son, congregate to await Titian's death and speak about his influence on their lives and on life in general. They feel late-comers, unable to share his creative power. But Titian, the great artist, is an example. He taught them to approach life with open eyes to see things as they really are. He gave life to life itself. For he had seen beauty steadily and seen it whole. Because he possessed the power to do so, each moment was for him one of fulfilment. But he did not live merely for himself. The power of his art and of his life extended to them as well. They would have spent their empty lives in twilight, but for him. They indirectly partake of beauty, and their life thus acquires meaning.

> Er aber hat die Schönheit stets gesehen,
> Und jeder Augenblick war ihm Erfüllung,
> Indessen wir zu schaffen nicht verstehen
> Und hilflos harren müssen der Enthüllung . . .
> Und unsre Gegenwart ist trüb and leer,
> Kommt uns die Weihe nicht von außen her. . . .
>
> So lebten wir in Dämmerung dahin,
> Und unser Leben hätte keinen Sinn . . .
>
> Die aber wie der Meister sind, die gehen,
> und Schönheit wird und Sinn, wohin sie sehen.[40]

The great artist, by his existence and achievement, thus serves as proof that life is meaningful.

These ideas recur in Hofmannsthal's lyric poetry together with the others discussed in his essays. Above all, one of them recurs: the poet's awareness that language is inadequate, inner experience evanescent and communication, therefore, virtually impossible; yet the poet is none the less able to cast a spell on his readers.

On the one hand, the poet is seen as a homeless wanderer, a deceived deceiver who is confronted with doubts about the meaning of words. They seem merely empty and ineffectual formulae. Poetry seems to be incapable of being efficacious. On the other hand, poetry is, by definition, an exercise in the use of words. And words do affect men. Indeed, a poetic work may say much as is suggested in 'Ballade des äußeren Lebens' ['Ballad of External Life']. A poet, like God, can keep all enthralled. He is the keeper of the secret which forms the basis of existence. In 'Gedankenspuk', a poem appropriately endowed with a motto from Nietzsche, Hofmannsthal sums up the whole problem in an image which signifies that poetry is like an incandescent fire:

Vernichtungslodernd,
Tödlich leuchtend,
Lebensversengend
Glüht uns im Innern
Flammender Genius.[41]

It symbolises the joy of life, but – alas! – in order to be given form it has to be subjected to constraint; Venus the goddess of joy and love is, as the image suggests (H – G, pp. 477f.) married to Hephaestus, the God who, sooty from his work as a smith, is the very prototype of inadequacy, even of negation. So the poet is like Hamlet, he lives both in the realm of dream and the real world. His craft compels him to compromise. He is a Titan-like Faust and a poor servant like Sganarelle. Inspiration and torment are both his. And yet however poor, worn and soiled, the word truth – shining with the clarity of a crystal – cannot be entirely concealed (H – G, p. 477f.). Thus, for Hofmannsthal, the prophetic stance that came so easily to George seemed inappropriate. In this poem he says that, on the one hand, a poet like George can exercise great power by telling us of our unknown aspirations and the unconscious forces within us, of the secret locked up inside us, but, on the other hand, poetry can also be merely seductive.

There are other hints, too, telling about Hofmannsthal's view of the poet's task. In *Der Tor und der Tod*, his most famous early drama, a lyrical playlet of remarkable poetic power, Hofmannsthal exposes the pointlessness of a life of mere aestheticism. The hour of death here reveals that a life devoted to aesthetic pleasure is selfish, lacks moral character and must be condemned. Here it expresses his own fear, the fear of a poet not doing justice to life since he was 'a chamaeleon-like figure who, as Keats [whom he quotes with approval] put it, has no identity, he is continually in for, and filling, some other body. . . .'[42]

By criticising the aesthete in *Der Tor und der Tod* Hofmannsthal criticised aestheticism which worshipped *l'art pour l'art*, a movement characteristic of *fin de siècle* Europe and particularly of Vienna. Implicitly he distanced himself from George's own praise of the supremacy of art, while at the same time he also implicitly agreed with George's moral attitude: for he perceived the ambiguity in George's stance. But above all he depicted the fear of having his poetic development stunted by the worship as well as the creation of mere beauty. In portraying the aesthete he revealed the dangers confronting the poet who failed to master life and to convey the need for unity and wholeness, thus becoming a prey to decadence, characterised, in the words of Nietzsche, by the lack of these very qualities.[43] The poet, by implication, fails if he does not live up to the moral challenge of art and life, for the basis of all aesthetic experience is morality (H – A, p. 101).

Likewise in *Der Schwierige*, a superb comedy,[44] Hofmannsthal emphasises how the use of conventional words, clichés or concepts produces petrifaction:[45] it makes man fall a prey to prejudice and preconceived notions or forms of thought and so makes him fail to do justice to life. Its hero, Hans Karl Count Bühl, is able to become engaged to Helene Countess of Altenwyl whom he loves precisely because he distrusts words and he is helped to bridge the gulf created by speech between him and others, and, for a while, even between him and her, because he can rely on her understanding and love which transcend language. But those who, unlike the hero of *Der Schwierige*, are not able to cope with the limitations imposed by language because they are unaware of them, are joined in failure by another of Hofmannsthal's figures, the adventurer.[46] There are many adventurers in his work, for instance, Florindo in the comedy *Christinas Heimreise* [*Christina's Homecoming*] or Baron Weidenstamm (apparently a pseudonym for Casanova) in *Der Abenteurer und die Sängerin* [*The Adventurer and the Singer*] (1898); Baron Ochs von Lerchenau, in *Der Rosenkavalier*, is an adventurer without sparkle, a merely seedy example of the type. Each time the moral failure, the inability to commit oneself to another person, the refusal to love truly and to live beyond the moment, thus impairing or even destroying the social order,[47] point to the demands which Hofmannsthal made of man and of the poet. For himself, as a poet, Hofmannsthal tackled the problem by turning away from mere aestheticism or the pure fleeting concern with himself and contemplation of beauty to explore wider issues: love, marriage, social responsibility and action – all forms of responsible living, thus avoiding impoverishment, decline, petrifaction which would have been his fate if he had continued writing in his youthful solipsistic manner. But this is not easy: Vittoria in *Der Abenteurer und die Sängerin*, for instance, has to learn, after years of sorrow, to break the spell cast upon her by the happiness which she enjoyed with the adventurer. But when she does, and is able to find her way to emotional stability through commitment to conjugal love she is able to make full use of her art as a singer, a proof of the true sources of mature art.

Hofmannsthal here, as in *Der Schwierige* or in *Der Unbestechliche* [*The Incorruptible Servant*] shows that these dangers can be overcome. He took a positive view of the poet's task. He believed that the road was arduous, but he showed by his mature work that the poet could meet the challenge. By turning to the powerful sources of Austrian literary tradition – to comedy and to the festival play – he proved that the ideas developed in his essays were not empty rhetoric, but truly alive for him. The power of his work is the proof of their validity.

5 Rainer Maria Rilke (1875–1926)

From his early youth onwards, Rainer Maria Rilke felt himself to be a poet and, for him, this was no mean thing. He had no doubts about his poetic vocation, though frequently, despite all his facility in writing verse, he had grave doubts whether he would be able to satisfy his own poetic standards. He never hesitated, however, to take all the necessary steps to accommodate the needs of his poetic genius. If poetry served his ends, it did so not merely for selfish reasons – and a powerful streak of narcissism or emotional solipsism dominated his approach – but on account also of his conviction that art mattered for the world at large. For Rilke not only vocation and personal ambition, but also metaphysics and aesthetics were inseparable. Poetry was a meaningful activity; it also provided the answer to the riddle of the universe.[1] It came to usurp the place of religion and philosophy.[2]

Thus, poetry, and the writing of poetry, became the pivot of his life and he tailored his life to it. He used it to express his feeling, to convey his grappling with ideas, to get on in the world, and, in the first instance, as a young man, to revolt.[3] He rebelled against the orthodox Christianity of his family, particularly of his mother, and against the restrictions imposed by middle-class life; but his revolt was only in rare moments extreme and for all to see, as in the *Christus Visionen* [*Christ – Visions*], (1896–98), published only after his death. As a rule, it was concealed beneath a veneer of gentleness and even submissiveness. The desire to assert his individuality, the Nietzschean injunction taken over from Pindar 'become what thou art'[4] – and there is a strong streak of Nietzscheanism in Rilke[5] – became for him the goal of poetry. His devotion to the task, the mental and emotional energy he expended, are apparent, but discernment did not come to him easily. His facility was unbounded – and at first he published in order not to perish, apparently unaware of the weakness of much or most of his verse. When, in later years, precision mattered to him above all, he regretted, and was even ashamed of what he called 'his lyrical superficiality' and his 'cheap *à peu près*'[6] based on lively but undeveloped feelings; and he agreed with the strictures of Stefan George, who had reproached him, on the occasion of their only meeting (in the Boboli gardens in Florence in April 1898), for publishing too soon[7] and had recommended patient work.[8] In later years he became fastidious, and his desire to get his poetry absolutely right explains in part the long gestation period (1912–22) of the *Duineser Elegien* [*Duino Elegies*], his major poetic cycle.

Although Rilke developed his ideas about the primacy of art early in life and gave a full account of them in the *Florentiner (oder Toskanisches) Tagebuch* [*Florentine (or Tuscan) Journal*][9] which he wrote in the spring of 1898 at the age of twenty-two for his friend (and then mistress) Lou Andreas-Salomé, but published only posthumously, there are shifts and changes in his attitude. He did not so much recant his early beliefs, as develop, elaborate, and refine them. Indeed, even his reviews and essays on literature before 1898 do not tell a substantially different story. Throughout his creative life he saw the artist as an aristocratic figure – an individual singled out from among others by dint of the power of his perception [*Anschauung*][10] and his creative capability. Not that art itself is for the few only – a mere leisure-time activity for the rich or aristocrats; on the contrary, it can and ought to be widely appreciated, but the artist must stand above, or outside, the common multitude; his task is therefore essentially a lonely one.

Indeed, Rilke's picture of the artist sometimes sounds as if he were cast in the mould of Nietzsche's superman. Yet, despite Rilke's anti-Christian convictions, the artist is characterised by an aura of religiosity.

For Rilke, the question of the nature and purpose of art not only gave rise to theoretical reflections, however, but was also organically embedded in his work. It is a central theme of his poetry itself, and it also becomes the means by which Rilke explores the many personal and philosophical problems that exercised him as well as his age. Rilke was concerned with ideas, but he looked upon them as a poet and developed them in his poetry.[11] But poetry by its very nature is rarely unambiguous. This is particularly true of modern poets, such as Rilke, who cultivate ambiguity and make it the centre of their mode of writing. But readers only too frequently desire certainty and want to read a poem from one point of view only even when uncertainty is built into the very structure of the work and multiple perspectives alone produce an adequate reading. These unrealistic demands have given rise to the many metaphysical and quasi-theological, frequently even hagiographical, interpretations of Rilke's work which have bedevilled so much of his reception and which, despite the onslaught of reputable scholars, led by Eudo C. Mason,[12] have never been entirely exorcised. And the present-day tendency to blame him for his lack of social and political commitment is only high-flown metaphysical adulation in reverse, however hotly its advocates are likely to deny this charge.

I

Rilke's early views on art[13] reflect his attempt to discover himself as a poet, to tell the story of his devotion to his art and to understand, with some precision, the nature of the relationship between art and life, between the artist and the world in which he lived. Yet his starting-point was not the world, but his own yearning to be an artist and his supreme regard for poetic achievement.

A good introduction to the ideas of his early years is afforded by his book-reviews, essays and lectures, of which, in the first decade of his creative life, he composed a comparatively large number. And, of course, his letters are, as always throughout his life, an invaluable source for understanding his poetry.[14] The following ideas emerge from them: the artist had to devote his whole life to art, otherwise he would not be an artist at all.[15] At that time, art, for him, was closely bound up with feeling. Misunderstanding Lessing, he invokes his authority to criticise those poets who are concerned with depicting objects from external reality which, for him, is the realm proper to painting (R, v, p. 292). Since poetry is about feeling, good poetry should be the most personal expression possible (R, v, p. 301). Rilke found this view confirmed in the poetry of Detlev von Liliencron (1844–1909), the German Impressionst poet whose lyric poetry excited him very much at that time, in the early nineties. Since he felt attuned to Liliencron's poetry he took it as a model for his own work. Liliencron's art seemed to him 'the new art'; it was an art that did not pay primary attention to the material chosen by the poet, but was based on the 'eternal wisdom of the world: perceive, enjoy, love' (R, v, p. 319). This conviction anticipates important features of Rilke's concern in later years: the need to perceive (Anschauen), the emphasis on the act of perceiving and mental assimilation of what has been perceived. This task of coming to terms with what had been perceived should, in principle, be mastered by way of a positive reaction, here defined in terms of enjoyment and love.

Even the young Rilke is too much of an artist not to know that perception, enjoyment and love by themselves are not enough; the experience has to be given form, for content alone does not suffice. Indeed, art has to be very different from anything else in the world. In its difference resides its very nature and significance:

[Art] gains its importance through form, i. e. through the manner in which it is delimited against the multifarious and the alien.[16]

It is precisely because art is different from ordinary life, that Rilke, echoing Nietzsche and Stefan George, attacks the Naturalists' conception of faithfully imitating external reality.[17] Equally he is opposed to writing poetry about current affairs or topical matters since these events are basically insignificant. It is no more than 'rhymed or painted journalism' which may have 'pedagogical or cultural value', but 'it is not art.[18]

These ideas are summed up in the early essay Moderne Lyrik [Modern Lyric Poetry] written on the eve of his departure for Italy in spring 1898. This essay contains his first important statement on art. Like George, Rilke is critical of the conventional fashions in poetry and attacks those poets whose work is a mere pose. But, unlike George, he does not condemn most contemporary poets: on the contrary, he praises many of them, provided he feels their poetry to be genuine since they appear to understand all things, 'the smallest, as well as the largest' (R, v, p. 365). Art can be viable if art and life are intertwined. Therefore, Rilke inveighs against the gulf that has arisen between art and life as a consequence of the intellectual tendencies of the age. This gulf, particularly noticeable in Germany, is in fact a symptom of a chronic disease (R, v, p. 363). But the genuine artist can bridge the gulf and, by implication, eradicate the disease. In doing so he must reject all principles of utility applied to art or aesthetics (R, v, p. 363). A movement realising some of these ideals is already afoot; for silently, so he believes, a new unconventional art has grown up which is 'healthy, great and strong' (R, v, p. 364). Rilke thus feels that despite many aberrations in contemporary cultural life there is no need for despair. Indeed, there is ground for hoping that a literary and cultural revival will come about, though he never sets out any convincing reasons for this hope. Yet at this juncture, art, for him, transcends the individual's concerns; it is not merely the personal affair of the artist, but affects the many, indeed, it governs their feelings. Rilke even postulates as the aim of art that the conception of beauty [Schönheitsbegriff] should not belong to the few alone, but to the many.[19] In other words, the impact of art on culture should be profound; as Nietzsche had claimed, it ought to pervade the whole of culture. But nowhere does Rilke say precisely how this influence should operate. Nor does he spell out his cultural aims in detail.

Rilke's concern is different. He emphasises that it is the cultural intention of all poetry to confess the poet's deepest innermost process of finding maturity.[20] Admittedly this confession will be understood only in an age aware of this need to confess.[21] Moreover, the task of art is to apprehend the external world, all the things of whatever size and importance found in the external world; at the same time, it must, through this dialogue with the external world, draw on, or come close to, the 'ultimate silent sources of life itself,'[22] sources which will apparently be revealed by and found through the poet's approach to the reality of the outside world. But the poet must not only direct his gaze on the outside world, he must also turn to his inner life if he wishes to achieve originality, the most important criterion by which to judge genuine poetry, a point for which he invokes Dante's poetry as proof.[23] Indeed, a poet can become a true poet only if he succeeds, amidst the flood of fugitive events, in 'finding himself'[24] and listens 'to the deepest recesses of his mind until he hears what has not been said and what is truly new', which begins with his work.[25] Thus, from the beginning he is seeking to define the artist's need to mediate between the inner and outer worlds and seeks, through poetry, to grasp and convey the unity of all life. However, without the poet's full commitment to his task good poetry cannot be written, for mere virtuosity, however brilliant, is not enough, nor does the judicious choice of subject-matter [*Stoff*] suffice. What is really necessary is to possess a 'genuine artistic intention[26] If a poet has that, all other things will fall into shape; this doctrine is of course appropriate to a poet for whom to convey feelings is of paramount importance. The artist's personality also determines the character of his work, but he will have to find a new form for anything new which he has to say.[27] But he cannot say anything new and avoid mere imitation unless he is sincere. Yet art, at least at that stage in his career, is for Rilke not an end in itself. It is the way to an end;[28] Rilke does not, however, make it absolutely clear what the end is. He seems to suggest that it is found in the artist's endeavour to appropriate the secret nature of things and to merge his deepest feelings with these things so that they can speak for his own yearnings. He claims that 'the rich language of these intimate confessions is beauty.'[29] In the last resort, the aim of poetry is, then, to express personal feelings, but also at the same time to assimilate external reality to these feelings. Poetry alone can do justice to these two needs of which at this stage the expression of feeling can still claim primacy.

The *Florentiner Tagebuch* contains Rilke's only full-length discussion of his attitude to art. In this work his formulations are more extreme and more ecstatic than in his earlier writings, which were of course intended for publication and were not a private record of feeling and reflection. Whatever the reason however, whether it was the influence of Italy, or some other experience, Rilke speaks with a novel note of self-assurance. Indeed, the most striking feature of this collection of reflections on art is the stridency of his tone, which is particularly noticeable after the new beginning on 17 May 1898, following a break in the entries, a break perhaps occasioned by his encounter with George.[30]

What Rilke proclaims above all in the *Florentiner Tagebuch* is: firstly, an emphasis on the need for the artist to go his own way to achieve perfection in his art, and secondly, the primacy of art which overrides any concerns that may be imposed by the external world. He uses almost mystical language to describe art as the 'most sacred fulfilment (R – Tb., p. 30'). Not unlike Nietzsche, he praises great periods of art, though he does not specify what they were. And he attacks false attitudes towards art and the prevailing educational practice as hostile to the development of aesthetic sensitivity (R – Tb., p. 32). Art is, for him, a form of self-liberation and self-fulfilment, it is his road to freedom (R – Tb., p. 33). The experiences gathered by the artist become so powerful that he cannot contain them within himself; this urge gives him a singular power which turns his life into an act of creation. Art is thus a means by which the artist realises his hidden depth resulting from his experience both of himself and of the world. There are indeed moments when his vision is powerful beyond the ken of normal experience and he sees the causes of all things (R – Tb., p. 70).

Rilke however not only gives primacy to art over other modes of experience, but for a while he even goes to the length of believing that as an artist he does not need the external world for inspiration. He conceives the artist as someone able to live in complete emotional isolation and thus propounds an extreme emotional and intellectual solipsism. The artist does not create works of art for others; he creates them for himself alone (R – Tb., p. 33). Every artist is, so he believes, a stranger in this world. In contrast to George, and probably in opposition to him after their encounter, Rilke rejects the community of artists (R – Tb., p. 39). In his view, artists have to preserve their solitude since they are a danger to one another. Even if all genuine sincere art is national,-art goes from one solitary person to another,[31] leaving the multitude that cannot attain these heights in the depths below. Therefore, the artist must be concerned with self-development. For culture is a matter of personality (R – Tb., p. 104), and art can further only the culture of the creative artist, not of the world at large. Consequently, the artist is bound to ignore the common crowd if he wishes to achieve profundity. But this isolation and solitude has its rewards. It enables the artist to create order out of ephemeral experience, whatever this experience may consist of – be it 'his lonely suffering, his vague desires, his anxious dreams and those joys which will fade away' (R – Tb., p. 34). Art transcends these experiences to reach a higher plane. Experience ceases to be ephemeral, for art partakes of eternity; indeed, Rilke even goes so far to claim that it is eternity (R – Tb., p. 35).

Art stands above religion, for religion is merely the art of those who are not creative themselves (R – Tb., p. 38). Indeed, God is not a being who exists by himself in eternity, but one who has been created by the artist, that maker of legends. However, the God created by earlier artists is now in a derelict state, a badly preserved ancient monument, merely the oldest work of art (R – Tb., p. 47). It is a matter of sophistication or education to talk about him and to have looked at the remains, but, by implication, Rilke suggests it needs a new great artist, such as doubtless he aspired to be, to create a new God valid for himself and perhaps, through his poetry, for others. Though whether he wanted to benefit others by his creative experience is not entirely clear, since his main concern is with his attempt to define the status of art and the artist. The achievement of art is greater than that of religion, indeed, it constitutes the greatest possible achievement. Consequently, the artist stands in a rare, dignified and splendid isolation.

But this does not mean that the artist does not have an impact on others. This impact is produced by the artist's personality as revealed in his art. If it is genuine art it is appreciated because the artist has submitted to higher laws. So the artist's work, although relating the story of personal experiences told by him to a few close intimate friends in hours of sacred twilight, has a higher significance.

These strange ideas, revealing an artist struggling to express his self-regard and to build up self-esteem, are further elaborated in an important

essay *Über die Kunst* [*On Art*][32] written in the summer of 1898, in which art is
defined as an approach to life, similar to religion or science. It differs,
however, from all the other ways of thought and experience through not
being tied to the age in which it is created; for it is the philosophy of the
timeless truth. God, then, becomes the last and deepest fulfilment of the
artist. Again he states that the artist has virtually created God. It is his duty
to make it possible for God to find collective fulfilment. The artist can do so
only because of his spontaneity, which is child-like. Indeed, he is close to
children because of his sense of piety towards everything and every
experience. Art is indeed deeply rooted in childhood.[33] It springs from the
child's desire to fashion something new since he, like the artist, has not yet
come to terms with the outside world. Through the act of genuine creation
the artist is able to penetrate into depth of truth. Rilke cites Maurice
Maeterlinck as a striking example of this ability.[34] But the artist must avoid
a false realism. Through the creation of a new world which is not a mere
copy of the existing world the artist is alone able to eschew his own
subjectivity.

Thus, Rilke has taken his extreme claims on behalf of art one stage
further. Even if art often contradicts or criticises contemporary life[35] its
concern is not with the past or the present; it looks towards and tells us of
the future. Works of art do not belong to their own age; they are even
untouched by it. They are things of the future;[36] they are perennial, perfect
things, and, as such, contemporaries of God whom men have been creating
from the beginning. Art foreshadows the future union between life and art
to be experienced by all.

Such claims are as unusual as they are extreme. They tell in a poetic,
exaggerated formulation of the poet's attempt to proclaim the autonomy of
art, an autonomy arising from its nature as a distinct mode of experience[37]
or existence. But they also convey Rilke's hope that through art man would
be able to grasp the wholeness of life and then find spiritual fulfilment. This
autonomy makes special demands on the artist. He has to live a life
conducive to artistic creation simplifying the multiplicity of life and
reducing it to a whole, to one, experiencing unity first in his life and then
expressing it in his art. Only then does beauty arise, beauty which is but
another word for the autonomy of art.[38] The artist's creative power which
only he among adults possesses marks off genuine art from mere
explanation or description or criticism of the world. We cannot judge a
work of art by referring to its impact on the world or by any extrinsic
criteria, for in doing so we could miss its real significance and bring about
confusion. The significance of a work of art exists in its being not a way of
thinking, but a fact or a mode of being. And, in the wake of Nietzsche's
Geburt der Tragödie, Rilke proclaims an aesthetic view of the world which is
to vindicate the very existence of the world and of man's activity.

However, not all that claims to be art is art. And even genuine art is
easily misunderstood. Fame is indeed 'the sum of all misunderstandings

that accumulate around a new name.[39] Like many artists before him, Rilke inveighs against analytical criticism which, since it is merely an intellectual activity, inhibits the development of personality[40] and consequently artistic work. These obstacles to the growth of art are very strong indeed in the present age, an age that lacks maturity, since, in contrast to a genuine artist like himself, most people experience art and life as separate entities.

Rilke's early poetry confirms these ideas so profusely and extravagantly expressed in the early essays and the *Florentiner Tagebuch*. His earliest poetry, written in Prague before his departure for Munich (1896) and even that poetry dating from his stay in Munich (1896–7) is marked by the influence of Impressionism and mainly reflects personal feelings. And so does even the much more substantial *Stundenbuch* [*Book of Hours*] (1899–1903; final version published 1905), the work that first established Rilke's fame. Rilke here uses a language borrowed from religion to depict the efforts and problems of the artist. God is seen as the highest symbol of artistic creation. Art is what matters – and the poet, in the guise of a monk or pilgrim, sings of his solitude or pilgrimage – of his attempt to transmute loneliness, particularly when encountered in poverty and death. Art tells of the response to the emotional strain and stress of modern urban life.

The poet does not depend on divine inspiration or help, but God depends on the poet and cannot exist without the poet's creative activity and support. Rilke's usage of the word 'God' is frequently ambiguous.[41] When using it he often, in fact, denotes art and not a transcendental Being. This use of the term 'God' is an attempt to emphasise the spiritual significance of art and to reject materialism and natural science. Indeed, a world conceived in terms of science appears empty, and art provides an antidote to that sense of emptiness. The monk or the pilgrim is a symbol of the potentialities of Rilke's mind[42] which he raises and intensifies to an independent poetic, but only poetic existence; for, in the last resort, the *Stundenbuch* turns on the question of the artist's vocation. As Rilke put it, 'there is nothing more jealous than my vocation',[43] and throughout the work, most strikingly in the third book of the cycle, *Das Buch von der Armut und vom Tode* [*The Book of Poverty and Death*], the poet imagines variations on the possibilities of the artist's vocation. They are presented as poetic realities, but as poetic realities only, and any claim to actual truth is, like all other statements and poetic utterances, incapable of being tested for truth in terms of science or history. In the last resort, the poet throughout speaks about his own emotional reaction to the world as a poet. So he states in the first book of the cycle, in *Vom mönchischen Leben* [*Of the Monastic Life*]:

> Ich glaube an alles noch nie Gesagte.
>
> Ich will meine frömmsten Gefühle befrein.
> Was noch keiner zu wollen wagte,
> wird mir einmal unwillkürlich sein.[44]

II

Rilke went to live in Paris in 1902 where he met and worked for Rodin for some years. With this move to Paris a new phase in his approach to art starts. He himself claimed to have changed his mind about the nature of poetry soon after arriving in Paris and falling under the spell of that great city and the great sculptor, but these claims are not entirely true; for the development of his thought was more gradual and less dramatic than is often asserted. His own poetry did not reflect this change of thought until *Neue Gedichte* [*New Poems*] (1907–08). Indeed, the third part of the *Stundenbuch*, which was composed in Paris, does not reveal it at all. Rilke's friendship with the Worpswede colony of painters, with Otto Modersohn, Paula Modersohn-Becker, Heinrich Vogeler and Hans vom Ende, as *Worpswede* (1902), his essay on these painters, makes abundantly clear, prepared this change before he met Rodin and before, in the *salon d'automne* (1907), he studied the paintings of Cézanne, the second great artistic influence in his Paris years.

What were, then, these new ideas which inform many of the letters of this period, particularly those to his wife Clara (herself a painter of the Worpswede school) and his friend Lou Andreas-Salomé, and which are foreshadowed in his books on the Worpswede painters and on Rodin, *Auguste Rodin* (1902–07)? They are summed up by a statement of Malte, the hero of his strange novel *Die Aufzeichnungen des Malte Laurids Brigge* [*The Notebooks of Malte Laurids Brigge*] (1910): 'He was a poet and hated that which is imprecise.'[45] The change in the direction of his thinking is in some ways little more than an elaboration of his early position, a shift of emphasis rather than a radical reorientation. Observing the work of painters and sculptors made him desire to endow his work with greater precision. The things of nature had to be most carefully observed and studied again and again. Art had to do even better than nature. It ought to attain an even finer precision. It is imperative not to imitate, but to create art-things based on things (of nature), indeed, even to recreate things. Things matter rather than feelings. In doing so subjectivity can be set aside and objectivity can be attained.

In a well-known passage in a letter to Lou Andreas-Salomé of 8 August 1903 this new position is most strikingly conveyed:

> The thing is precisely defined, the art-thing must be even more precisely defined. Above all it must be deprived of the accidental and be given space. It has become lasting, capable of eternity. The thing to be modelled *is semblance*. The art-thing *is* – .
>
> (Br. R – LAS, p. 84)

The terminology here betrays the influence of Rodin's thought although Rilke interpreted Rodin's theory in his own peculiar way.[46] For Rilke

Rodin's thought and work was a process of maturity which meant a 'mastership in the things of the spirit, particularly in art'.[47] Indeed, art had to be more than the result of mere inspiration. Rilke was convinced that the great medieval cathedrals – 'these mountains and mountain-ranges of the middle ages' – would never have been completed if they had arisen from inspiration. The cathedrals were – and all great works of art are – the products of worthwhile work. Therefore, Rilke preached the gospel of hard work which he believed he had discovered in Rodin.[48] And he sought to apply that discovery to his own poetry. Thus, he wanted to find, as he wrote to Lou Andreas-Salomé on 10 August 1903,

> the tool of his art, the hammer, his own [my] hammer so that it may become master and transcend all noise. There has to be a craft below his art, too; faithful, daily work which makes use of everything must be possible here too.
>
> (Br. R – LAS, p. 97)

Craftsmanship is needed, a craftsmanship which can alone do justice to the things which are to be modelled. In Rilke's view, Rodin succeeded in turning things of the external world into some kind of perennial space. Rodin did not speak about art; he did much better; he made reality by creating works of art which belonged to a calmer and less endangered realm than the world which we know. In fact, Rodin's works possessed spiritual qualities. To quash all the doubts that assailed Rilke continuously about a poet's – and in particular his own – ability to rival a sculptor in realising and creating works of art of similar stature Rilke worked at mastering his medium. He did so relentlessly and even studied Grimm's dictionary to learn to know his medium, language, better and thus to find more precise ways of depicting things.[49] Rilke spoke of his *métier*, and that meant for him experience, knowledge, ability and exactitude and a rejection of anything imprecise or uncertain.[50]

Rodin's work was not the product of a whim of the moment, or of the impulse to play, but of patience.[51] But devotion of this kind cannot be achieved without great sacrifice; for all other concerns, even personal happiness, have to be subordinated to it. Moreover, the example of Rodin was also capable of imparting other truths. Because he was aware of the significance of his work he was indifferent to all else that, by comparison, seemed unimportant.[52] However, a conflict inevitably arises between the demands of life and those of art, a conflict which he portrayed most powerfully in the longish poem *Requiem* [*Für eine Freundin*] (1908) written to commemorate his friend Paula Modersohn-Becker, the great German Expressionist painter. At times Rilke feels that, on account of his devotion to art, he is awkward in dealing with life;[53] at others this gaucherie does not seem to be of much consequence. He is torn between the belief that art is apart from life and the desire to accomplish a synthesis between art and life which is, however, difficult, if not impossible, to bring about. Yet whatever the difficulties, for the sake of art, an artist must not flinch from living an experience through to the end; indeed, he must be aware that things of art result from having experienced danger,[54] and that art, in the last resort, must prevail. Otherwise an artist cannot do justice to the singularity of experience which art must convey. Rilke here reverses the position of classical aesthetics; art is not semblance for him. On the contrary, it is reality, and the external world is semblance.[55] Consequently, there is more reality in a poem than in human relations.[56]

The artist is a creator. Thus, his work is like that of nature. And he, too, is in tune with nature[57] to which he listens with utmost conviction. He divines its secrets. But more than that. He also fulfils an intention of nature itself[58] and his work is therefore a product of necessity.[59] Only if he recognises this dimension of his work can he rid himself of his doubts about his status as an artist. In looking back on that period, Rilke rejects the language of his youth which, in retrospect, appears to him merely an emotional outburst. Language, so he thinks as a mature poet, ought to become fuller, denser and firmer than it was in his early poetry. If a poem possesses these qualities it alone represents an unmistakable, assured and pure achievement which is the mark of genuine poetry.[60] Yet, despite all self-confidence, Rilke still harbours the suspicion of the artist's inability to live up to his responsibility. He presumes that, in the last resort, art is beyond the living. Or, in other words, it is life itself which no one, not even the greatest artist or the oldest sage, can encompass; for even those who have reached great age are only beginners.[61] And yet, such is the paradoxical situation facing the poet, true life can be found in art alone.[62] But art also makes its impact on the artist. It profoundly changes him as a man through the act of artistic creation.

Cézanne confirmed Rilke in the attitude towards art developed and defined by him under the impact of Rodin. The experience of his paintings dominated the second phase of his Paris period just as Rodin and his work had dominated the first. In Cézanne's work he saw, quite rightly, a turning-point in the history of European painting: he hoped to bring about a similar revolution in poetry by his cycle *Neue Gedichte* [*New Poems*].[63] Whether he succeeded in accomplishing this revolution in the history of German poetry may well be doubted despite the great and unusual quality of his work, but it is certainly true that these poems constitute a revolutionary change in his own poetic practice. Yet this goal was not really a major reason for his new poetic style. Rilke does not seem to have worried about posterity's view of his work nor did he care much about his place in literary history or about the course of literature in general. He was too self-centred and self-reliant a poet for that. What mattered to him always was his own poetic development and his own artistic satisfaction, though he seems also to have basked in the praise of his close friends, many of them of aristocratic birth and way of life.

Cézanne, so Rilke believed, had discovered a great truth, a truth which Baudelaire had already adumbrated in his poem *Une Charogne*. He had recognised that the artist needs to search for a meaning to existence amidst the terrible and seemingly ugly experiences and features of life and to turn them into something beautiful.[64] In doing so Cézanne, like Rodin, had proved that the artist could still be a hero even in an unheroic age. For Rilke, Cézanne was a hero because he created a new, a heightened and indestructible reality by bringing out the relations between colours, relations which had always existed but had not been perceived.[65] Cézanne discovered them and made actual what had so far been only potential.[66] This act of telling us how to see the world as it really is Cézanne called '*la réalisation*'. Rilke sought to emulate Cézanne in his own poetry by describing relations in objects which he believed he perceived and he asked his reader to accept his description as just and right.

'*La realisation*' is however not a conscious process; rather, despite the artist's necessary unceasing work, it is an unconscious one.[67] The painter (or sculptor) must make progress without understanding the nature of the process that brings it about. Rilke here endows the activity of writing with some kind of mystic power which he uses to explain his (alleged) refusal to pay attention to comments on or reviews of his work, an activity he thought as distasteful as the task of collecting other people's comments on the woman whom one loves. But by ascribing mystic quality to language Rilke shirks the issue. Perhaps wisely and understandably, he avoids saying anything of substance about the nature of the creative process. As usual, he plays with ideas rather than setting them out in a consistent and coherent manner of giving a precise or comprehensive account of his views.

Of the creative works written during the Paris period *Das Buch der Bilder* [*The Book of Images*] (1902–6), more a collection than a cycle properly speaking (although Rilke paid some attention to the order of the various poems), does not add anything of importance to our understanding of Rilke's approach to art. But in the *Neue Gedichte*, his next great cycle, the new ideas were given poetic form.[68]. The central theme of this cycle is the status and function of art and the artist.[69] Each of the books opens with poems about Apollo. Each time a statue is carefully described and its impact on the beholder is analysed. The impact leads to a reversal [*Umschlag*][70] bringing about a reorientation of the artist's attention which is now devoted to the object depicted. This object may be either an artefact, a work of art or an edifice, or a work of nature.

Some poems, ostensibly about natural objects may, in fact, be about works of art. It is, for instance, by no means certain whether 'Blaue Hortensie' ['Blue Hydrangea'] (1906), a key-poem which Rilke had at one time thought of putting at the beginning of the work, is about real flowers or about a painting of flowers. But this poem, like many others, describes the ephemeral character of nature and experience and the possibility of renewal, a renewal of experience through art.[71]

BLAUE HORTENSIE

So wie das letzte Grün in Farbentiegeln
sind diese Blätter, trocken, stumpf und rauh,
hinter den Blütendolden, die ein Blau
nicht auf sich tragen, nur von ferne spiegeln.

Sie spiegeln es verweint und ungenau,
als wollten sie es wiederum verlieren,
und wie in alten blauen Briefpapieren
ist Gelb in ihnen, Violett und Grau;

Verwaschnes wie an einer Kinderschürze,
Nichtmehrgetragnes, dem nichts mehr geschieht:
wie fühlt man eines kleinen Lebens Kürze.

Doch plötzlich scheint das Blau sich zu verneuen
in einer von den Dolden, und man sieht
ein rührend Blaues sich vor Grünem freuen.[72]

Many poems, such as 'Der Turm',[73] – 'Quai du Rosaire'[74] and above all
'Die Gazelle[75] are concerned with reflection on the power of art. Ryan's
account and Herman Uyttersprot's earlier analysis of this poem dem-
onstrate convincingly that its subject-matter, as of many other poems, is
both art and nature. The poet points to the impact which art can have on
life, particularly on the life of the artist, as had indeed been foreshadowed
by the 'Apollo sonnets' – 'Früher Apollo' ['Early Apollo'] (1906) and
'Archäischer Torso Apollos' ['Archaic Torso of Apollo'] (1908).[76] Rilke is
seeking to show that by responding to art with proper empathy we are able
to enter the magic world which it creates, a world which forces us to
reconsider our way of life and asks us to look for a resurgence of our
spiritual power. Indeed, a good work of art involves for the artist and, at
one further remove, for the reader, a surrender to the subject. Yet the artist
does not stop at this act of self-abandonment to the experience, an act
which goes to the point of self-denial, but he seeks also to recapture this
process itself in order to create art.[77]

Great art, too, has important consequences for other artists; for all things
created by a master like Rodin[78] make the artist turn to nature and to
works of art and force him to study them with greater interest. He is able to
experience the impact of art, especially the reversal of what it can or ought
to produce in his mind, as a form of revelation (or epiphany in the Joycean
sense of the word). Art is, in fact, a mode of cognition leading to a different
view of reality, to a new apprehension of the world, not only for the poet,
but also for the reader.[79] To apprehend the world it is necessary to
transmute earlier experiences, as does the artist in the creative process. An
experience constituted by a blending of feeling and thought can, then, be

recreated and retained in art. The artist, in fact, succeeds in giving permanence to the flux of life – stepping outside the fold of mortal finite men and thus acquiring a higher god-like power. This esoteric doctrine informs the poetic practice of the *Neue Gedichte* and is embodied in some of its most striking poems, such as the 'Apollo Sonnets'. The most striking portrayal of this impact is in the second of these sonnets:

ARCHAÏSCHER TORSO APOLLOS

Wir kannten nicht sein unerhörtes Haupt,
darin die Augenäpfel reiften. Aber
sein Torso glüht noch wie ein Kandelaber,
in dem sein Schauen, nur zurückgeschraubt,

sich hält und glänzt. Sonst könnte nicht der Bug
der Brust dich blenden, und im leisen Drehen
der Lenden könnte nicht ein Lächeln gehen
zu jener Mitte, die die Zeugung trug.

Sonst stünde dieser Stein entstellt und kurz
unter der Schultern durchsichtigem Sturz
und flimmerte nicht so wie Raubtierfelle;

und bräche nicht aus allen seinen Rändern
aus wie ein Stern; denn da ist keine Stelle,
die dich nicht sieht. Du mußt sein Leben ändern[80]

Yet despite all their claims to spiritual power the role played by the sensuous element in Rilke's poetry must not be underrated;[81] it makes the poet fix his attention always on the concrete objects in the external world.

Rilke does not however, merely describe an object, for description, in his view, entails an inner process represented outwardly through a poetic form: the interplay between the object depicted and the subjective experience, between the outer and inner world is also intimated. It is Rilke's aim to say everything in this poetry with relentless matter-of-factness and coldness of presentation while yet reflecting an inner event.[82] He summed up the whole process of thought when he wrote to his wife on 8 March 1907:

Gazing is such a wonderful thing, about which we know little; in gazing we are turned completely outward, but just when we are so most, things seem to go on within us, which have been waiting longingly for the moment when they should be unobserved, and while they are happening in us, intactly and strangely anonymously, independently of our consciousness, their significance gradually grows in the object without, a convincing, powerful name, their only possible name, in which we joyfully and reverently recognise the happening within our soul, without being able to reach it, only quite gently, quite remotely comprehending it under the symbol of a thing that immediately before was quite strange to us and in the next moment is again estranged from us.[83]

This passage conclusively sums up his thoughts on art during his middle period during which he was seeking, under the impact of the example of Rodin and Cézanne, to come to terms with the poet's relationship to external reality. He did so by describing the impression made by external objects, or even more frequently by works of art, on the poet's sensitive mind. The impressions recorded are usually not what would normally be expected, for Rilke's perspective, while not actually falsifying the object depicted, gives it a very peculiar slant. Indeed, his work at first sight even seems not to satisfy the correspondence theory of truth, but relies on the power of internal coherence – and does not permit refutation by an appeal to the object depicted. Yet what he sees is not wholly imaginary; it resembles at least some facets of reality, even though his view is not at all conventional. His account can always be corroborated by an appeal to the facts, but in part only; his preoccupation with renewal and resurgence is always associated with a highly selective description of facts. It is as if Rilke sees the poet's task as consisting in a challenge to the conventional view of the world, the poet's aim should be to replace this view by a novel and more searching one, thus carrying out in poetic practice what great artists have always sought to do, viz. to modify or change our view of the world by creating the new reality of their works. For a new great work of art, just like a new scientific theory (or set of theories), changes our conception of the world by forcing us to reassess our presuppositions and our perspective.

From the years before 1910 – the watershed, as Rilke called the year that was marked by the completion of the *Neue Gedichte* and *Die Aufzeichnungen des Malte Laurids Brigge* – a more or less clearly delimited set of ideas on art and the artist emerges. After 1910 this is not so; there is very much less material available, apart from the poetry itself, to be quoted in evidence for his views on art. His 'theoretical' comments are very sparse indeed. He did not review books any longer and he wrote hardly any essays, and those which he wrote yield little information. Even his many letters do not contain full accounts of his views, as do his great letters about Rodin and Cézanne. For a tentative account we have to rely on occasional remarks and on interpretation of his poetry.

This reticence is perhaps not surprising. He was intensely dissatisfied with the course of his poetic development as he had never been before. He wondered why this should be so. *Malte*, so he suggested, had virtually exhausted him.[84] Most of his previous convictions began to appear dubious. He was assailed by doubts about his own ability to write. Likewise, he was uncertain about the function of art and the artist. Various personal experiences probably helped to bring about this state of mind – his quarrel with Rodin, his Don Juanism which increased more and more in pace, the war – all played their part. These doubts were, however, not merely hindrances to poetic production, but were also fruitful, since from that <u>soil</u> sprang the *Duineser Elegien* and the *Sonette an* ⤦ *Orpheus*, Rilke's major achievements; but until he had completed both works in 1922 he felt that he was not writing the poetry he wanted to write, although he was by no means unproductive however much he liked to complain about the truancy of his poetic genius.

What do his views in the years after 1910 amount to? First of all he felt it necessary to reorientate his approach, for he wanted to take stock of what he had done and of what he could hope to do now. He felt he had allowed his impressions to have too much sway over him. He felt: 'I stay too long before them. Au lieu de me pénétrer les impressions me percent.'[85]

Secondly, at times Rilke even believed that his inability to write amounted to an emotional and spiritual crisis that was the symptom of a mental illness, an illness which was growing more and more acute and in turn became part of his work itself. Nostalgically, he looked back on his earlier Paris days, especially on the period of the *Neue Gedichte* when he would never (so he alleged) have expected setbacks of that magnitude.[86] He now felt at the mercy of the powerful forces to which artists have to submit and he was unable to ascertain the directions in which they were propelling him. He did not even know whether his work was making progress or declining in power.

Thirdly, – and this was the most difficult of all to bear – he was, although he had passed the zenith of his life, still without a vocation which he could exercise continuously;[87] for he now alleges that poetry is too intermittent an activity to constitute a proper vocation. He was unjust to his poetic creativity which, in fact, never ceased, and he was perhaps even putting up a pretence, but he was preoccupied, indeed obsessed, with his inability to complete the *Duineser Elegien*, his major task in hand ever since their inception in 1912.

In that very year 1912 Rilke complains bitterly that all his experiences had combined only to make him a failure. There even seemed little point in being an artist: in a mood of despondency he remarked to Katharina Kippenberg, the wife of his publisher, that 'art is superfluous, can art heal wounds, can it take away the bitterness of death? It does not assuage despair, it does not feed the hungry or clothe the shivering.'[88] These doubts were not new,[89] but, at this stage of his life, he felt them with peculiar intensity. Art, so he believed, was not only a dubious, but even a sinister pursuit. Its capacity to delude seemed too great, for it pretended to establish certainties which the artist himself did not possess and was thus incapable of conveying. It was therefore questionable whether anyone had a right to be an artist. On 28 August 1911 he summed up these doubts in a letter to the Princess of Thurn and Taxis:

I think nobody has ever experienced more clearly than I have how much art goes against nature; it is the most passionate inversion of the world, the return journey from the Infinite, in which all honest things meet one advancing in the opposite direction! . . . Yes, but who is one, that one dares to go in this direction against them all, in this eternal retroversion whereby one deceives them into believing one has already arrived somewhere, at some final point, and now has leisure to come back again.[90]

On account of these misgivings, Rilke looked for change, for a new beginning,[91] an experience he sought to crystallise in the poem 'Wendung' ['Turning'] of 1913, but although this poem was an important one, until the completion of the *Duineser Elegien* in February 1922 he doubted continuously whether he could succeed in achieving this new beginning in life and in poetry.

The 1914–18 war made Rilke feel even more despondent. After a first uncritical bout of enthusiasm not so much for war, but for the emotion which it unleashed, he was filled with horror.[92] He was highly sceptical of all propaganda and profoundly distressed by the suffering which he felt to be beyond endurance.[93] And the few months spent in the Austrian army, as a conscript, even if he served them not at the front, but in a clerical capacity in Vienna, were predictably a great shock to his sensitive mind. In his view, the most that any one could hope for during the war was that spiritual death would be avoided.

After his release from Austrian war service, brought about by the intervention of highly-placed friends, he lived in Munich where the Bavarian Revolution of 1918/19 was, in principle, welcomed by him. But he quickly felt that it did not seem to answer the need for that real and profound change which he felt to be necessary.[94] He wanted a new beginning, but, in his view, this could succeed only if man's inner life was shaped entirely anew.[95] The poet alone could show how this reorientation of man's spiritual aspirations could be brought about. Rilke therefore rejected all political programmes since they did not appear to touch the real problems, which were, for him, spiritual problems. Therefore, he was not concerned with political and social change, but with the development of his own inner life and with his ability to transmute his own personal experiences into poetry.

Not too much should be made of his rejection of politics, nor of his later ignorant and foolish (to put it mildly) approval of Italian fascism, an unimportant episode in his life.[96] Neither amounts to a considered statement of a political creed, let alone to a political philosophy. There is no doubt that he was, throughout most of his life, opposed to any form of narrow nationalism, even the *Fünf Gesänge* [*Five Hymns*], written in the first flush of war fever on 2/3 August 1914, do not alter the picture; for they describe his awareness of the elemental force of war rather than they praise it.[97] And he was certainly highly critical of German and Austrian militarism, of German chauvinism and of its aspirations for European hegemony. The collections of his letters so far published do not however give a reliable picture of his political sympathies[98] since they exclude references to his connection with leaders of the Bavarian revolution, such as Kurt Eisner and Ernst Toller, nor do we learn from them that accusations of communism and the searching of his flat by the counter-revolutionary police were among the reasons for his leaving Munich for Switzerland in 1919. They also do not tell of his relationship with critics of German nationalism, such as Alexander Prince Hohenlohe or Walther Rathenau, one of the leading statesmen of the Weimar Republic.[99] But Rilke had no consistent political views. It was more often people rather than political ideas and convictions that impressed him. Indeed, Rilke was always a European in outlook, though undoubtedly his political attitudes were full of contradictions and his call for total, profound inner revolution is full of hazards since it is capable of being exploited by extremists at either end of the political spectrum. Likewise, his longing for a pre-industrial world poses many dangers, though his criticism of modern technological civilisation often goes to the heart of many abuses of modern urban life.[100]

Yet, in the last resort, it remains true that politics never really mattered to Rilke even if, from time to time, he took an interest in them. His political judgement was poor, a characteristic which, of course, he shares with many, if not most, people. His interest lay in cultivating his inner, emotional life and in recording that experience – and here, although himself of Roman Catholic origin, he followed a powerful German Protestant tradition going back at least to Pietism, if not to the Reformation. In that respect, he was yet another representative of Western individualism. This attitude may or may not call for reprobation: indifference to politics is certainly a limitation but so is overestimation of its importance. Lack of interest in politics is certainly found among men and women of widely differing political views and background, and is certainly not restricted merely to conservatives or crypto-fascists. To condemn his poetry or even his views on art on this account is sadly mistaken. It amounts to asking the wrong question to get the desired answers, for poetry is not science or philosophy or history, and poems cannot be falsified like statements in these disciplines.

Rilke was looking for a new way of writing and hence for a new approach to art. Not that he completely rejected his earlier beliefs, but he wanted to build on his achievement up to date in order to find an even more adequate way of dealing with his experience of the self and the impact of external reality. What he had so far achieved seemed no longer valid. His doubts made him wonder whether he was able to write valid poetry at all. Rilke returned to the problem which he thought he had solved in the *Neue Gedichte* of whether poetry can adequately and objectively sum up or evoke experience or must always be subjective. Or, in other words, he was grappling with the epistemological question of whether it is possible to have an objective experience of reality and of oneself, a question for him always to be tackled by way of poetry.

In the *Neue Gedichte* he had sought to record change by depicting the process of how 'things' impinge on the mind, but, in fact, in doing so he was merely depicting 'things' as a pretext for a confession. He had looked in the external world for concrete equivalents (which could either be natural objects or works of art) to denote emotional experiences, but he now began to recognise that 'things' or, for that matter, the descriptions of 'things', were incapable of recording inner experience adequately. Admittedly, the description however ambiguous had none the less offered some tangible record of reality, but it had not been a comprehensive one.

Rilke had been shifting his point of view. However important 'things' and craftsmanship remained for him he no longer wished merely to record his emotional response to the external world. His aim was now different: it was, as he wrote to the Expressionist playwright Reinhold Johannes Sorge on 4 June 1914, 'the making visible of the spiritual realm' (R – Br I, p. 498). Art had to solve two problems simultaneously. It had not merely to depict the impact of the external world on the inner life, it had at the same time to find images in the external world which were to express inner experiences. However, it is not merely this two-way traffic which is at work: the poet continuously encounters the limits of the unsayable and seeks to transcend it.

The attempt to go beyond these limits entailed the necessity of understanding and conveying the experience of death, a problem with which he wrestled throughout his life.[101] As he put it in his famous letter to his Polish translator, Witold von Hulewicz, of 10 November 1925, death is 'the non-illuminated side of life, the side turned away from us' (R – Br. 1921 – 26, p. 332). He believed that the artist can, through his work, bring within our orbit that which is normally assumed to be beyond our experience, or, in other words, he wished to push the limits of mental experience further than is normally assumed possible. This aim springs from his conviction that there exists a transcendental sphere which lies beyond the empirical realm as well as from his desire to convey this conviction to a secularised world. The artists are, he wrote in the same letter, 'the bees of the invisible' (R – Br. 1921 – 26, p. 335). As Rilke suggested in a letter to Dieter Bassermann in the last year of his life (5 April 1926), they discover, record and hand on spiritual tradition; they put into poetry that which they have seen in 'the countless signatures of creatures of the past, found in the skeletons, in the yesterdays – in all their changes of being' (R – Br. 1921 – 26, p. 384).

In conveying spiritual experience poetry again shows that it belongs to a higher sphere, a sphere which is still closely connected with the artist's own being. For it was a central belief of the later Rilke that the artist is able to encompass the whole world within himself. To this experience he gave the strange name of *Weltinnenraum* (literally 'the inner space of the world'), a term that defies translation.[102] The set of beliefs surrounding this word is so idiosyncratic as to make it impossible to accept it as a reasonable and plausible cosmological theory; yet it springs from the time-hallowed belief that life is unity and that 'we differentiate too much',[103] that we neither achieve wholeness as men nor see life as a whole, but allow analysis to prevent synthesis.[104] But like Goethe[105] and Schiller before him, Rilke aimed at a synthesis that did full justice to individual phenomena and experiences. His poetry was not to record fragments of experience, but to convey an experience of the world as a whole, to depict the world not as a series of individual instances but as a nexus of interrelations. Rilke's aim is to convey an experience of the world as a whole in his poetry. To record fragments of experience no longer suffices. The world is, so he claims, depicted in his poetry not as a series of individual instances, but as a nexus of interrelations. These interrelations exist in the mind of the poet as a set of mental relations and images: it is his task to find the appropriate words and images to convey them in his poetry. In doing so an imaginary world is constructed which does not have an anchor in the outer world, but is none the less real and even perennial. For him, a work of art can convey the underlying unity of existence since it can comprise the past, the present and the future and, through its imagery, allow them to exist simultaneously in space. Thus, a work of art is capable of transcending ephemeral experience and making tradition live within us. This ability gives a special dimension to art and explains why the perfect work of art has no other task save that of surviving us.[106]

To create art is however difficult. Modern machine-made technology – of which North American society offers the most advanced instance – impairs artistic sensitivity.[107] As a result, artistic creativity suffers. It cannot flourish in an arid spiritual climate. Indeed, the spiritual climate has deteriorated so much that living itself has become harrowing for a sensitive mind and particularly for the artist.[108] And since art feeds on the artist's life it appears to be a mystery that art can be produced at all. Rilke's own age may, so he believed, be the last when it will be at all possible to create art and in this desolate world, he himself may be the last of a long line of artists.

The growth of modern technological society certainly frightened Rilke, but, to a very large extent, by putting these fears to the fore he merely externalised his own inner problems. He felt uneasy in the modern world because he felt apprehensive about new ways of living. Also, his self appeared to be divided within itself.[109] Moreover, poetry could not, so he felt, serve his purpose as readily as the plastic arts.[110] Painting and sculpture are able to appropriate the external world more adequately since their medium allows them to do so in a more tangible manner. In his childhood Rilke believed he had been able to respond spontaneously to the world as an artist ought to. For an artist should absorb the world without noticing the fact of this absorption, like an anemone which, as Rilke once observed, had been open all night and was unable to close its petals in daytime.[111] Children have this capacity of achieving renewal and transformation which is so necessary to him in order to cure him of his tensions, but which now appears beyond his reach.

At the root of Rilke's predicament was his emotional solipsism, which, though intensely desired at some time, never satisfied him. Narcissism did not deliver lasting contentment[112]. The external world, and in particular other people, remained an obstinate fact that could not be ignored. Thus, others impinged on his solitude and prevented the desired autonomy of mind and feeling. To withdraw into one's inner world, however complex it might appear, was inadequate. His art was also unable to help others; for Rilke felt that he did not himself possess the certainty which many of his readers desired and which poetry should convey.[113] The poet's approach had to be different. He is a magician who turns into song that which he is unable to cope with. For he is also a conjurer creating myths, recreating legends that need not necessarily carry objective or universal validity. What he is able to do is less comprehensive, and yet significant. Again, he states his fundamental conviction; the poet is able to create a reality of its own that can be placed alongside other realities. While doubts might not be banished from the poet's own mind the act of creating poetry could and should mean that these doubts are transformed into poetic statements and, through the poetry, the world as a whole could then be accepted and even praised. This meant accepting and praising even those aspects of the world which appeared repugnant to the poet, such as modern technological civilisation[114] or Christianity. Rilke therefore liked poetry which overcame doubts and praised the world.[115] He wanted to follow the example set by his great predecessors who had written that kind of poetry.

This magic power which Rilke attributed to poetry did not however mean that he believed that poetry could solve all problems. He was too uncertain for that. His room for manoeuvre appeared limited and poetry seemed his only weapon to protect himself against the warring forces that afflicted him:[116] the God within him and the splendour or horror of the world without. Poetry alone allowed him to develop his inner life within the small space at his disposal. If he did so he could give his art the necessary balance of outer world and inner life. To write poetry, like living itself, was a most precarious activity, threatened at every turn; it had to be tackled with sincerity, with a fastidious regard for words and themes, and with the desire to praise the attractive and the repellent, joy and fear, triumphs and failures, the insights and the uncertainties offered by life. In the last resort, it was a complex activity reflecting a complex view of the world. No wonder that Rilke's poetry is most complex, too.

IV

These ideas form the basis of his later poetry, in which Rilke's concern with the writing of poetry, or even with the composition of the next poem or cycle of poems, plays a major part. Like all artists he wanted to discover and create a form of art which was peculiarly his own. To do so entailed creating a language of his own. As he wrote in his essay on the painter Otto Modersohn: 'Everything that is individual requires, if it is not to be silent, a language of its own. It is nothing without it.'[117] Only thus could the artist endow his art with the power and the force, and consequently with the reality which all art needs.[118]

In his early poetry Rilke had wanted to tell the story of his feelings, but in his later period he thought that very little can be known of feelings. What can be told has to be told in a complex and even elusive manner in order to do justice to the baffling emotional experience. But, in this period of his life at least, Rilke did not want to separate the recording of feelings from the discussion of ideas. Indeed, both feelings and ideas had to become assimilated one to the other in the poetry. What he has to say is as much the story of a *felt* response, as it is that of an *intellectual* response, to experience and ideas.[119] Poems are, he maintains, more than either feelings or ideas; they combine both and become experiences themselves for the poet and, at one further remove, for the reader as well. As Malte stated in a famous passage: 'verses are not feelings – those we have early enough – they are experiences' (R, VI, p. 724).

Since Rilke felt life to be precarious in a world where traditions were threatened and nothing was arising to replace them poetry was his sole means of spiritual support. However critical he was of tradition and orthodoxy he was convinced that without a framework of tradition culture was incapable of survival and the individual's spiritual development was stultified. Therefore, he cherished the outward form of those traditions in which he did not believe: he did so since he thought that there was nothing available to replace them and these traditions made the world more hospitable than it would otherwise have been. Poetry needed them too. Rilke knew that we cannot live without values; if the values inherent in tradition have become jeopardised or even obsolete, they have to be replaced by new values. But to find them was not easy. For instance, he sought to develop a new doctrine of love (*Liebe ohne Besitz*) which meant that lovers had no claim on the physical presence of each other, once their love had been established – a doctrine which might, without being uncharitable, be called a convenient device for his Don Juanism, but which could also be said to be an offshoot of the well-established tradition of unselfish love.

Loss of tradition meant change, and the poet had to come to terms with a changing world. The only adequate way of describing the process of his emotional and spiritual adjustment to that change was, for Rilke, to depict or intimate relations between things and experiences, and *Bezug* [relationship] is appropriately a key-word of his later poetry.[120] The hope remained that, though words by themselves are inadequate to do so, poetry would provide intimations of how to cope with the uncertainties of life. Since Rilke's own doubt and sense of uncertainty were always closely bound up with his struggle to write, the completion of successful poetry necessarily solved part of this problem, if indeed it did not provide the feeling – or illusion – of a total solution.

Rilke, then, even in his later poetry, returns to his beginnings, or at least to the question which preoccupied him in his youth and which is summed up in the *Florentiner Tagebuch*: what can the poet say and how can he say it? In *Malte* or in the early prose tale *Ewald Tragy*, the main figure is a poet whose attempts and failures as a poet are depicted. The question is always asked whether the poet can transmute both inner experience and external reality through his poetry into a meaningful and adequate pattern which is more than an accumulation of mere words and subjective impressions. In the *Duineser Elegien* all these doubts are reviewed. Are words adequate? Can they say the unsayable? As he put it in one of *Die Sonette an Orpheus* (T, 10)

> Wissen wirs, Freunde, wissen wirs nicht?
> Beides bildet die zögernde Stunde
> in dem menschlichen Angesicht.[121]

Are fragments of experience meaningful? How can we live when we are uncertain about values and traditions, and do not know the direction and purpose of our lives? Or, to use the peculiar terminology of this great cycle, how can the poet reach the figure of the angel who possesses the unity denied to man, who has perfection but appears to live even beyond the poet's reach? And how can the beautiful, how can art make an impact on us? And how can we bear its impact? Is beauty only the beginning of the terrible – of the experience of the angel – or can it help man? The very first lines of the *Duineser Elegien* pose these questions:

> Wer, wenn ich schriee, hörte mich denn aus der Engel
> Ordnungen? Und gesetzt selbst, es nähme
> einer mich plötzlich ans Herz, ich verginge von seinem
> stärkeren Dasein. Denn das Schöne ist nichts
> als des Schrecklichen Anfang, den wir noch gerade ertragen,
> und wir bewundern es so, weil es gelassen verschmäht,
> uns zu zerstören. Ein jeder Engel ist schrecklich.[122]

In the *Duineser Elegien* the poet then speaks about not being at home in the world and not being at ease with other people's interpretations of it. He is not sure of his mission, or even of his function. Unsure of his way he follows the dictates of the moment, but cannot find any refuge or rest. Experience remains ephemeral, and he finds himself unable to transcend this condition. Unable to grasp life as a whole, like all human beings, he relies too much on reason, on analysis, and on distinctions. He desires order, but encounters dissolution and chaos. Yet all is not lost. He can learn to speak as a poet. He can stand out against the fashions and trends of the age, he can be opposed to and detached from the *Zeitgeist* and transmute his experience of the world into poetry, thus overcoming his own sense of inadequacy.

This bald summary, like all summaries, is inadequate, but it may point to the central questions raised in the cycle. And Eudo C. Mason certainly carries conviction in arguing that the theme of the *Duineser Elegien* is the fate of the poet, and not that of man,[123] though it must be added that the poet appears to be a symbolic figure.

In the *Duineser Elegien* Rilke transcends, through the writing of poetry, his problems as a poet, though not necessarily as a man, even if the creative act may well have given him personal comfort.[124] If in the *Elegien* the road to this stance of affirmation is depicted, in *Sonette an Orpheus*, the companion-piece to the *Elegien* written in the month of their completion (February 1922), affirmation itself is the theme.[125] The poet sets out to praise the world; even when it appears menacing and detestable. Saying itself has become existence:

> Ein Gott vermags. Wie aber, sag mir, soll
> ein Mann ihm folgen durch die schmale Leier?
> Sein Sinn ist Zwiespalt. An der Kreuzung zweier
> Herzwege steht kein Tempel für Apoll.
>
> Gesang, wie du ihn lehrst, ist nicht Begehr,
> nicht Werbung um ein endlich noch Erreichtes;
> Gesang ist Dasein. . . .[126]

The poet, as the cycle tells us, has to pursue experience to its very limits. He has to abandon the thought of self in the quest for the whole, but like Orpheus he has to return to the here and now – to praise the whole of life. In the seventh sonnet of the first part the poet gives us the answer

> RÜHMEN, das ists! Ein zum Rühmen Bestellter,
> ging er hervor wie das Erz aus des Steins
> Schweigen. Sein Herz, o vergängliche Kelter
> eines den Menschen unendlichen Weins.
>
> Nie versagt ihm die Stimme am Staube,
> wenn ihn das göttliche Beispiel ergreift.
> Alles wird Weinberg, alles wird Traube,
> in seinem fühlenden Süden gereift.[127]

And the poet has to praise at any price, even if it means abandoning his beloved. In song all discrepancies and difficulties are accepted, for poetry allows us to grasp the world as a pattern of relations, even of necessary relations. Through the magic of art time and space are suspended, the beautiful and the ugly, the seductive and the menacing are mingled, the differentiation normally practised by man which impedes understanding ceases. Poetry becomes the goal of life which the poet – and, by way of analogy, the reader – must pursue steadfastly and ruthlessly. In that sense, art, for Rilke, is here the answer to the ills of the world, not because it solves any practical problems or even induces an attitude of mind through which man becomes inclined or conditioned to solve such problems. It manifestly does nothing of that kind. But art suggests how the underlying unity of life can be reconstructed in the work of art itself. Art thus reveals to us how we can avoid damage to our spiritual and cultural life. It also endows life with a spiritual, transcendental dimension by pointing to, or even testifying of, something that goes beyond the bounds of sense. It seems to tell of regions which cannot be spoken of. This creed seems to be mystical, but Rilke was no mystic. Nor was he a saint as his maternal friend, the Princess Marie of Thurn and Taxis-Hohenlohe,[128] pointed out to him. His concern was, whatever pose he may have adopted at times, with this world, but he was loath to accept a purely materialist or naturalist conception of the cosmos, and desperately looked for a transcendental explanation. Yet he was able to find an answer to the riddle only in his own peculiar vision. He wanted to give form to that which is unsayable.[129] Yet he can only express his own insight. Rilke always wanted to achieve the impossible – to find the meaning of the world through art; but this, by its nature, art is precluded from achieving. For art can give only form to a meaning which the artist has already found. It is magic, and as such it can cast a spell, but it cannot perform the miracle of producing a meaning where there is none. Thus, Rilke can sing in praise of life, accepting and revering it, but he cannot establish a faith. But why should a poet be expected to do so? It is not his province. Art cannot be a substitute for religion. And Rilke's hagiographers who claimed that it was did him a disservice, even if at times they seemed to be encouraged by the poet's own words or attitudes. The Romantic claim to raise the world to a higher level through poetry may sound appealing, but it is an illusion. In the end, the poet must face the reality of self-deception. Poetic magic may amount to no more than a cloak for the mating-call, as Rilke himself admitted in his poem *Magie*, written in August 1924 after the completion of the last two great cycles of poetry'.

> Aus unbeschreiblicher Verwandlung stammen
> solche Gebilde – : Fühl! und glaub!
> Wir leidens oft: zu Asche werden Flammen;
> doch, in der Kunst: zur Flamme wird der Staub.

> Hier ist Magie. In das Bereich des Zaubers
> scheint das gemeine Wort hinaufgestuft
> und ist doch wirklich wie der Ruf des Taubers,
> der nach der unsichtbaren Taube ruft.[130]

None the less, the biographical fact does not tell the whole story either. It does not nullify the power and truth of poetry whose spell may create a reality of its own. And Hofmannsthal spoke for many when he told Rilke that he had, in *Die Sonette an Orpheus*, succeeded in wresting a slice of land from the frontier of that which can still hardly be said;[131] using, of course, a demonstrably more cautious formulation than has been employed by those who claim that Rilke has cast his glance beyond these bounds from which no traveller returns.

Still, the sense of dubiousness remains. The poet is both a creator and yet a part of creation; he is the man aspiring to the heights and yet he possesses feet of clay. He belongs to the world and yet is alien to it. Poetry is seductive, it may reflect man's carnal, selfish nature, but it also tells us of his hopes and expectations, of his seeking to reach beyond the bounds of self. Poetry is both a joy and a lament, both pure and dubious. Such is at least the nature of Rilke's poetry. It tells us of the poet's voyage to sound the clarion-call of poetic power, but also of his failure to reach a definite goal as he discovers that uncertainty is his lot. But his poetry is none the poorer for this discovery. From this source, too, springs his refusal to be unambiguous, definite and clear, and his continuous resorting to the nuances of meaning. This ambivalent attitude towards that which can be said in poetry also contributes to the difficulty of his poetry and the inconsistency of his thought. Rilke's poetry offers a kaleidoscope of impressions and meanings, fascinating and absorbing, but also often baffling and contradictory. No firm conclusions can be drawn from his poetry nor can they even be inferred about his poetry. This is why there have been so many different interpretations. In the last resort, Rilke did not commit himself either on the ultimate question of existence or on the problems of his emotional life. Uncertainty lingers on – despite all praise of life and championship of art. It is, in fact, built into the very structure of his work because he wishes continuously to shift his meaning or perspective. A multifarious pattern of ideas alone could encompass the experience of both the here and now and that which may transcend it. This intellectual pluralism reflects the plurality of values to which men subscribe in a world no longer dominated by a single creed or a uniform tradition. But art must give form to this complex, elusive, multi-perspectival experience. On this uncertain ground, then, Rilke rests his case for the supremacy of art, that fragile, but only reed of support to which he could clutch in life. But however sceptical we may remain of the philosophical validity of his ideas – and he certainly did not produce a profound aesthetic philosophy – they remain of great interest as the personal statement of a modern poet, and a great poet at that. Moreover, the ambiguities of Rilke's philosophical position do not detract from the value of the poetry, for unlike philosophy, art does not have to provide a consistent argument. Poetry lives on the strength and compelling power of the impact which it makes on the reader, and Rilke's best poetry has certainly succeeded in deeply affecting many sensitive minds. As a result, his ideas – and particularly his views on art and the artist – have mattered to many and repay attention. To chart the development of these ideas is to depict a great poet's attempt at self-discovery by way of thinking about poetry and composing it. The poet's struggle to understand his own artistic task is also a symbol for a sensitive mind's endeavour to cope with the uncertainties created by the continuous erosion of traditional cultural and religious values in a technological age. Thus, Rilke's thought and poetry become a poignant reminder of the difficulties in store for sensitive and creative minds in the modern world.

6 Thomas Mann (1875–1955)

Probably no other twentieth-century writer has conveyed the central ambiguity of the artist's place in the modern world as forcefully as Thomas Mann. Three of his major works, *Tonio Kröger* (1903), *Der Tod in Venedig* [*Death in Venice*] (1912) and *Doktor Faustus* (1947) have an artist as hero while in others, such as *Buddenbrooks* (1901), *Königliche Hoheit* [*Royal Highness*] (1909), *Die Bekenntnisse des Hochstaplers Felix Krull* [*Confessions of Felix Krull, Confidence Man*] (1954) and *Joseph und seine Brüder* [*Joseph and his Brethren*] (1933–43), the hero is a man of artistic sensibility who symbolises artistic aspirations. Indeed, from his earliest stories onward the relationship between artistic sensibility and day-to-day bourgeois reality, between intellect and life, mind and nature, is a central, if not *the* central, theme.

The choice of this subject-matter was no accident. It arose from the author's own situation and from his attitude to literary tradition. Born in the ancient Hanseatic city of Lübeck, into a patrician bourgeois family, Thomas Mann always felt guilty at having strayed from the path of bourgeois virtue. He did so not merely because he saw himself as a bourgeois who had gone astray but also because he no longer felt able to accept traditional values – in the realm of art, morals or religion. Not that he rejected these values outright, but he found he had to subject them to scrutiny and doubt. For he had imbibed too many Nietzschean ideas not to regard all statements, attitudes of mind and intellectual positions with extreme scepticism. Indeed, his scepticism was so radical that Nietzche's /sc own thought was not spared. And he soon drew conclusions from the work of his mentor which Nietzsche could not have agreed with.[1] He claimed that he never accepted Nietzsche's intellectual position, but found his work challenging and felt always compelled to differ. In principle, Mann's criticism extended to several areas: firstly, he questioned the prevailing literary tradition, i.e. realism as exemplified in the Naturalist movement still in vogue at the turn of the century; secondly, he wondered whether the Western intellectual tradition was decadent or not; thirdly, he asked whether art could claim any value or validity whatsoever in the modern world. The last problem made him also doubt whether art was able to convey the truth or whether the artist was not a charlatan. Moreover, it made him reflect on whether he was a representative of his age or merely a peripheral figure of no consequence. Mann wrestled with these questions all his life, but he was too creative an artist merely to discourse on them. He gave expression to them in his imaginative work. Almost inevitably, he changed his point of view in the course of time. As he grew older he became more and more aware of the individual's relation to the world around him and he began therefore to consider both the criticism and the defence of his own position as an activity which concerned the whole of culture. Indeed, he went further: he began to use critical enquiry to defend not only his own creative enterprise, but also culture itself against the forces that threatened it. By vindicating his art he sought to rally people to the defence of culture, and, to the best of his ability, to justify its existence. At the same time, his range widened; he saw himself as the champion of German national culture, and as such thought he must speak for the freedom and creativity of the European mind. But political events made him change his perspective. The German nation and its culture had to be judged in terms of the tradition of European freedom and of Western civilisation. The demons which had so disastrously usurped political power in German and which pretended to speak for German culture had to be exorcised; barbarians had overturned right in favour of might and debased humanity itself. They had therefore to be exposed and destroyed so that the German nation could develop once more its culture within the rightful European tradition of freedom, law and humanity.

In order to understand the historical situation, Mann analysed his own presuppositions and those of the society in which he lived. He sought to separate the wheat from the tares, to distinguish what was valuable in life and art from what was pernicious. To do this meant that he had to know himself as an artist. For him art was dubious. Nonetheless, he took it very seriously; for he *felt* most seriously about it. He was too much a scion of the North German Protestant bourgeoisie not to feel that whatever one did in life had to be done with conviction, even if it was a non-bourgeois, bohemian activity, such as art. Also, he was a man who increasingly wished to lead a responsible, good and even exemplary life. However, he was always saved from being heavy-handed and stuffy by his sense of irony, detachment and humour. His concern with the status of art and the artist rarely stopped him for long from pursuing his artistic task, though at least twice in his life – at the end of the first decade of the twentieth century and during the 1914–18 war – he interrupted his creative writing in order to clarify his ideas on the role of art and the artist. His doubts about the value of the artist's task never ceased. He himself summed them up humorously:

> Those who have glanced through my writings will recall that I have always regarded the artist's, the poet's mode of living, with the greatest distrust. Indeed, I shall never cease to be astonished at the honours which society bestows upon this species. I know what a poet is, for I am one – and there is proof of that. A poet is, to sum it up, a fellow who is absolutely useless in all fields of serious activity, whose only aim in life is

fun and games, who not only is of no use to the state, but even regards it with a rebellious mind; he does not need even to possess special gifts of intelligence, but may be of such slow and imprecise intellect as I have always been. Also, he is a charlatan, at heart childish, inclined to wasteful living and suspect in every respect, who should not expect anything from society but quiet contempt – and indeed basically does not expect anything else.[2]

Yet these doubts were fruitful, generating a tension that fostered and enlivened his fiction.

Mann's views on the role which art and the artist ought to play in the world can be distilled from his many essays, notebooks and letters. Like Schiller a highly intellectual writer, he felt it necessary to accompany his imaginative works continuously with discursive writing, partly to clarify his own ideas, partly to get rid of material for which he had no space left in his fiction, partly to elaborate ideas which he had merely adumbrated there.

Mann wrote much: he was also much in demand as a lecturer, and, indeed, many pieces among his discursive writing are lectures. He was a superb performer and his lectures often sounded much more attractive than they read; any one who has ever listened to him lecturing is likely to remember the scene vividly – the address steeped in irony, but none the less delivered with intellectual passion, though without any recourse to obvious rhetorical devices, the lengthy, often involved, yet carefully poised sentences, the vivid scenic descriptions with which the argument was enlivened, the detached vision which none the less revealed a deep personal commitment to literature, to culture and to humanity. It was like a conjuror's act and yet at the same time an appeal to reason.

However striking the individual pieces, however interesting the main argument or description, however unmistakable the voice, the cumulative impact of his discursive writing none the less leaves one in no doubt that Mann was *not* a powerful analytical thinker. Not that he did not deal with important or interesting ideas and think about them seriously; but his essays have none of the thrust of a Hobbes, Kant or Lessing, nor do they have the elegance of a Montesquieu or Hume. He had a philosphical bent, but he was not a philosopher. Nor did he claim that status; for he did not analyse or clarify, let alone solve, any important philosophical problems. Rather, he raised interesting intellectual issues and explored them in a highly personal manner; his style is unmistakably his own; it is often attractive; but not always; for it can be rather involved. His work is not free from repetition, some of which was brought about by his desire to view an issue from different angles. This mode of writing is not without appeal, but it also has its hazards. It can become tedious. Moreover, his style frequently lacks edge; but his urgent concern for the issues raised often makes itself felt. His writing is never as crisp as that of Lessing nor as wide-ranging as that of Nietzsche, nor as capable of the sustained weight that characterises Schiller's philosophical essays, nor does it have the logical rigour required for philosophy proper as possessed, for instance, by Kant; still, at its best, it has a compelling tone of its own. As an essayist he does not compare with Bacon or Montaigne;[3] for he does not achieve their power and he wrote too many minor incidental pieces, many doubtless prompted by financial exigencies; perhaps this was inevitable in times of inflation and exile when he had to support a large family and help relations and friends. There are also noticeable contradictions in his work, but he did not, like Nietzsche, put them forward in order to shock his readers, or because he lacked circumspection, but rather because he tended to look at a problem from different angles, stating somewhat different positions at different times. He was not so much concerned with treating universal problems, as with questions that exercised him personally as a writer, believing, with remarkable self-confidence, that these questions had wider significance, a belief that was frequently widely, though by no means always, or universally, shared. His argument is often couched in terms of polar opposites which, like *Geist* and *Leben* or *Geist* and *Kunst* seemed to mesmerise him at times, but which did not further precision of thought.[4] But it is, in principle, mistaken to interpret him in terms of his own terminology which would, for critical purposes, in any case be an inappropriate meta-language. An examination of his thought that steers clear of these elusive terms removes much that seems otherwise paradoxical and contradictory. At least it will be found much less contradictory than that of his mentor Nietzsche, whose flamboyance he also (for better or for worse) lacks; for he was far too scrupulous to indulge in intellectual fireworks, particularly if used only for their own sake.

I

Thomas Mann recognised the need to bridge the gulf that separates the intellect from nature. The experience of this gulf was very real to him, and in the wake of Nietzsche, he postulated an antithesis between life and mind, but viewed the problem differently. He gave a complicated twist to Nietzsche's antithesis of the Apolline and Dionysian by linking the Apolline with Nietzsche's conception of decadence. He, then, at first sight, appears to endorse Nietzsche's condemnation of modern culture as a product of decadence developed after his break with Wagner. Only in an age of the decline of vitality could sophistication and refined sensitivity flourish. But Mann never fully accepted this position. He was willing to explore any perspectives resulting from it, but at the same time he also sought to discover how a modern artist could overcome the danger of decadence. On the surface, the artist is at worst pathological or even criminal. At best he is a magician or adventurer. But this does not tell the whole story. Other perspectives emerge. The artist can also be seen in a positive light; he can be said to represent the feelings and aspirations of the many to whom he speaks – and their genuine feelings and legitimate aspirations at that. The modern artist does not necessarily stand for a decadent age, he can also symbolise man's desire to cope with decadence and speak of men's hopes, expectations and dreams.

Could the line between charlatanism and genuine artistic work be distinctly drawn? Wagner, so Nietzsche had proclaimed after he had turned against his erstwhile friend and mentor, was a striking example of the entertainer [*Komödiant*], the prototype of a decadent artist. Mann never saw himself as a mere entertainer, though he did feel that he was just having his fun ('*Allotria*', as he called it);[5] yet, as he sardonically put it, it was fun that surprised him on account of its success with the public and because it bestowed respectability. But even respectability did not assuage his spiritual discomfort; he always felt his work to be close to a confidence-trick.[6] Moreover, he claimed he had become a writer because he was 'incapable of doing anything else'.[7] Yet he also knew that writing entailed complete commitment, a loving, passionate surrender to the theme in question or the object portrayed.[8]

These two positions (positive and negative) seem mutually exclusive and hence contradictory. How could this paradox be resolved? Mann was puzzled. The answer did not come easily to him, as is shown by his contemplating the problem ever and ever again, fruitfully in his fiction, less *Lo lo* so in his discursive prose. His solution is ingenious and imaginative. Art could appear dubious, even a confidence-trick, because the artist needs to transgress the limits set by convention and common usage; for his realm is freedom. The need and the ability to exercise imaginative freedom allows the artist to appeal to the imagination of those whom he is addressing. In so far as he succeeds in rousing the imagination of his public, he is their spokesman and representative and could be said to stand at the very centre of society. But though a representative of his public, perhaps even of a nation or an age, he still remains inevitably an adventurer of feeling and mind. He is an adventurer because he enjoys a mental freedom from the constraints of ordinary life, a freedom which he cherishes for the purpose of artistic creation, though for that purpose only. The artist is an eccentric, an outsider, but not irresponsibly so; he is both serious and light-hearted; for, after all, tragedy and farce have the same origin. The artist can thus be both an entertainer and a moralist; he can educate others so very much more effectively by combining teaching and pleasure than by way of merely didactic and moralising writings; for in his dual role he is able to reach deeper levels and wider ranges of experience.

Mann faces the same problem that preoccupied the German classical aesthetic theorists[9], but, unlike Schiller, he views the aesthetic experience as treacherous, the commitment to the world of sense appears immoral; yet pure moralising also repels him. Nietzsche's influence is patent and Mann discusses the problem mainly in Nietzschean terminology. The world is semblance and to depict semblance is hence necessarily a dubious enterprise.

As an artist, Mann felt himself an outsider, but was not content to stay one. He viewed bourgeois culture with unease; yet he wished to belong to it and claimed to regard the normal bourgeois with envy. But we must not be deceived by this stance. He never wanted to be a normal philistine bourgeois. Like many gifted youths he rebelled against conventional culture and, though he esteemed the solidity of bourgeois life, he was prepared to be only a bourgeois, provided he could be a bourgeois with a difference. He succeeded in regaining access to the bourgeois world from which he stemmed on account of his material success and public esteem, a feat that also earned him envy and censure, and still does, especially on the part of less successful or less respected writers. Once Mann had achieved success his attitude became self-assured. The rebel – for the early Mann rebelled against bourgeois culture which seemed for him to be philistine – had become established. He was surprised, and pleased to find, that his books, published by the leading German literary publisher of the day, S. Fischer, were acclaimed by sensitive critics (even by Rilke who, at that time also making his reputation, praised *Buddenbrooks*). (R, v, pp. 577–81). What mattered to him just as much, his novel sold well. Gradually he became financially independent and seemed vindicated by success. A love-match with a daughter of an extremely wealthy Munich professor, the heir of a very rich Silesian industrialist, also helped to reinforce his self-confidence. Yet success, though it did not come overnight, exacted its price. He became uneasy on other grounds, worrying about the accusation of being too intellectual, too cold a writer; for his sceptical temper of mind had made him turn to irony, with a rather sharp edge at first. This manner of writing aroused much criticism at the time, and perhaps still disturbs some readers. Ironically, Mann's own attempt at overcoming decadence, i.e. ending his alienation from life, was called 'decadent' too. His critics, in the main, came from two camps – firstly, there were those who, following Nietzsche, thought that we live in a decadent age, and found all modern literature (of which Mann's was but one example) wanting. Secondly, there were those who took simplicity and health to be what German literary and intellectual tradition required. There is no need here to elaborate or refute these misunderstandings, but Mann was also attacked from yet another quarter – the Naturalists, who felt that his irony and symbolism, woven into his stories within a realist, if not naturalist, setting, represented a betrayal of their aims. It is almost surprising, and at least a sign of his commitment to his work and of his personal pertinacity, that he survived all these attacks, if not unscathed, at least with undiminished creative vigour. It is also proof of his own basic self-confidence that he did not swerve from his path as an ironic writer. Inevitably, he protested against the view that he was too detached, even too frosty a writer, and that to analyse feelings of fictional characters without showing any apparent emotion necessarily entailed hostility to life. In his defence, he maintained that an author's emotional life must not be gauged by the intellectual stance that he adopts. Nor does interest in the pathological aspects of life mean that the author himself is diseased. Mann was not able to shrug off these attacks and misunderstandings easily; for otherwise he would not have returned to them so frequently.

What were the reasons for his concern? They appear to have sprung from his own apprehension, deeply felt in his early years, that the intellect or indeed mind itself (*Geist* is the elusive German term) was inadequate in the face of life. It could neither do justice to it nor could it command sufficient weight to counteract life's demands. To create art, the product of the mind, was therefore a second-rate activity in comparison with any whole-hearted committal to life (whatever that may mean – there is no question that Mann, like Nietzsche before him, here enters the nebulous, not easily charted, realms of metaphysical speculation). But the *felt* consequences are clearer: In Mann's view, the artist is thus a seducer inducing men to stray away from the right path, that of living a full life. Artistic sensibility impairs the will to live and produces weak, endangered individuals. But Mann did not give in. He used this experience as material for his work and he sought to analyse it again and again. He found it an inexhaustible source of ideas to be used in his imaginative work. He also reflected on it in his letters and essays, and above all in his uncompleted treatise *Geist und Kunst* [*Mind and Art*] (c.1910). This work was to be a twentieth-century counterpart to Schiller's classic essay, 'Über Naive und Sentimentalische Dichtung' ['On naive and sentimental poetry'] (1795), but he abandoned it and then ascribed it to Gustav von Aschenbach, the hero of *Der Tod in Venedig*. Yet he did not merely show the weakness of the artist and the dangers which intellect and art posed to life. And, finally, in a later lecture on 'Nietzsches Philosophie im Lichte unserer Erfahrung' ['Nietzsche's Philosophy in the Light of our Experience'] (1947) he stated it as his conviction that it was wrong to praise life at the expense of mind: 'as if it were necessary to defend life against mind? as if the least danger had ever existed that mind would prevail in this world!' (TM, IX, p. 696).

The first full-scale defence of his standpoint was the essay 'Bilse und ich' ['Bilse and I'] (1906) where Mann set himself against Fritz Oswald Bilse, whose novel *Aus einer kleinen Garnison* [*From a Small Garrison*] (1903) had had some success, but was, in fact, hardly more than a reportage of real events somewhat rearranged or fictionalised. As a genuine artist, classicist in the literary tradition of Goethe, even if on a lowly rung of the literary hierarchy, Mann availed himself of artistic freedom. The ability to do so set him far above third-rate writers; it allowed him to use everyday reality (and that included models from real life, such as he had used in *Buddenbrooks* and *Tonio Kröger*) for his poetic purpose. The exercise of freedom is the genuine artist's birthright and the right use of freedom is the mark of the true artist. Mann took issue with those who had accused him of

modelling his characters on real persons or incorporating slices of reality in
his work and thus showing lack of respect to those on whom he appeared to
have modelled his characters. His defence was simple and decisive: an
author of standing like himself does not copy from reality – that is far too
naive a view of his practice – he transforms it by giving the characters a life
of their own. A fictional character is not identical with any model on which
it is based. On the contrary, an author seeks to create a personality; for he
has appropriated the model by an art of subjective deepening. Consequently, there exists always a profound difference between reality and a
work of literature (TM, x, pp. 16). This reply carries conviction. He
follows those theorists who rightly interpret Aristotle's term *mimesis* to
mean more than mere imitation; and he thus differs from those who, like
Bilse, simplify complex issues, such as the relationship between art and
reality. Moreover, the reality depicted in his work belongs to the realm of
art which is, in principle, different from the realm of the real world, and
each of the two realms are autonomous. A writer may well appear to
criticise, and therefore seem to be hostile to, the world which he depicts,
but this is only a stance which he adopts. At least this was so in Mann's
case and in that of many other kindred writers influenced by
Nietzsche – they pretended or appeared to be hostile to the society in
which they lived in order to give full rein to their desire to analyse and
understand it. Analysis requires detachment which looks like coldness of
heart. But appearance is misleading. This may appear to be narcissism, but
it is really an attempt to discover himself and his place in the world. What is
more, the attempt is amply justified by its issuing in the production of
imaginative writing. He was perhaps not fully aware that this attitude
formed a rather narrow basis for writing.[10] Yet it gave rise to some
remarkable works. His self-criticism had all the appearance of a criticism of
the age, or at least of certain important tendencies thereof.

II

The work in which this theme is most fully explored is *Tonio Kröger*, one of
his great *Novellen* (longer short stories), to use this virtually untranslatable
German term. It belongs to Mann's early, though not earliest, phase.
Space permits only a brief analysis of this seminal story.[11] Suffice it to say
that here we are given the portrait of an artist as a young man and we
witness his development into a poet. Tonio feels alienated from life, from
normal bourgeois existence – he is not able, nor does he wish to lead the life
of the unthinking ordinary man. Yet he feels drawn to it, despite his
knowing that an abyss separates him for ever from ordinary men and that
his whole demeanour makes him appear different from them, unmistakably so. Tonio is the artist with the guilty conscience of a bourgeois who
feels that literature is a curse and writing a dubious, indeed almost criminal

activity. He reflects on his experience of the world, but to reflect means necessarily to drift apart from others. It entails solitude against which he rebels. Since his sensibility and imagination are married to an analytical mind, he becomes aware of the origin of his predicament and then revolts against all awareness. He speaks of *Erkenntnisekel*[12] [disgust at knowledge] to characterise this situation. But his tenacity of purpose and the toughness of his artistic gift allow him to overcome this disgust with life; he turns experience and perception, feeling and thought into art. Yet he can never rid himself entirely of his sense of doubt as to the value of art and as to the legitimacy of the artist's endeavour. Tonio is not merely suspicious of both intellectual analysis and artistic imagination, he also fears the consequences of self-awareness and creativity. To be prone to reflect and to have an artistic temperament apparently makes men stray from the path of strict conventional morality. Tonio appears to be so suspect a person that he is almost arrested in his native city. He himself thinks that the accusation of being a confidence man engaged in criminal counterfeit activity is not all that far off the mark. He escapes arrest since he can establish his identity by producing the galley-proofs of one of his books. But Tonio shares the policeman's doubt whether a piece of imaginative writing can be considered as adequate proof for the purpose of establishing someone's identity and innocence, even if he does so for far subtler reasons. The ironic temper of the *Novelle* may well, in the end, militate against our accepting Tonio's view as valid. Indeed, Tonio may not do so himself. But it is suggested that this affinity with criminality is part of the price which art exacts from the artist, just as suffering is the necessary consequence of awareness. Tonio pours scorn on those who believe that the artist can do without it. Yet he learns to value this situation and to turn despair, loneliness, introspection and a seemingly excessive concern with himself into worthwhile art and thus saves himself from self-destruction. Tonio learns self-knowledge and self-control just as the artist learns to turn his suffering into creative activity and thus into joy. Thus, he overcomes his isolation and is cured both of his yearning for a more natural, ordinary life and of his belief in the intrinsic sickness of the artist.

In *Tonio Kröger*, then, Mann turns away from extolling decadence although he continues to be intrigued by the seemingly close relationship between art and disease. However unambiguous his *Novelle* may appear to be his doubts concerning the role of art and the artist are not allayed. Mann does not exorcise them by casting them into artistic form; he merely gives them a life of their own and in the process of doing so he learns to live with them.

By the act of artistic creation and by acquiring a public the writer transcends his isolation and overcomes the tug-of-war between life and art. Whatever view we take of Tonio's experience, his is not the only possible view of the artist's nature as revealed by the story. Lisaweta Ivanowna, Tonio's Russian friend and confidante, is also an artist – and she does not seem to be at all assailed by the doubts and apprehensions that beset Tonio; on the contrary, she appears healthy and self-confident although she by no means belongs to the conventional bourgeois world. Yet in one respect both middle-class ethos and the needs of the artist coincide: success in either sphere requires discipline – even if the discipline needed by the artist must always be self-imposed. The antithesis may, to some extent at least, be more apparent than real; in any case reality always seems elusive to Mann, a form of semblance capable of an infinite number of interpretations.

This (relatively) insubstantial theme of the artist's experience[13] dominated Thomas Mann's work for a decade and was resumed even in later works. In *Krull*, in a humorous way, the trickster is portrayed as a practising artist, suggesting that the artist, too, is a confidence-man. Like the operetta star, Müller-Rosé, whose performance Krull watches, art appears to the outside world as an ideal, pure and glamorous alike; however, behind the scenes, in the dressing room, it all looks different, tawdry and tarnished.[14] Yet man needs this illusion of art; for it only reflects life itself which is an illusion.

> He [Krull] has learnt from tricking the world and makes himself into an ideal, a stimulus to life, a power of seduction in face of the world – and she falls into that trap. Every one flies into the flame as moths do. The world, that lascivious and stupid whore, wants to be tricked – and that it is a divine ordinance, for life itself rests on deceit and trickery, it would dry up without *illusion*. The vocation of art.[15]

So much for *Krull*, a riotously entertaining tale of the adventurer and the education of a confidence trickster. We are tempted to see in Krull a portrait of the artist and consider art as deception to be a central theme of the story. And understandably so; for there is much of the artist in Krull – he is certainly an artist in the art of tricking – but we must be careful not to overstate that point. For Mann is an ironic writer, and Krull is also a parody, even a caricature, or half-brother, of the artist.[16] We may, thus, rightly assume that the novel does not tell the whole story of art, but only an aspect. For art has not only to do with form but also with content of which Mann never thought lightly. *Der Tod in Venedig* and *Doktor Faustus* are proof, if proof be needed, of Mann's serious-minded exploration of the theme of the artist in travail. For the immense power of self-destruction is exposed.

Indeed, Krull in the second part of the novel also stands for Hermes, not only the god of thieves, but also the god of all relationships and of beautiful semblance as well as illusion.[17] Thus, the positive side of the artist's activity is intimated even in *Krull*; indeed, his very name Felix speaks of the good fortune which Mann – and there are allusions to indicate it – associated with Goethe just as his narcissism, his self-love, is seen as the basis of all autobiography, if not of art itself.[18]

III

For Thomas Mann another major theme was that of semblance and reality. Art was an illusion, but so was reality.[19] The task of art was to make, or as Mann more cautiously puts it, to help to make life bearable. The impact of life was itself paradoxical. It was not merely repulsive, but also seductive. It excites and blinds men. It also springs from a deception of the senses – here the debt to Schopenhauer is clear. Are not our views about right and wrong, good and evil, indeed, all differentiations, part of our inability to see the world as it is, as a unity produced by our will? But Mann never accepted Schopenhauer's thought fully, any more than he did Nietzsche's. 'The veil of Maja' may envelop man and the world, cloud his vision and prevent knowledge of truth. Yet however sceptically Mann viewed man's endeavour to attain knowledge or truth, he was too committed to the world not to ask how man had throughout history been able to cope with this basic uncertainty. For him the artist's response to this general human question was paradigmatic. The question appeared first and foremost in this form: could art, though an illusion, still have any purpose in the world? Or, to put it in Nietzschean terms, how did art succeed in making life bearable? For if it were mere entertainment it would not satisfy more reflective minds. It certainly would not have satisfied Thomas Mann, who was too serious-minded, too moralistic to be content with being a mere entertainer; he had to be an entertainer with a purpose.

Thus, if art was a dream, was it merely a dream? Did it have any moral and social purpose? Did it have any claim to truth in so far as truth could be conveyed? Did it possess any validity? Or was it merely a dreamer's idle fancy, i.e. mere delusion?

Again, Nietzsche's impact makes itself felt. For Schiller, art was indeed semblance but one which constituted an autonomous realm securely grounded in reality and therefore not merely illusion. But for Nietzsche, as we have seen, art had a dubious existence whose validity or moral purpose was uncertain.

Mann's success as a writer did not quench these doubts as to the purpose or validity of art. Could art be taken seriously in the world of everyday life where man faced so much injustice? Mann grappled with this problem throughout his life but never gave a dogmatic answer, such as George, for instance, had done. Nor did he expect as much from art as Rilke or Kafka did. He was too much of a Nietzschean and too much of a sceptic for that. But while he recognised art as an illusion he criticised Nietzsche by asserting that semblance did not necessarily mean deception. Art gave order to the chaos of life through form. Nietzsche, the champion of the 'Apolline', would hardly have quarrelled with that, but probably with Mann's view that to have achieved beauty is proof that the artist is in tune with nature, and that his work is therefore worth while. His emphasis on the Dionysian 'elemental forces of life' would have made him differ, and differ strongly.

To achieve the mastery that alone can justify a work is a continuous struggle. It has to come from the very depth of one's personality. Even entertainment can be a very hard taskmaster, how much more so was genuine art. And there was always the artist's fear that he had failed to produce worthwhile art.

Thomas Mann, thus, fought a continuous battle against the 'still small voice' within him that told him that art was both useless and meaningless. Yet he never embraced nihilism. How did he win the battle against doubt? He conquered because he grasped that art presented a paradox: it is both light-hearted and serious. It pleases us *and* makes us ponder. It is a jest that matters. The words which Goethe applied to *Faust II* '*diese sehr ernsten Scherze*' ['these most serious pleasantries'] sum up his own attitude[20] For him they are 'the definition of all art'.[21] And in this approach he is again more a discipline of Goethe and Schiller than of Nietzsche – starting from the belief that art contains a moral element but imparts morality indirectly. It is, so to speak, entertainment with moral consequences.

Yet if the artist does not have any real knowledge of what morality is, how can he speak about it? If he does not have any objective knowledge of the world how can he claim objectivity for his work? A taxing problem. How can it be solved? Mann was of course averse to making high-sounding claims. His temper was far too sceptical for that. This sceptical turn of mind made him turn to irony as his favourite mode of writing.[22] In a striking phrase Erich Heller has called Thomas Mann 'the Ironic German',[23] a term not inappropriate to characterise his attitude of mind. Mann's use of irony allows him to avoid the Olympian posture, to eschew pompousness and to be free from heavy-handedness. It can also provide, by the very criticism and distancing which it creates, a counterbalance to any possible subjective bias and hence brings about a degree of objectivity. His critics always took him to task for the ironic temper of his work. His irony hurt some – for he seemed to treat themes sacred to them with disrespect – while others believed that it revealed a refusal to commit himself to any point of view and allows him to achieve objectivity.[24] It looked to them so very much like an attempt to be all things to all men. But Mann's defence is vigorous. For him, irony expresses the artist's re-cognition of his responsibility to truth.[25] It allows him to preserve his freedom without which art cannot flourish. It does so by providing an exercise in self-discipline, poise and artistic dignity.[26] Mann rebuts the charge that his irony proves that he does not take a stand; on the contrary, it enables him to affirm life as well as to assert and defend human freedom. But the ironic artist knows that this is better done by eschewing solemnity and by doing it lightly and with a grain of salt. For irony is the antidote to complacency. It prevents grand gestures or affectation. It stops the artist – and the reader – from taking himself too seriously or from being uncritical. It springs from the spirit of criticism. It connotes a philosophical purpose and even spiritual activity, but it does so with a question mark.

Mann goes still further; in the last resort, he makes large claims, even though usually in the guise of modesty – claims not all that far removed from those made much more stridently by George or Rilke. Art, he suggests, effects a unity of mind and matter, morality and truth. It reflects the fundamental human striving for truth.[27] More than that: art can give rise to a new conception of humanity. To claim that can easily sound pretentious. It means occupying a position which may well be untenable; and claims of that magnitude – the artist as a prophet or harbinger of a new humanism – can easily jeopardise an artist's work. Mann was aware of this danger. After all, he is never naive, always on his guard. Doubt saves him from complacent optimism. Only if all assertions about the value and meaning of art and life are continuously called into question can the artist be true to himself and his art. An artist may hope that he can say something that matters to all and may even hope that he can intimate more than that – a mystical striving for God perhaps. But the purpose of art remains doubtful; for art cannot say any more than the artist, consciously or unconsciously, knows and has put into his work. And if he does not know or is not sure of his knowledge, he can ask only questions and take a sceptical view of what can be known. Thus, his work necessarily leaves us with questions and not with answers, and irony is the appropriate, perhaps even the necessary mode of expression.

IV

This conception of art is a major theme in *Der Tod in Venedig*, Thomas Mann's most famous *Novelle*. It offers particular difficulties of interpretation. The author's all-pervasive ironic style should warn us against assuming that the hero's death spells a negative verdict on his art and that art is fundamentally hostile to life. Far from it: all that we can safely infer is that art and disease are closely linked. Art threatens the artist's morality because of its intrinsic illusory character. The earlier novel *Königliche Hoheit*, written in a much lighter vein, is about illusionism.[28] Art appears to be semblance of semblance, a view in tune with Nietzsche's conception. It does not seem to be an autonomous realm in which reality has been re-created, as German classical writers on aesthetics maintained, but an illusion deluding us into believing that it is like reality. But is this really Mann's position? Of course, as always, he does not entirely side with Nietzsche's view; it may well be argued that, in the last resort, he rejects it. Yet the dangers inherent in the practice of deceit by the artist are great; they are liable to threaten the emotional balance of its practitioner. This theme is woven into *Der Tod in Venedig* as Mann portrays forces which may at any time destroy the artist.[29] Its hero, Gustav von Aschenbach, has eaten from the tree of knowledge and is, like most modern artists, no longer able to create spontaneously; hence he is engaged in a perennial struggle to render experience and knowledge into art. His work has been the product of self-discipline, a victory of moral order, of will over chaos, but the writer has had to pay a heavy price for this constant effort; his inner resources, both physical and spiritual, are being eroded. Not that Aschenbach is not aware of these problems, but, unlike his creator, Thomas Mann, he does not analyse the psychology of the artist; rather his work reveals moral revulsion at doubts about the moral purpose of art. But his attempt to achieve dignity, harmony and severity of form, to produce works of art steeped in the spirit of classicism, does not make him immune to spiritual disease. The attempt to be Apolline, to use Nietzsche's term, must fail if it is not grounded in a successful mastery of Dionysian stress and strain. Or, in more mundane language, man is not entirely rational; thus, the attempt to rely entirely on reason and to ignore the needs of instinct is bound sooner or later to fail. Mann, of course, puts this truism much more impressively; he unmistakably alludes to Nietzsche's conception of the Dionysian chaos beneath the veneer of civilisation by making use of a passage from *Psyche* by Nietzsche's friend, Erwin Rohde, depicting Dionysian orgies.[30]

None the less, it would be wrong to take the story as nothing but the psychological account of a writer's failure to keep in tune with nature and of his consequent loss of strength as his mind wages relentless war on his body. This is of course only one side, the psychological side, of the problem. For the story combines 'psychology' with 'myth',[31] a technique that Mann thought characteristic of his later work, but which he is already practising here. Aschenbach's decline is set against a background of myth of the world of ideas that prevailed before science and philosophy took over. Myth presents itself naturally to the mind of the hero steeped in Greek thought; for references to Greek mythology, Plutarch's *Erotikos* and the Platonic dialogues – the *Phaedrus* and the *Symposium* – abound.[32] For Plato, beauty was the visible manifestation of the Divine, an outward symbol of the realm of ideas which otherwise eludes the grasp of men. For Mann, art necessarily also contains an erotic element. Eros is a companion for all artists, but a jealous God and a dangerous friend to harbour; he can easily turn into an enemy able to destroy the artist. Or rather Eros is, like all myth, like all art, fundamentally ambivalent. Aschenbach's development may be an error leading to disaster, but it can also be interpreted as denoting the artist's sacrifice to higher truth, a positive act which does not however rule out the other possible interpretation, viz. that it is an act of self-indulgence by a man whose self-control has become whittled away by fatigue caused by an excessive regard for duty. The story, since it is cast in an ironic vein, suggests that both interpretations are admissible. And in order to understand Mann's conception of art and the artist properly we must take account of both.

Der Tod in Venedig, then, tells of beauty as a perennial value, as Socrates had suggested in the Platonic dialogues, and of the dubious psychological condition that gives rise to it.[33] Art is Janus-faced; it partakes both of the eternal and the temporal; hence its essential ambiguity. For the artist is the guardian of tradition, of values and of beauty whose impact is lasting, but he is also involved in the here and now. Eros allows him to apprehend a higher spiritual realm, yet also leads him astray; it arouses passions which can be both creative and destructive. Eros also brings forth illusion; the beauty of the Polish boy Tadzio for whom Aschenbach falls is not immaculate[34] and is thus deceptive. Yet in this *Novelle*, genuine, lasting art is achieved whose value can, despite all inherent dubiousness, be asserted. Semblance, so the *Novelle* suggests, gives rise to reality and illusion, to solidity and deceit. *Der Tod in Venedig* is an example of the ambiguity of art which has to be grasped if justice is to be done to the work. Thus, even the end, Aschenbach's death, is ambiguous. It can be seen as an apotheosis; for he dies admiring the beauty of which Tadzio is an evanescent symbol. Yet at the same time Tadzio's beauty always eludes his grasp; Aschenbach's love is never consummated and there is also an element of sordidness about the whole story.[35] And Aschenbach's death can also signify failure: the failure of art to sustain life. It overtly spells the final stage of continuous moral corruption and physical decay. Does this ambiguity not even call into question the apparent moral teaching of the *Novelle*? Are we not thus left with the possibility of an infinite regress of interpretation, perhaps a necessary consequence of any work of literature about literature, of a work that constitutes semblance at three removes?

V

Scepticism was the order of the day for Thomas Mann. Yet on what resources did he call to gain strength so as not totally to surrender to doubt? He looked for sustenance to literary and cultural tradition. Yet even here he feared that he was no more than a late-comer [*Epigone*] who had inherited a tradition, but was no longer sure whether or to what extent it was possible to write within this tradition. Could the decay be arrested? Could the decline be reversed? And if so, by what means? Much of Mann's writing is about that. He wanted to make tradition valid by embodying it in his work. He became more and more aware that he had a duty, both to the present and the future, to safeguard and hand on valuable traditions of thought.

Mann was in fact always conscious of his debt to tradition.[36] In art he saw (as he argued at least in the *Betrachtungen eines Unpolitischen* [*Reflections of a Non-Political Man*] (1918) a conservative force opposed to progress. It was the artist's task to revitalise tradition at a time when bourgeois culture was declining. Yet as always he perceived ambiguity; art was revolutionary, too. It cannot exist without freedom, and freedom entails the possibility of revolutionary change. Art, thus, is capable of liberating man by making him aware of his potentialities. The artist then has two tasks: by preserving tradition he guards continuity; by criticism of tradition and by consequent innovation he paves the way for new ideas and approaches. He is, as Mann believed, a conservative rebel, one who preserves the past by way of innovation, one who brings into being a new humanism that combines the old with the new by blending myth and psychology, by returning to the sources of Western culture and using them in a modern fashion. At least these were the aims of his art, first intimated in *Der Tod in Venedig*, but fully displayed in *Joseph und seine Brüder*. Through the medium of art, and with the help of psychology, myth was – in these novels – to become a living force again. Mann was even convinced that he had, by means of the *Joseph* novels, taken myth out of the hand of fascism and given it a humane focus;[37] (though this formulation reveals that he overrated Alfred Rosenberg's notorious book *Der Mythus des Zwanzigsten Jahrhunderts* [*The Myth of the Twentieth Century*] (1930).[38] This was so because, in later years, the desire to portray 'the merely individual and particular experience, the singular case', disappears.

> That which is typical, for-ever-human, for-ever-recurring, the timeless, in short, the mythical begins to occupy the foreground of interest. For the typical is the mythical in so far it is the archetypal norm and form of life . . . [39]

To do that it had, of course, to reach the public at large, the people itself: the new humanism could be fostered only if it made a powerful impact on a sufficiently large number of readers, a demand to which the 'Joseph' novels hardly live up. The goal to which the new humanism might direct artists was ambitiously set: works of art were to be created which would no longer deal with the artist's alienation from society since, as a consequence of the new humanistic art, that gulf would have disappeared and the artist would be firmly enmeshed in the life of the community. This aim is of course utopian. It does not differ much in kind, even if it does in degree, from what Brecht envisaged, as we shall later see. Mann was looking forward to the future. But what of the present? He never became so utopian in outlook as to ignore it. Rather he knew that in practice as an artist his wings were clipped. His own immediate task was modest. He could do no more than avail himself of what he found valuable in tradition, use it with discernment and with a sense of what was practicable in his own time. But to do this he had to be fully aware of belonging to the whole of the European cultural tradition. For this view he found support in T. S. Eliot's essay *Tradition and the Individual Talent* (1919) which he cited with approval.[40] Mann's concern with tradition earned him the reproof of looking backwards, of having produced work heavily laden with reference to works of earlier writers and of having thus written for a cultivated elitist public only. Yet is this charge just? Many of his works have after all attracted a wide reading public, and not only in German-speaking countries. Mann is not a highbrow author in the narrow sense of the word, writing for an esoteric, self-styled elite alone. The wide sale of his books proves the contrary. (Some of them have been turned into films!) Of course, to write books as if one had an encyclopaedia at one's elbow[41] invites readers to stock up and savour their own learning. But is that so very wrong? Is it mistaken for a novelist to stimulate his reader's interest in history, the literature of the past or mythology, for instance? In any case, Mann's books can be enjoyed at several levels. He did tell a story which can be enjoyed by uninitiated readers. Yet those would-be literary detectives wishing to unravel the many allusions and references can have – and have been having – a field-day as well. Yet Mann's learned manner should not deceive us. His mistress was not science or history, but art.

Mann's sense of detachment also created problems. To be excluded from the crowd, to feel both superior and guilty at feeling superior, was an uncomfortable experience, even if, as we have seen, it provided material for his creative writing. Mann yearned to be a different kind of artist, one who is in tune with life, with nature and society. Or at least this was the kind of writer with whom he wished to identify himself. Like Nietzsche, as well as Goethe and Schiller before him, he looked to great literary figures of the past as models. But unlike them, he did not turn to the Greeks, but found his masters nearer in time, notably in Goethe and Tolstoy.[42] The art of these two writers, so it seemed to him, was not the product of an intellect hostile to nature, but of a refinement of nature: it had far deeper roots than mere intellectual knowledge could provide. Nor did they experience guilt at knowledge having estranged them from life; on the contrary, whatever knowledge they had was used to serve life. Like Schiller, he knew, he could not be like Goethe (and Tolstoy), but like him too he felt Goethe not merely to be a rival, but also a source of fruitful inspiration. Admittedly, the artist who had relied much on his will and on his intellect, the sentimental artist in the Schillerian sense of the word, suffers from the burden of uncertainty and guilt. But it was wrong to condemn him for not being able to write in a spontaneous manner. Indeed, in his final tribute to Schiller, *Versuch über Schiller* [*Essay on Schiller*] (1955), Mann summed up the view expressed intermittently throughout his life; Schiller proved the contention that the reflective or intellectual (sentimental) artist, too, could be a useful member of society and create genuine works of art. Thus, Mann stubbornly defended intellectual art in face of criticism from many quarters, including his own. The reflective artist, he thought, can, as Schiller did, achieve masterpieces equal, or almost equal, to those of spontaneously creative artists. An artist writing in the reflective mode would seek to harness the intellect to life; and the example of writers such as Goethe and Tolstoy[43] whose genius had given them different, more original gifts, supplied the strength to impose discipline on his own art. This is of course an autobiographical statement, of a kind whose truth as a subjective account it is pointless to question. (Mann did not claim to have produced works equal in stature to those of Goethe or Tolstoy. He knew that his range was more limited, and he did not rank himself among the greatest masters of literature. But despite all humility, appropriate to his scepticism and self-criticism, he knew that he had an assured place in German literary history, and he did enjoy, in every sense of the word, his international reputation and relished being a citizen of the world.) His further conclusion is of a different brand altogether; for he claims that art has a discipline of its own that surpasses that of science, or at least differs from it. As a result of his experience the artist is able to convey intellectual knowledge, as well as sensual, mystical awareness.

Indeed, art is able to convey psychological truth: it can reveal what goes on within the human soul. So it is not surprising that Mann once noted down a passage from Tolstoy's diary which states:

> The main purpose of art is to tell the truth about the soul, to reveal and express all secrets which cannot be said with simple words. Art is a microscope which the artist focuses on the secret of his soul and which reveals to men *the secrets common to all of them*.[44]

The artist cannot ignore fact, particularly if he lives in the modern world reared in scholarship and science. But art is fiction, not fact. An artist does not establish or communicate scientific or historical knowledge. So Mann is able only to create the impression of that kind of knowledge, of creating a world that could be set alongside that produced by scholarship or science. Consequently, he was searching for exactitude; he wished to use precise knowledge about reality whether it be historical or scientific, and to incorporate it within his work. On the other hand, he knew – for he had learnt it from Nietzsche – that, since he was neither a scholar nor a historian, his historical and scientific knowledge was superficial only.

But is it enough to pretend to knowledge? Does pretence not breed impostors? No, it does not. The artist is not an impostor; he only appears to be one. His concern is not with the content as such, but with form. This awareness allowed Mann to find an ingenious solution to bridge the gulf between knowledge and art: his method of montage.[45] It allowed him to create the impression of knowledge and realism necessary to make his fiction convincing. He used information and knowledge not for its own sake, but subordinated them to his art, by systematically embodying them in his work so that they had a definite artistic function. Indeed, for him the writer's task was to produce the semblance of reality[46] in order to make his work credible.

Mann took great pains to get his information correct and to convey a sense of accuracy, even precision. He consulted experts and scholarly treatises, as well as handbooks, encyclopaedias and works of reference; he also relied in general on the harvest of his catholic reading. But he did not become an expert in any field of science or scholarship. His knowledge was always a veneer which he put on his work. He was neither a scientist nor a physician, neither a musicologist nor a professional historian, though he was interested in the problem of knowledge, albeit not in the manner of a professional philosopher. On the whole, scientists and physicians do not seem to have worried; perhaps because they do not indulge in literary criticism, more probably because they do not expect scientific enlightenment from fiction whose mode is too far removed from the realm of science and medicine. (Though one physician at least has told me that *Der Zauberberg* conveyed to him the *feeling* of being a medical man.) They are content with having the feeling conveyed of what the practice of medicine or science is like. With historians it has been different. They – or rather some literary critics dressed up as historians or sociologists – have taken Mann to task for his treatment of history. When *Doktor Faustus* appeared the attack was mainly from the right; of late it has, inevitably, perhaps come from the left.

These attacks are of course sadly mistaken. The imaginative writer's task does not consist in creating works of art that can be falsified by reference to science or history or practical life. What matters is the power to convince, the ability to make us believe in his point of view. In other words, Thomas Mann as an imaginative writer was not a historian, but he communicates to us a feeling of what the world of nineteenth-and twentieth-century Germany might have been like. He succeeds, as T. J. Reed has argued, in conveying the emotional temperature of the period by making us believe that we know how people felt in Germany at that time, an experience that too often eludes the historian's craft.[47] Of course, he cannot tell all; he must select, but the segment of reality that Mann depicted was to be representative of the whole of historical reality. Moreover, a multiplicity of perspectives was to ensure a sense of variety of views and experiences.

Does this approach to writing mean that Mann the artist seeks to have the best of all worlds? Perhaps. But it is legitimate for him to do so; it is not the act of a charlatan or confidence man. For it is not his task to provide a system of thought. He is neither scientist nor historian nor philosopher. Lessing and Moses Mendelssohn, in their classic exposition of the problem in *Pope ein Metaphysiker!* (*Pope a Metaphysician!*) (1755) settled that issue convincingly two centuries ago. And like Pope (and Goethe, for that matter), Mann appropriated much from others. For, like Krull, an artist is a thief, but, like Mercury, the God of thieves, he is a divine thief, he has the right to steal anything and from anyone whenever it pleases him provided he has the gift to use his loot with skill and conviction.

This borrowing or thieving leads us to another problem, his attitude to tradition. From early on his literary and philosophical debts are patent. Nietzsche, Schopenhauer and Wagner left their mark unmistakably on *Buddenbrooks*, but that was only the beginning. In later works he draws on

/s

an increasingly catholic reading. In *Der Zauberberg*, for instance, beside the thought of these old friends, allusions to Freud and Georg Lukácz, the ideas of the enlightenment, not to speak of medical and biological knowledge, are woven into the narrative pattern.[48] In *Doktor Faustus* the allusions to German theology, philosophy, history and musicology, to reality and to myth are manifold – all are merged, and the action, as many interpretations have shown, takes place on several levels and thus makes a multiple impact.[49] Medieval literature supplies the sources for *Der Erwählte* [*The Holy Sinner*],[50] but as in *Doktor Faustus* an amalgam is constructed that only a skilful literary detective can unravel (indeed, without recourse to Thomas Mann's posthumous papers even as imaginative a literary detective as Herman J. Weigand was unable to discover everything; and even now new associations may still await discovery.) The mythological and prehistoric sources of the 'Joseph' novels are manifold; even *Krull* offers much. As Hans Wysling has shown in a brilliant analysis, in the dining-car conversation between Krull (disguised as the Marquess of Venosta) and Professor Kuckuck, the palaeontologist, shades of at least seven heroes of Thomas Mann's reading make their bow.[51] First of all, a number of scientists, perhaps seven, are merged into the figure of the biologist Professor Kuckuck, whose name was in fact taken from a real biologist, Moritz Kuckuck. In addition, other intellectual ancestors – Schopenhauer, Nietzsche, Wagner, Freud and Goethe from history, Zeus, Hermes and Mephistopheles (for the Devil) from mythology and literature – are presented in the course of the conversation, a narrative technique which Mann had learnt from Theodor Fontane, the late nineteenth-century German novelist, (1818–98) particularly from his novel *Der Stechlin* (1898), and through him from the great European novelists.[52] Behind all these figures lurks that of the author himself, thus blending tradition with his own personal experience.

The most comprehensive summing up of the challenge which tradition issues for the artist is however found in two works – *Lotte in Weimar* and *Doktor Faustus*. In the latter great novel Mann analyses how an artist succumbs to and symbolises a tradition of irrational and hence dangerous, if not pernicious thought and action – this will be discussed later in the context of Mann's political attitudes – while in the earlier *Lotte in Weimar* he depicts in Goethe a great artist capable of mastering the irrational.

By writing fiction about Goethe, whom he had already considered in some of his best essays, Mann reappraises his own view of the artist and shows what tradition means for him.[53] The dangerous pull towards self-destruction need not, so he suggests in this novel, lead to disaster: it can be mastered even if both the artist and those whom he encounters cannot entirely escape hurt.

The artist may well have to suffer and inflict more pain than he or anyone may wish. Goethe appeared to Mann the paradigm of that truth. To avoid making him appear merely Olympian or stuffy he portrayed him and his entourage in *Lotte in Weimar* (1939) with irony and with humour. He emphasised Goethe's success as a poet and man, a success due to self-mastery, but bought at the price of renunciation, even self-sacrifice and of lack of consideration for others. Goethe is drawn with love and scepticism; he is portrayed warts and all. He towers over the circle of men and women that surround him, but he is also guilty of egocentricity. The artist, by pursuing his artistic task, neglects his responsibilities as a human being. He sacrifices others to his needs. The case against the artist is grave, and all the admiration lavished on Goethe by Weimar society cannot nullify the indictment of an artist who treats others as means and not as ends. Nor can all the adulation lavished on Goethe blind Lotte, his returning beloved whom Goethe had wooed in vain forty-four years earlier as a young man in Wetzlar and whom he had immortalised in his first novel *Die Leiden des jungen Werthers* (1774). She takes the view that Goethe has evaded his human responsibilities in order to pursue his art. His whole entourage – family and friends, secretaries and servants – all are made to suffer, for Goethe's powerful personality impairs their freedom by keeping them spellbound within his orbit, and his demands brook no refusal. Goethe dissents from this verdict, however. His very words, according to Mann, explain the process: just as he, the God, is the final sacrifice, so the artist too is at first and last a sacrifice. (TM II, p. 763).

Art is, then, a hard taskmaster. It hurts, lames, even destroys those whom it captivates. Mann felt, so it would seem, enslaved by it. He had to pay his due by his daily surrender to and struggle with writing from which there was no escape. But that is only one side of the picture. The truth is with him always many-sided. For the artist also enjoys freedom as no one else does. And this gives him power, raises him above others and makes him an exemplary figure, a man who can be detached from the life of ordinary men. Goethe can afford to stand above the fluctuating opinions of the day, deliberately avoiding involvement in the to-and-fro of daily opinion, wishing to take a long-term view of events and ideas; for as an artist his concern is with culture – with *Bildung* – a most characteristic German pursuit. (The term denotes both self-cultivation and education; and its pursuit has become an important aspect of the German national character.[54]) It is worth noting that at the very time when Mann thought it his duty vehemently and unambiguously to oppose and publicly denounce Hitler, he also reasserted in fiction his conviction of the timeless function of art and the artist. But in doing so he no longer naively assumed that the artist could ignore politics; events forced him to become more and more aware of the artist's social responsibilities. He recognised that however unpolitical an attitude of mind might appear a political element was still latent within it. Unlike other *poètes engagés*, however, he did not lose his sense of proportion, but was saved by his sense of humour, as *Lotte in Weimar* proves; he thus avoided the uncalled-for stuffiness or solemnity of which Goethe himself was so frequently accused, and against which Mann, in the last resort, successfully defended him in the novel – and in defending Goethe he defended the artist – and, of course, himself.

In any case, Mann never mistook his work for philosophy. He always treated philosophical problems, like all ideas, as part of the story itself. Realism is blended into symbolism. Not merely facts are used, but also ideas. Further complexity and ambiguity results. The work's scope becomes wider, for social and cultural history, biography and autobiography, as well as the history of ideas, are included, making his work a genuine tribute to and reappraisal of tradition.

VI

Many critics have shown how Thomas Mann's sense of tradition specifically meant, in T. S. Eliot's phrase, 'to write not merely with his own generation in his bones but with a feeling that the whole of the literature of Europe from Homer and within it the whole literature of his own country has a simultaneous existence and composes a simultaneous order.'[55] They have also analysed how he expressed this awareness in his work through montage.[56] We do not need to recapitulate their findings. Any brief glance at Mann's practice would, however, confirm that it is in accordance with his theoretical views.

The more Mann wrote about himself the more did his vision encompass the world around him. Growing maturity forced him to recognise that preoccupation with his own feelings no longer sufficed. He had to come to terms with the artist's wider responsibilities. For he found that, emotionally and intellectually, he was becoming increasingly involved in the world. The germ of this concern with wider issues is already latent in his early thought. He felt, already as a young man, that he spoke for others. In the second half of his life nothing less than being the champion and defender of German – and later even of European, if not Western, culture would do. But for his constant self-criticism and irony, for his irrepressible sense of humour, it would have looked like the posture of a megalomaniac. Not that he did not take his role very seriously. His manner was not entirely free from solemnity, though he eschewed pompousness. Some critics, ignoring his own continuous sardonic self-criticism, have reproached him for appearing self-important, just as others have objected, even more vehemently, to his irony. But Mann was a complex writer. To fasten one's glance on one side of his thought is to misinterpret his work. To claim to speak for a whole culture is an act of confident self-assertion, not unworthy of Mann's own mentor Nietzsche, who saw himself as *the* critic of German, nay, European civilisation *and* as *the* harbinger of a future cultural renaissance. Doubtless, this act of self-assertion was but the other side of his constant self-criticism, another way of justifying his mode of life as a writer, and yet equally ambiguous. Here is one of the reasons why he has been attacked so much. To claim superiority of mind may seem arrogant, if not ludicrous. But by assuming the role of a representative figure, a role endorsed by continuously growing success, first in the German-speaking world, later on in the international arena – this claim seemed, even though extremely self-confident, by no means absurd. To some extent, perhaps even in large measure, it was widely accepted. Many considered him primarily *the* representative of twentieth-century German culture. Needless to say, those who disputed this claim only grew angrier on account of the adulation showered upon him and questioned his self-assertion even more hotly. Mann came to adopt this stance, not by way of affectation, but quite naturally. Still, he regarded it with irony; for how could so suspect a figure as an artist mean anything to others? Yet already, as a young man of not yet thirty, at a ball in the mansion of his wealthy future father-in-law, the author of *Buddenbrooks* saw himself as a representative figure, that of the successful novelist, as he admitted perhaps somewhat sardonically in a letter to his brother Heinrich.[57] At about the same time the writer of *Königliche Hoheit* claimed that a prince in Imperial Germany – still the highest representative figure – would be the appropriate symbol for the writer, implying that aloofness, detachment and distinction were all necessary for either role. Moreover, these qualities helped to make the novelist the representative literary figure. Indeed, Mann believed strongly that this was so – and he said so to emphasise its significance when denouncing Nazism for the first time in public: for the novel combined 'consciousness and criticism, music and knowledge, myth and science, human breadth, objectivity and irony'.[58] Furthermore, Mann believed that the writer was the representative of the age;[59] indeed his power could be such that:

> the novelist moulds life not only in his book, but he has frequently moulded it *through* his book and if I am asked who or what existed first – nineteenth-century French society as we know it from Balzac's work – or Balzac, I should not at all be disinclined to reply: 'Balzac'.[60]

This stance invites criticism. There has of course been plenty, much of it based on misunderstanding. Mistaken judgements – both from the right and the left, so to speak – have been made about his political attitudes. Oversimplified judgements have ignored the complexity of his relationship with his country both in politics and culture. At first, until a few years after the rise of the Weimar republic, he believed, in contradistinction to his elder brother Heinrich, also a successful novelist, that an artist should steer clear of politics. Mann cited Goethe in support of this position. It would harm, indeed destroy his poetic powers.[61] But he also followed his own personal urge: he wished to safeguard his freedom as an artist, that precious gift, by avoiding embroilment in day-to-day politics and alignment with partisan doctrines. However, to represent German culture imposed obligations, personal and political. At first, he wanted to do his bit for

Germany when the 1914–18 war broke out and, like many German intellectuals, he was swept into a nationalist enthusiasm which quickly became undifferentiating and repulsive.

Mann's first political phase is indeed anything but pleasing. He had, so he thought, to speak out as the cultural representative of Wilhelminian Germany defending the cultural and spiritual superiority of the German nation over the Western world, particularly over the French. That there had been much that is good in German culture hardly any one will deny. But neither the *Kulturpolitik* of the pre-1914 German authorities nor the officially endorsed culture itself were, to put it mildly, attractive. Nietzsche showed greater foresight when he said, in 1872, just after the end of the Franco-Prussian war that 'a great victory spelt a great danger' in the first of his *Unzeitgemäße Betrachtungen*, 'David Friedrich Strauss: Der Bekenner und Schriftsteller' [*Untimely Reflections*, 'David Friedrich Strauss: the Confessor and Writer'] (N, 1, p. 137). Mann would have been wise to heed his mentor's warning. But his political attitude at that time expressed his own yearning to belong to the bourgeois world from which he came. The outsider always wished to return from his self-imposed exile. He wanted to safeguard the artist's freedom by linking himself with the community, with the nation.[62] Mann saw himself to be a true conservative, standing for tradition, for 'profundity', allegedly a German virtue discovered by the Romantics,[63] for a refusal to bow to the destructive forces of liberalism, particularly in politics.

The political problem from that time onward occupied Mann deeply. He put aside work on the novel which he was writing at the time (from 1913 onward) and which later became *Der Zauberberg*; he had to discover what he thought of the artist's relationship with politics. The book into which he poured his thoughts, *Betrachtungen eines Unpolitischen*, is an ungainly work. It is tedious and rambling.[64] There is much repetition. Nor is its tiresome style redeemed by its content. It is certainly not a profound treatise on politics. As a defence of conservativism it cannot be ranked in the same class as Burke's *Reflections on the Revolution in France* (1970)[65] on which, as its title suggests, it may have been modelled. Nor is it as powerful an onslaught on the ideas of the Enlightenment, on liberalism and democracy as Nietzsche's *Unzeitgemäße Betrachtungen*[66] which is a more likely source of the title; for like Nietzsche, Mann saw himself a man-out-of-season who was polemicising against prevailing fashionable trends.

However, the *Betrachtungen* is basically a reply to and an attack on his brother Heinrich's political radicalism – a radicalism which however, in this case, had common sense on its side. This is not the place to analyse Thomas Mann's defence of non-involvement in politics, of German conservativism and even nationalism.[67] Fortunately, this disagreeable phase was transitory. By writing down these ideas he was able to free *Der Zauberberg* from much material which would have perilously encumbered it and by the time he concluded the novel he had changed his position. The

turning-point was for him the murder in 1922 of Walther Rathenau,[68] then
foreign minister of the Weimar Republic, an industrialist, writer and
would-be philosopher, the prototype of the intellectual in politics. For
Mann that murder was an act of senseless irrationalism, and he had not
wished to glorify irrationalism in the *Betrachtungen*. From now on he set out
to defend the Weimar Republic and thus became reconciled with his
brother Heinrich, who had championed it from the beginning. But
Thomas Mann still did not become an active politician. Day-to-day
practical affairs were not for the artist. To avoid politics, however, he
recognised, was a political act, too. The artist ought to speak on general
principles and issues in order to defend individual liberty and, thus, the
artist's freedom as well as humanism itself. Self-interest left him no choice.

Reason and order are not against nature, Mann claimed in his lecture
Deutschland und die Deutschen [*Germany and the Germans*] (1945) but rather
they can – and ought to – arise organically from it. Barbarism (or Nazism)
spells a perversion of reason *and* nature. It is culture gone wrong. Bad
Germany was not the bad half separated from good Germany, but good
Germany fallen on evil days (TM XI, p. 146). There are not two
Germanies, an evil one and a good one, but only a single one whose best
character has, by means of diabolic cunning, been turned into evil (TM XI,
p. 146).

On the surface, Mann's changed attitude is a volte-face. His later views
appear, so it would seem, completely at odds with his earlier ones, which he
did indeed regret and reject. But there is a distinct connecting link. It is not
some undiscriminating conservativism which always defended the *status
quo* until Hitler made it impossible to do so. The common ground lies far
deeper. It is Mann's concern with the writer's freedom to write as it pleases
him and with the cultural ideal in which he believed.[69] When he saw this
basic right and the final aim of his endeavour threatened he protested. For
like reasons he condemned McCarthyism in the United States in the fifties.
And that is the reason why he was unable to tolerate Nazism and never
agreed to compromise with that evil regime although attempts were
secretly made by others to procure such an arrangement despite his Jewish
wife. Of course, the misdeeds of the Nazis cried to heaven. He felt therefore
compelled to speak out against the evil of Nazism vigorously, though he did
so only in 1936, more than three years after the beginning of his exile.[70] He
was of course right in doing so. Yet he was blamed after the war for
attacking Nazism from abroad, for having as an exile claimed to speak for
German culture. (As if culture had never before relied on exiles for defence
and survival.) But he was not merely criticised from the right, but also from
the left who attacked him for defending bourgeois culture. Still, if he had
not spoken he would have been quite justly condemned for his silence.
Mann knew that by taking a stand in politics he sacrificed, to some extent at
least, the artist's freedom to stay *au dessus de la mêlée*. But he saw that he had
no choice. The issues at stake were too serious. When Nazism had come to

its end he did not return to political indifference, though he was glad to be able to avoid political commitment or partisanship. Conciliation seemed a more appropriate task, for which the artist's ability to see the complex issues from different angles was of great help. Thus, he wished to bridge the gulf increasingly separating the two halves of Germany, the Western part from the Eastern. He leant to the left because the Western world was moving to the right. As a man of the centre he wanted to restore the equilibrium in order to be able to fulfil the representative role that was his calling.[71]

In his later years, then, Mann became more and more convinced that the writer ought to guide, foster and defend the culture which had nurtured him, to which he belonged and which he ought to hand on to later generations. He had no right to shirk this task and he should be seen to carry it out. In order to do so he had to understand his native culture and embody this understanding in his imaginative work. Only in doing so would his work become truly representative and reflect the true humanism which he thought it the artist's duty to espouse. In order to be effective this new humanism ought however not to be a pale insipid product of the intellect. Although requiring a rational understanding of life, it ought to entail a passionate commitment to art and to life involving the artist's personality as a whole and demanding mastery of the self. For Mann, the problem of humanism was, in the last resort, the problem of being an imaginative writer. He knew well that the writer's first and foremost task is to write. To create and foster culture he had to write and to capture an audience by his imaginative work, but that task meant making an impact on the whole man, not merely by an act of introspection, but by seeing the writer in the culture, in the society, indeed, in the whole world in which he lived.

VII

For Thomas Mann, it was, then, a duty to discover one's political presuppositions and, if need be, to correct them in the light of one's knowledge of what was right in politics. Could the artist help in this task? Certainly. But how? It was not merely a matter of making speeches on political issues as Mann did where he stated political principles and attacked the violation of freedom. In his work he ought also to place politics in a social and personal setting and show how political attitudes and individual experiences interacted. Mann gauged the emotional experience of German politics. He did so implicitly in *Der Zauberberg*, revealing the hazards facing German society and showing the way to overcome the threats of irrationalism. Hans Castorp, the hero of *Der Zauberberg*, was only a sensitive, middle-of-the road young man. He is exposed to many intellectual discussions. Liberalism, the philosophy of enlightenment, is preached at him by Settembrini, an Italian rationalist and humanist, who uses much of the language employed by Mann's brother Heinrich, while conservative or even reactionary solutions are advocated by the Jesuit Naphta,[72] an irrationalist with collectivist leanings, who utters Romantic views as well as some of those expressed by Thomas Mann in the *Betrachtungen*. Hans Castorp stands between them – and so in the end does Mann. For he treats extremes ironically. Naphta, indeed, appears less attractive than Settembrini; for *Der Zauberberg* is meant to be a criticism of traditions which are dead and hence dangerous. Hans Castorp seeks to achieve harmony. What he aims at is meant not as 'an "idyllic" convention' standing for an 'ideal community in classical terms', but as a counterblast 'to the pervasive Germanic obsessions of the day'.[73] To the irrationalism he opposed the classical tradition that was a peculiar part of European man. He is looking for a Europe free of dogmatism and facile slogans. But however subtle Mann's analysis of the underlying political problem of Germany, indeed, of Europe, and his prescription for the solution of its ills were, by the time the novel appeared they were already outdated; for the election of Hindenburg to the presidency had revealed the weakness of the republic and forecast its likely doom. In *Der Zauberberg* Mann rightly claimed to have spoken with the same voice as the author of *Von der Republik* [*Of the Republic*] (1922),[74] the speech in which he championed the Weimar republic. Yet this novel, like any work of art, was unable to affect public thought in an age that demanded manifestoes, though it took Mann another decade before the rise of Hitler to power made him draw that conclusion and attack Nazism directly and unambiguously through speeches and pamphlets. But never permanently. He remained an artist and wished to analyse his age through art.

Mann did so in *Doktor Faustus*, his last great novel. Here the artist's fate does not illustrate the victory of reason over irrationalism, but reveals how irrationalism could, albeit temporarily, triumph over reason. To depict that event was of course in keeping with the times. It is Mann's comprehensive settling of accounts with Nazism. Audaciously, he ventured to explain the rise of Nazism.[75] At first sight the task would appear well-nigh impossible, but Mann, by a bold stroke of genius, used the decadence and self-destruction of an artist as a symbol for the moral and spiritual decline and the self-destruction of the German nation. By looking into the dangers which he saw lurking in his own path (and which he successfully overcame) he was able to tell the story of how irrationalism can triumph. The portrait of the artist becomes the portrait of the nation. The roots of social coherence and of art are located deep down in the collective or personal unconscious respectively.

The novel's hero, Adrian Leverkühn, is a composer whose artistic genius becomes tainted by disease. He recognises the irrational sources from which music springs, but instead of learning to master them he seeks, dissatisfied with tradition, by way of dangerous means to rekindle his dwindling inspiration. A modern Faust, he concludes a pact with the devil – just as Germany did; as a result, he has to forswear love. Like Nietzsche, on whose life his is partly modelled, he becomes infected with venereal disease. In Leverkühn's case the infection is deliberately contracted – he consorts with a prostitute (*hetaera esmeralda*), in an act of perverted love, choosing sickness in order to be creative. This act of infection symbolises the signing of the pact with the Devil. Leverkühn's decision to choose evil, to choose a spiritually depraved way of loving, has been prepared by the spiritual disease to which he has succumbed. For he is guilty of the sin of pride nurtured by theological studies divorced from genuine faith and undertaken in a spirit of arrogance. The step from theology to music is an easy one for him to take; for music is a characteristically German activity. But music harbours many dangers. Mann sees it as the most irrational form of art, a form that cannot accommodate moral purpose. Moreover, Leverkühn affords the most striking example of an artist who needs abnormal (or diabolical) stimulus[76] for inspiration. In this novel, then, it is not a scholar like Faust in search of knowledge, but an artist looking for creative power and a rebirth of art who transgresses, with the aid of the devil, the boundaries of morality as well as of ordinary experience. He turns away from convention, but his adventure destroys both himself and others. Any pact with the devil must exact its price. All the power and originality of Leverkühn's music cannot conceal the central flaw in his art. Since the composer has been denied the capacity of loving, his work perforce lacks the power that love alone can give. His art hence lacks spiritual force. However fascinating and intellectually challenging Leverkühn's work may be it will still fall short of genuinely great art; for it is art depraved. The mistaken attempt to avoid decadence only ensures it. The artist, if he wishes to be true to his calling, cannot evade moral responsibility. The parallel with politics is patent. However ambivalent the artist may feel about life and art, he must, as an artist, love life and inspire his art with love. Likewise, he cannot escape the challenge of politics; he must take a stand against the forces of hatred and unreason. But to assume that Leverkühn champions the intellect against the heart and the spirit would be to ignore Mann's irony; however powerful Leverkühn's intellect he also betrays it; for he turns his back on reason. To do so is to abuse the intellect. An evil cause is espoused. Leverkühn thus cuts himself off from ordered and civilised existence, finally bringing about ruin. The parallels with *Volksbuch vom Dr. Faust* [*The Chapbook of Dr. Faust*], with Nietzsche and with German political history need not be drawn out here as they have repeatedly been examined elsewhere.[77] Nor need all the various allusions, references, parallels, prototypes and models be here enumerated. However, the dangers lurking in the path of the artist are made clear: in Mann's view, they symbolise the defects inherent in the German (national) character as well as the errors of German history.

The verdict passed on the artist is, then, severe. But this verdict must not be mistaken for a wholesale condemnation of art. Leverkühn is not Mann (though there is much of him in that character) nor does *Doktor Faustus* tell the whole story of art. It depicts only the corruption of art – and shows how, as always, the corruption of that which is best brings forth the worst. And one side of Mann is also found in the narrator, Serenus Zeitblom, a humanist teacher, who is writing the biography of his friend Leverkühn as best he can. Although he is frequently taken in by Leverkühn's conduct and ideas, he is by no means completely deceived. Although he does not see all the parallels which the novelist through him intimates to the discerning reader, he warns against evil and seeks to protect humanity and art against evil and seeks to protect humanity and art against abuse and corruption. Admittedly a mere schoolmaster-historian, he lacks profound historical insight as well as the serenity which his name suggests, and on which Mann prided himself as a writer, but his final words are a prayer for grace, a prayer repeated by Mann himself at the end of his lecture *Deutschland und die Deutschen* . This prayer is as characteristic of Mann as his (almost obsessive) preoccupation with decadence and his indictment of evil. For like Zeitblom, Mann is a moralist who wished to champion goodness and truth. Yet he knew that to strike postures is not enough. An artist must also understand and convey this understanding. For his was a subtle enough mind to recognise that the appeal to goodness might, in a sophisticated age among men uncertain of their values, only too easily appear banal[78] (as indeed, the too frequently invoked quotation of Hans Castorp's vision in the snowstorm[79] has become). Of course, goodness or morality are not devalued by being truisms, but to preach sermons is only too often counterproductive. The appeal to reason can rally supporters but it may create as many more enemies. Not that it should not be tried. But for the artist, there is better way out through his art. For this reason the rather superficial humanists Settembrini and Zeitblom are portrayed with irony. Moreover, if the writer clothes whatever answer to human problems he may find (however tentative it may be) in the garb of humour his impact can be the stronger. To have produced *Krull* as his last major work was not as inapposite as its author feared when he thought this kind of light entertainment inappropriate for one who was almost an octogenarian.[80]

VIII

To look for an author's final summing-up of his intellectual position is always hazardous. Yet it is a temptation to which, with some reservation, we may yield in Thomas Mann's case. For in the last year of his life, in his eightieth year, he produced two essays, *Versuch über Tschechow* and *Versuch über Schiller* in which he distilled much of his thought. Walter Muschg, a well-known Swiss professor of German literature, had assailed him in a powerful passage in a widely read history of literature – with a catchy, but, in principle, illegitimate title *Tragische Literaturgeschichte* [*A*

Tragic History of Literature] (Berne, 1957) – and reproved him on moral grounds (p. 254A.).[81] In Muschg's view, Mann had failed to give an answer to the ultimate questions concerning the meaning and purpose of life. This attack touched a central nerve in the near-octogenarian; for otherwise he would hardly have replied so tellingly. He did so when writing about Chekhov, in whom he saw a kindred mind facing the same predicament. An allusion – he used the name Katja, the name of a Chekovian character *and* that of his own wife – leaves no doubt that it was also a personal statement:

> Writing, faithfully, indefatigably writing to the end knowing that we do not have any answers to the ultimate questions, writing with the bad conscience that a writer deceives the reader, remains a strange 'None the less'. It is nothing else but saying: we entertain a doomed world with stories without providing it with a saving truth. To the question of poor Katja· 'What shall I do?' we can answer only with the words: 'Upon my honour and conscience I do not know.' We work none the less, we tell tales, give them form and entertain a needy world in the dark hope, almost in the confidence that truth and serene form are able to make an impact which grants spiritual freedom and that they are thus able to prepare the world for a life which is better, more beautiful and more appropriate to the human spirit.[82]

As in Chekhov's case, this attitude was the quintessence of a lifelong struggle. Although so many questions in life appeared to be intractable and although so much that is claimed for the value and significance of art is incapable of proof, Mann did not, like Schopenhauer, maintain that the impulse to artistic creation was a desperate, pointless exercise of the will, or, like Nietzsche, that it was a mere camouflage of or consolation for a meaningless world. He refused to give dogmatic answers since he distrusted misguided seriousness. Not that he was not serious, but humour was a more effective weapon. Indeed, it was a divine gift. And it helped to realise the aim of all art, to give joy to mankind. We could not expect more in this world.[83] In the exercise of these talents human freedom resided. This conviction was matched by the ample and skilful use which he made throughout his creative life of his own talents of irony and humour. For it is these talents that made his work convincing and appealing in a sceptical age unsure of truth and of the value of humanism.

But the aesthetic achievement is also a moral one. Such is the message of Mann's final masterpiece in essay form, *Versuch über Schiller*. Schiller's work corroborated that insight, and perhaps it was Schiller, rather than Goethe or Tolstoy, who, as a primarily reflective artist like Mann, served him as example. In a short story, *Schwere Stunde* [*Grave Hour*] (1905) Mann had, half a century earlier, praised Schiller's fight against disease, which, by dint of perception and unremitting strength of purpose, had enabled him to conquer adversity and create art. Mann had seen in Schiller a model of conduct; for Schiller succeeded in achieving greatness as a poet the hard way, a greatness which Goethe, a man more happily endowed by nature, attained spontaneously. In his last great essay he describes how Schiller's moral seriousness triumphed because, through hard struggle, he transformed his experience of life into art. At its best his art was mature mastery of his material and medium, and his achievement expressed 'man's will to beauty, truth and goodness, to morality, inner freedom, art, love, peace and to man's saving reverence for himself' (TM, IX, p. 950). He thus attained a goal aimed at and attained by Mann too. Mann admired and emulated Schiller because Schiller too had learnt to live with disease. He had compelled his perception to control nature, and through his work had furthered morality, self-cultivation, spiritual freedom and the aesthetic judgement without which no social improvement was possible. This insight into the interdependence of morals, politics and aesthetics in the life and work of Schiller, conveyed by Mann in a lecture given to rapt audiences in both parts of Germany, in Stuttgart and Weimar a few months before his death, was his final public message concerning the writer's task. Like any artist, the writer had to tread an arduous road – full of hazards and misunderstandings. Yet Schiller's example proved that the task could be well worth while. More Mann felt unable to concede. But were the writer's efforts therefore of no account? However much Thomas Mann cherished his doubts he did not like to think so. And, in the last resort, 'art is not some form of school homework or a tiresome exercise, not something that is done à contre-coeur; no, it will and should produce joy, entertain and thrill the reader.'[84]

To entertain, to thrill, and thus to give joy to others is no mean end to pursue, but still there must, as we have seen, always remain the nagging doubt that, in face of ultimate questions, it will, when weighed, be found too light. But that question is not the only one in the author's mind; for he wonders whether there is not a further purpose in art: 'would he have gone to so much trouble if he had written for his fellow-men only? Art is said to strive for perfection. And is that not something that is not entirely of this world?' Thus Mann in a letter written just over a year before his death.[85] Yet on that occasion too his ironic temper precludes his ending on this somewhat solemn note; for he adds that for the author of *Krull*, a work into which he has just put a lot of nonsense, reflections of this kind are out of order. Still we must not be deceived by the irony: it does not rule out Thomas Mann's ultimate assent to the value of art, an assent not easily achieved, but the more powerful and authentic as the outcome of a continuous deep inner struggle.

7 *Franz Kafka* (1883–1924)

Of all modern German – and not only German – writers of stature Franz Kafka is the most elusive. Interpretations abound: yet more frequently than not they disagree, indeed, contradict one another.[1] Not only do critics have different views of the meaning of his work; they also differ in their appraisal of what he is actually writing about. If they agree on anything at all they hold that his work is symbolic rather than allegorical. But most critics pay only lip-service to this insight, for in practice they rapidly succumb to the temptation of looking for a key to unlock the mystery of his work. This quest is fundamentally mistaken; though not all critics would admit as much. For Kafka's work seems to invite the reader to search for allegorical interpretations which invariably provide proof of the fertility of the critic's imagination rather than of his insight into Kafka's work. Thus, much of Kafka criticism has been mistaken, spreading confusion rather than light. For Kafka is elusive because he is deeply tormented, and this inner torment is writ large across his work. It springs from the depths of his personality, from his desire to fathom the meaning of the world *and* from his inability to do so. Kafka was driven by a most powerful urge to show how the world intrinsically hangs together, how it is a system of necessary relations. But all that he could achieve was to depict that this underlying unity could not be established while at the same time conveying the impression that it existed and that all experiences were related to one another.[2] This conflict between his spiritual desire and his intellectual understanding tortured him. But he felt unable to give a precise account of this torment and this failure again deepened his suffering and spiritual uncertainty, but it did not make him desist from this dogged pursuit of recording his attempts to interpret existence.

As a result, Kafka's attitude towards his writing appears ambivalent. While this ambivalence does not offer *the* key to the riddle of his work it has to be taken into account if false interpretations are to be eschewed. Kafka's conception of what might be expected from art and the artist is determined by this ambivalent attitude towards his own writing. It is precisely because he was unable to arrive at a conclusive view of the role of the writer and the function of writing that his work has become so impenetrable to criticism and so tempting for critics. His work is compelling because he seems to offer evidence for its interpretation which, on closer analysis, appears to consist of nothing but signs leading into culs-de-sac of thought. The cosmos of his work appears to be self-contained, but it is indecipherable. Kafka appears

to be concerned with meaning and interpretation, yet all interpretation is |
uncertain and his work defies any attempt to elucidate its meaning. So ,
many of the statements concerning his work seem, on reflection, implaus-
ible, unlikely to reveal the truth about a story or even the meaning of the
individual scenes or passages, on occasion even of individual words
(K – Erz., pp. 170ff.).

Kafka did not attempt any substantive treatise on aesthetics or art, nor
did he even define his attitude in essays. We have to search among his
diary-entries, letters, conversations and aphorisms for evidence to elaborate our view of his conception of art. Much territory remains uncharted;[3]
yet the overall picture that emerges reveals that Kafka's approach to this
central question of his writing was tortuous. He vacillated between
contradictory positions and based his view of art and the world on the
awareness of having to live with these contradictions.

I

Kafka was a radical writer. Neither in life nor in writing did half-measures
suffice. He saw himself as an outsider. A German-speaking Jew writing in a
Czech-speaking country he felt that he belonged neither to the Germans
nor to the Jews nor to the Czechs. More than that he felt alienated from his
family, indeed, from all others – he was aware of the sense of forlornness
that can assail man in a hostile, unintelligible universe which yet on the one
hand, promises to have a meaning, or which others claim it has. On the
other hand, it delivered nothing, neither sense nor salvation, but appeared
futile and frustrating. Indeed, the higher his expectations the more brutal
his disappointment.

Kafka's work is of a peculiar compelling intensity, but it is also
remarkably limited in scope. He penetrates to the core of the problems that
he raises, and he does not shrink from wrestling with the issues that agitated
him, but he does not paint on a broad canvas. In a sense, his work is
repetitive; it is focused on the same problem, the conflict between two
planes, the intelligible or realistic and the unintelligible or absurd.[4] He
seems to be exploring how what we believe we can understand can be
reconciled with what we do not appear to understand at all, and his work
seems impaled on the horns of a basic dilemma. It seems impossible to
distinguish between claims for human knowledge and human ignorance,
or, in other words, between that which, by convention and common
consent, can meaningfully be said and that which eludes the grasp of
meaningful statement. Yet the territory from which this incongruity rises is
never clearly defined. Still, many critics would agree that he is as much
concerned with himself as Rilke, for instance, was. He seeks continuously,
with a ferocious intensity and unceasing persistence, to come to terms with
the world in which he lives. The search for meaning, significance and
values, the quest for understanding the world perplexed and preoccupied

him, but he found he could not attain his goal by writing so that these probing intellectual questions also became questions about his ability or inability to write, as well as about the nature of his writing.

Kafka was as little satisfied with literature as he found it as were Nietzsche and George. He wanted to strike out on new paths and he succeeded in large measure, but however radically different from the work of other authors his own narrative pieces of prose appeared they did not satisfy him; for they fell short of his expectations. He had placed the whole burden of his life and thought upon his writing, and yet it did not, in his view, seem strong enough to bear so heavy a weight. At times, his criticism seems to concern his work only, but at others he appears to write about writing in general of which his own work served as an example.

From the beginning Kafka appears to have been steeped in scepticism; yet despite all despondency, he never fully despairs of hope. Not only writing in general, but the very medium, language, appeared to him to be inadequate, and its inadequacy made him deeply apprehensive; yet this apprehension itself was born of the high hopes which he placed on the potential power of language. In the very first extant piece of his writing, an entry in a friend's autograph album, he wrote as a youth of seventeen the following striking words:

> Words are poor mountaineers and poor miners. They do not fetch the treasures from the mountain-tops nor do they fetch them out of the mountain-shafts. But there is a living remembering that goes gently with a stroking hand beyond all values of memory. And if [when] from these ashes the flame rises, glowing and hot, powerful and strong and you stare into it bound by the magic spell, then . . . [5]

This image is astounding for a writer at the threshold of his career. It anticipates his later fears and hopes. It prepares us for the oscillation between the two modes of experience which gave rise to the uncertainty which marked his work. Since the power of language is here evoked in a conditional clause it might be more accurate to speak of its hypothetical rather than of its potential power. Triumph over the difficulties is not however entirely ruled out since the conditional clause is not in the subjunctive mood. Indeed, the conjunction could be temporal rather than conditional, pointing to his distinctly expecting the magic transformation created by language. Transmutation, rebirth, salvation almost is promised in the event of success. Failure, inevitably, would be all the more disappointing. Understandably, Kafka seeks to avoid failure by spelling out the limitations of language. For him language can speak beyond the bounds of sense only by way of intimation, but never, even approximately, by way of comparison (K – H., p. 45). It is the task of language to evoke rather than to state. Kafka is not an allegorical, but a symbolist (or post-symbolist)[6] writer.

Kafka's expectations of language are very high. He even called it an eternal beloved (J, p. 86). The more reason then to be dissatisfied with its inadequacy. Words are elusive. Only too often they do not accomplish what is expected of them and thus misunderstandings arise. They appear inadequate as symbols for conveying intentions. They may even be destructive and, as used by the author, do not match reality but create doubt and may even be messengers of decay and death.

Language is deceptive. Kafka is afraid of not being able to use words meaningfully or of not finding words sufficient for all that he has to say. He wishes to say so much that neither the time nor the space at his disposal suffice. But in the last resort he discerns the fault not in the medium, but in himself. And this dissatisfaction with himself, with being compelled to use a medium that does not satisfy him, characterises his work. In the last resort his writing is highly personal, for he was deeply committed to analysing his own position as a man and as a writer. As he said to Gustav Janouch 'Art is always a matter of the whole personality. Therefore it is basically tragic' (J, p. 30).

II

How overriding Kafka's concern with this personal problem was is reflected in his emphasis on the autobiographical nature of his stories. He rarely commented on his work, but in his comment on his story *The Judgement* (*Das Urteil*], in a diary-entry of 11 February 1913 (K – Tb., p. 296f.), he traces the relationships between the characters of the story, on the one hand, and himself, his father and his fiancée, on the other, in some detail. He states that the fictional characters and the persons in real life have the same number of letters in their names and possess the same initials, except that the suffix 'mann' in the hero's surname, 'Bendemann', is a strengthening of the first part of the name. As an explanation of the story this observation is of limited value, though it draws attention to the indubitable personal sources of much of his work. So does the striking remark in his *Brief an den Vater* [*Letter to his Father*] where he claims that 'all my writing is about you' (K – H., p. 203). While the autobiographical references do not exhaust the meaning of his work, they do reveal his incessant dialogue with himself and his incessant attempt to explore his own predicament as a writer. As with James Joyce, his work is 'a letter selfpenned to one's other' self.[7] But Kafka pursued even his own peculiar autobiographical mode of writing in a very special, limited manner. Life could not be seen as a whole. Emphasis had always to be laid on details, on fragments of experience, however small. He was neither able to build the edifice which he wanted to erect nor was he sure of having the strength to complete it; for writing itself, he found, could not be pursued wholeheartedly as he wished. There were always difficulties and obstacles to surmount which impeded and only too frequently frustrated him. Indeed, all too often he was left with an incomplete, unsafe structure and hence with a sense of failure, even doom and death.[8] Writing was an uncertain enterprise; it was even torture. Yet it was necessary torture; for without writing existence would become intolerable. To be deprived of the possibility of writing would condemn him to the situation of a madman robbed of his madness, robbed of his very essence and consequently absolutely mad.[9]

Writing, however, is not only necessary; it is a substitute for religion; it is a form of prayer.[10] Indeed, its aim ought to be to raise life to a higher plane, to raise to a realm of purity truth and immutability. To achieve this would at least temporarily satisfy him.[11] As he told Gustav Janouch, the writer is a prophet and a guide (J, p. 103). The purpose of writing was also to drag the writer, Kafka felt, out of the underworld and to give him peace.[12] Indeed, he esteemed creative writing so highly that all other activities and intentions were subordinated to it. He claimed that he hated everything else,[13] for it bored him. He knew of no compromise in the pursuit of writing. As Max Brod has testified,[14] he refused, for instance, to take up journalism since it would have entailed prostituting his talent. Even his professional life as an official in a public insurance company interfered with his work.

To expect so much from writing was to court disaster. The art of writing then caused unnecessary misery. The discrepancy between effort and achievement aroused terrible apprehension. Kafka captured the resultant dejection in an image revealing the incongruity between his hopes and reality. His fatigue is that of a gladiator after a struggle; his work was decorating a corner in an official's room (K – H., p. 42).

This discrepancy has further consequences, however; for it arises from and, in turn, increases Kafka's dissatisfaction with his work. His whole effort resembles the punishment imposed on Sisyphus (and Sisyphus, like Kafka, was a bachelor too, he noted in his diary,[15] indicating that he identified with him). Work seems unsatisfactory and the more it is continued the more unsatisfactory it remains. Whether he comes near completion or not the final achievement of creating satisfactory work always escapes his grasp. Whether the margin between intention and achievement is large or small, it always spells failure. Hope is never entirely quenched. None the less, it must always yield to frustration. Writing is eternal vacillation, sustained not by joy, but by torment, a continuous experience of uncertainty and suffering. There is no release nor respite; this is 'not like death, but like the eternal torment of dying'.[16] And the reality which he may set out to depict remains for ever elusive. All Kafka can do is to record his inner experience, a dream world in which everything, however tangible, appears insignificant. Indeed, the spell cast over him by the recording of his dream-like inner world renders the outer world and the experience arising from it less and less significant. But his strength does not even suffice to depict his dream-like inner life, for he is subjected to a battle between two opposing forces that are waging war within him.[17] He cannot reconcile these warring forces and thus faces self-destruction, an experience which he watches with careful and penetrating self-scrutiny; for he is the most self-conscious of writers and his art aids the process of an awareness that entails self-criticism. Writing is an assault on the self.[18] But writing is also a product of the self. Admittedly, art transmutes life (J, p. 32) and raises it to a higher level: yet at the same time the artist must look at his own artistic activity from the point of view of the critic. The more closely he observes himself the lower is his view of writing which necessarily must also appear to be of doubtful value.[19]

Kafka frequently referrred to the insignificant nature of writing, dubbing it mere scribbling (J, p. 13) and finding it repellent. He did not mince his words if need be.[20] He wished to tear up all he had written and he left instructions to burn his posthumous papers; for to write is to surrender to the devil; to abandon oneself to the dark forces of the nether world.[21] However sweet and wonderful the reward may appear in the sunlight, in the nocturnal hours of writing, it takes on quite a different guise; for then the writer is unable to experience anything but the eternal hell of all genuine writing[22] which consists of a whole solar system of vanity and self-gratification.

A further turn of the screw is Kafka's complaint that he does not even experience this hell. If writing promises deliverance from self it appears yet another tribute to the boundless cosmos of the ego. The mood of despondency when it prevails does not permit respite. Writing appears to further his self-indulgence, his vanity and other base desires. The more he writes the greater these desires become. There may be other worlds and other ways of writing, but, for Kafka, they exist only in dreams. At least so he frequently believes.[23] There is no escape. It is impossible to avoid writing; yet what he writes remains unsatisfactory, indeed, he feels unable to say what he wants to say. This inability to write is a profound experience of incongruity between what he is actually saying and what he wishes to say, an experience which deeply affects the subject-matter of his work. This incongruity is central to Kafka's work; for it reveals an inner conflict that obstructs knowledge and creates illusion as well as deceit. It does not give strength to life, but destroys it. The injunction to acquire self-knowledge turns first into the process of misunderstanding and eventually into the act of self-destruction.[24] Yet however powerful the impact of that experience it does not remain conclusive, for it is always ambivalent. There is always another side to the coin. To write is also to attempt to struggle beyond the limitations imposed by life. Writing can appear an assault on the ultimate frontier of experience.[25] Yet this belief may be yet another instance of self-deception; for what appears to be a cold, deliberate onslaught on the limitations imposed by life may be only another form of escape.[26] The dilemma in which he finds himself leaves him in no doubt about his position as a writer. He faces continuous frustration, compelled to write and yet unable to do so to his satisfaction; he is immobilised in front of his desk to which he is linked by the obsessive desire to write despite his persistent dissatisfaction with its product. What he writes then becomes a perpetual reproach. Literature does not clarify thought but obscures it. It distorts and impairs its perspective. Instead of conveying meaning and establishing significance his work sounds like 'the trumpets of nothing-ness'[27]. Indeed, writing makes him aware not only that he does not say what he wants to say, but that he does not even know what he wants to say. Thus, literature, which should be a voyage of self-discovery, only becomes a revelation of ignorance. Writing should arise from the root of one's being, but it appears to be merely a peripheral effort, tangential to the real task to be undertaken. As a result, all writing appears to be a mistake, an unfortunate stirring of the intellect. It amounts to creating something that is not genuine, but a forgery which, in the end, turns into a monster:

> What are we talking about? What is it all about? What is literature? Whence does it come? Of what use is it? What dubious things? Add to this dubiousness the dubiousness of your speaking and a monster arises. (K–H., p. 276)

Indeed, to write is not to speak the truth, but to convey falsehood or to pursue a false trail. A sense of something being wrong accompanies Kafka when writing.[28] There appears to be an unbridgeable gulf between an author's feeling and what he actually succeeds in writing down. His description of the world is at variance with his experience of the world. The result is incoherence in thought and writing. It also brings about a sense of inner insecurity which is matched by man's inability to see himself objectively; for any attempt to record one's introspection is necessarily inaccurate and hence misleading. Inner life can only be experienced but not described.[29] Still, to abandon writing would be even worse, for it is the sheet-anchor of his existence.

III

Kafka was convinced that there was something amiss both in his writing and in his life. The writer lacks substance; he commits treason against life, a notion reminiscent of Nietzsche and Thomas Mann. Lack of success in one of the spheres confirms his conviction of failure in the other. These experiences reinforce one another. The more he dedicates himself to the task in hand the more discontented he is.[30] But the resultant suffering is not the final state of mind either. However profound his apprehension and misery are he is at times able to find hope even in these dark moments. Admittedly, each word which he notes down seems to turn against its author. But he may draw comfort from the awareness that he too is not without weapons[31] to counter-attack. Yet this very capacity to attack only reveals his basic imbalance. For to concentrate entirely on literature and thought fulfils his desires, but also stunts his interests, activities and capacities. Writing becomes a substitute for living. But to restrict his experience of life so greatly means to limit severely what he can write about. Here is another reason for the flight into describing the dream-like inner world; for to describe the inner world appears the only possible course for a writer deprived of other experience.

But to concentrate on writing is a poor substitute for the richness of life. It is not only unsatisfactory, but fills Kafka with guilt. He is terrified by his own inadequacy as a writer and he is thus frightened by his apprehension of the uselessness of writing. But Kafka never remains addicted to one mood only.[32] He also believes, at times at least, that writing, despite all the *Angst* and wretchedness that it engenders, can have a purpose, a very important one at that. Characteristically he defined this purpose in a most unusual manner:

> The definition of a writer of that kind and the explanation of his impact, if there is an impact at all: he is the scapegoat of mankind, he allows me to enjoy a sin without guilt, almost without guilt.[33]

The writer can thus be of use to others by allowing them to experience suffering vicariously, a suffering which by the act of writing amounts to a firm conviction. On the one hand, Kafka's standards are too high, and he is incapable of adjusting them to the situation in which he finds himself. On the other hand, he takes too pessimistic a view of his own achievement, of his own capacity and of the nature of writing. Consequently, dissatisfaction and uncertainty result. They produce further dissatisfaction with his literary achievement and literature itself.

Kafka, then, was plagued by uncertainty about the meaning of the world and by his problem of giving an imaginative account of what he experienced and attempted to say about his experiences. It could be argued that he was all the time writing about his difficulties as a writer and that the ambiguity of his work arises from that perpetual attempt. Or, in other words, he was continually engaged in an endless dialogue with himself, seeking to discover firstly how he could say what he felt he ought to say, and secondly how he could know what could be said at all. This predicament may reflect his incapacity to see clearly what he wanted to say. His incessant concern with his inability to say something took the place of his desire to say something. The mysteriousness and obscurity of his work arise from his preoccupation with his supposed failure as a writer and his consequent inability to discover what he wishes to write about. For the art of writing should be the art of discovery. With Kafka, it becomes the art of self-accusation and self-torment because he is discovering and rediscovering all along his inability to say anything significant at all.

Art is by its nature elusive and ambiguous. Interpretation can only too easily become misinterpretation. Knowledge can only too easily turn out to be pretence and ignorance. The well-known words from Kafka's parable (if it can be called a proper parable) *Of Parables* [*Von den Gleichnissen*] (1922–23), 'All these parables aim at saying only that the unfathomable is unfathomable and that we knew all along' (K – Beschr., p. 96), sum up his approach to the problem of the validity of truth of interpreting his writing.[34] Yet even this statement is not as unambiguous as it may appear, for if the principle of ambiguity is applied, we discover that it reveals only part of the truth.

The world created by language is the world of Babel. It contains, or rather conceals, a multiplicity of meaning. For, in Kafka's work, ambiguity itself is not created in a manner which permits identification. On the contrary, all efforts to explain the world and one's place in the world by writing only create darkness. Yet even to enter subterranean depths does not exclude the possibility of creating some knowledge. At least so much may be suggested by Kafka's cryptic phrase: 'We are digging the shaft of Babel' (K – H. p. 387).

IV

Do Kafka's imaginative works bear out these conclusions? Given the multiplicity of apparent meanings which can be extracted from Kafka's work it would be very easy indeed to construct an interpretation that would corroborate our findings. But to do so would be mistaken; for it would be just another one-sided, misleading and inadequate account. Yet although these difficulties are unavoidable it does not mean that nothing useful can be said about Kafka. However mistaken it is to tie him down to a specific meaning it is possible to point to the main features of the human situation depicted by him. Complete agreement among critics may not be possible even then, but that is almost invariably so in any critical enterprise. Still, few critics would deny that Kafka is an author deeply disturbed about his inability to find a meaning for life and to have a sense of the unity of the experience. He focuses on the isolated individual seeking to understand the world but incapable of doing so, although he is continuously confronted with the problem of having to understand it. Indeed, the hero's powerlessness and his attempts to escape from this predicament usually form the nucleus of Kafka's plots, which are either briefly sketched or expanded but retain a dream-like quality, recognised by Kafka as corresponding to his own dream-like inner life.[35] The dreams are usually nightmares; for the hero in any story by Kafka is never certain what his place is in society or, indeed, in the world as a whole, and yet he is continuously trying to attain certainty or desperately arguing that however much he fails to do so he ought to be able to attain it. Perpetual intellectual and spiritual frustration is thus recorded. One source of frustration is that the hero's interpretation of the world does not tally with what others say about it. Only too frequently events prove others right and him wrong; yet even that cannot be certain; in any case the hero continues to probe into the question whether his account is correct. He appears convinced of being right; yet despite all appearances and statements by others to the contrary as well as despite all his own self-confident, often arrogant assertions of his claim, his own conviction is never fully sustained – doubts linger on. A feeling of guilt, often though by no means always suppressed, cannot be eradicated. But in the course of the story it never becomes clear which side is right. Is it the hero from whose perspective the reader has to look at the world or is it the world itself? Whenever the scales of the narrative seem to be weighed down on one side, a new look at the action, if action it can be called, forces us to revise our view, and the other scale seems to be weighed down instead. Why is everything so uncertain in his work? Why can we not know which view, if any, of the world prevails? We are not sure, because the reader is invited to identify life itself with Kafka's hero – who does not know either. His failure to know does not spring from some basic, easily discernible and describable ignorance like that of Cervantes' Don Quixote, but from an uncertainty as to the issues. Why is there this basic uncertainty of issues? It arises from the clash between two worlds – a world of conventional everyday life which is capable of being understood, but which proves to be inadequate and insufficient, and another world which seems at variance with what is normally accepted as customary and conventional. The collision of these two worlds or planes of experience gives rise to a basic incongruity which would be unacceptable to the reader if it were not accepted by the hero. Because he accepts the possible co-existence of these two realities they are indeed fused and become convincing for the reader within the framework of the story. And the reader accepts them because the hero's response appears so eminently sensible and plausible. Endowed with a lucid, searching intelligence, he has no compunction in asking searching questions, questions that seem to go to the heart of the matter and yet, on reflection, may well miss the point at issue altogether. Yet the quasi-scientific spirit of the hero's approach to the problem in hand gives the reader that reassurance which allows him to be enthralled by Kafka's grotesque and incomprehensible world.

It would be very tempting to interpret all of Kafka's works in the light of his attitude towards writing, but this is a temptation to be resisted at all costs; for it would be yet another mistaken attempt to supply a key to Kafka's work. But to rule it out as the sole explanation does not mean that his conception of the writer's task is not an integral part of the subject-matter of much of his work. Indeed, it must be paid attention to; more particularly since some of his stories can be interpreted in relation to reflections on his own writing. It is indeed plausible to contend, as Malcolm Pasley has done,[36] that the story *Elf Söhne* [*Eleven Sons*] (1917) contains comments on the collection of eleven stories, *Ein Landarzt* [*A*

Country Doctor] (1919) and that *Die Sorge des Hausvaters* (*The Caretaker's Concern*] (1917) discusses the fragment *Der Jäger Gracchus* [*The Huntsman Gracchus*] (1917). If Pasley's argument is accepted – and it does carry conviction – we may well be justified in bearing in mind Kafka's conception or perhaps rather his experience of writing when interpreting his other works. For the multiplicity of interpretations which his work has given rise to testifies not merely to the inventive power of the interpreters, but also to its essential ambiguity. The truth of the matter is: we do not know for certain what any story of Kafka is really about, except to say in general terms that he is seeking to interpret his experience of life and to record his spiritual torment in the face of this experience and his interpretation thereof. However, as soon as we believe we have found any specific answer we only discover ourselves lodged in the quicksands of speculation. For can we really say why Josef K. in *Der Prozeß* [*The Trial*] (1914) has been arrested? Can we be sure whether he is really tried by the court whose very nature and existence remains uncertain? Or do we know why he is apparently condemned and on whose authority he is put to death? And if there is a court, what are its rules and can the laws which it invokes and its administration of justice at all be vindicated? Or is it at all clear whether K.'s death is judicial murder, a miscarriage of justice, plain inexplicable murder by two thugs or henchmen sent by an anonymous evil authority or the imposition of just punishment? These questions could be multiplied. Much could be said on either side of any argument and no argument appears conclusive.

The parable *Vor dem Gesetz* [*Before the Law*] (1914) which forms part of the novel, but had been published earlier as part of the collection *Ein Landarzt* corroborates this point; for truth seems to be incapable of being established. Any number of commentaries seem possible, yet none may be correct or conclusive, indeed, no conclusion seems possible. The commentaries seem meaningless, yet necessary.

Das Schloß [*The Castle*] (1922) can be similarly interpreted. Again, we do not know whether any accounts of its officials and their procedures are correct or misleading. Neither do we know whether K. is a land-surveyor or not – all his efforts to establish his right to a place in the village and gain access to the castle seem nugatory, and yet we do not even know whether he has such a right. The relationship between the village and the castle is as uncertain as that between K. and his fellow-men. K. seems to proceed according to assumptions different from those of his fellows. Everything that happens seems to proceed according to rules and laws; and yet these rules are never made explicit or intelligible, and perhaps even the belief that they exist may be entirely unfounded. In the end, in the whole process of the novel, uncertainty prevails. For much can be said for any account and equally much against it.

Similar problems face any interpreter of Kafka's work again and again. For instance, the verdict passed on Georg Bendemann by his father in *Das*

Urteil [*The Judgement*] (1912) seems to bear no relation whatsoever to any misdemeanour committed by Georg – it is not treated as an act of pure fantasy but it is, most surprisingly, accepted by Georg who himself executes the sentence imposed upon him by a father who has no right in law to sentence him. Yet so compelling is Kafka's nightmarish narrative that we accept Georg's jumping into the river as reasonable.

To cite only one other major story *Forschungen eines Hundes* [*Investigations of a Dog*] (1922) as a further instance must suffice. The story tells us of an ever-failing investigation into the meaning of what are apparently the basic questions of the life of the canine race, questions which, though taken for granted by others, trouble the investigating dog who must yet, despite (or perhaps as a result of) all reflection, discover that knowledge of truth seems for ever to elude his grasp. All that remains is the discovery that all investigations only disclose ignorance and falsehood:

> The truth can never be discovered by such means – never can that stage be reached – but they [investigations of this kind] throw light on some of the profound ramifications of falsehood. All senseless appearances of life – and the most senseless ones in particular – can be explained. Not completely of course – that is the diabolic joke – but it suffices against inconvenient questions. . . . (K – Beschr., p. 262)

All search for knowledge, like all writing or, indeed, even all art, is elusive and ambiguous. As Kafka suggests in *Das Schweigen der Sirenen* [*The Silence of the Sirens*] (1917), art tells us only that whatever conclusion we draw about works of art or life we are likely to be mistaken since the very nature of art and of life is to deal with uncertainty, ambiguity, ignorance and falsehood, for that is what man's experience and understanding is made out of. In the short parable, too, in which Kafka gives his own version of the legend, we are told that Ulysses was saved only because he assumed that the sirens sang. He believed this because he saw the movements of their lips without hearing them singing. But this account may be false, for perhaps his cunning was even greater than had generally been thought. Perhaps he knew that the sirens were silent, but pretended that they sang, deliberately creating a false myth. So all art can do is to confront the reader with a never-ending series of surmises and falsehoods, thus closely resembling science and life.

V

The ambiguity of Kafka's work is, then, intrinsic and central. It seems as if he were continuously oscillating between two philosophical positions. On the one hand, he insists that we can know only something about the world of experience; even this knowledge is, in a sense, hypothetical, dependent on our perspective. Reality and truth exist, but they cannot be known. We can talk of them only by way of analogy, or we can communicate and know only lies. For even a partial truth falls short of the whole truth and is therefore a falsehood, 'Truth is indivisible, it cannot know itself; who wishes to know it must himself be a lie.'[37] All our cognition can reveal only untruth. Even if untruth were obliterated it would not help; for to see clearly would render vision impossible, 'Are you able to know anything else save deception? Once deception is destroyed you are not allowed to look back at it or you become a pillar of salt.'[38] On the other hand, this point of view does not satisfy Kafka either. Admittedly every step which man takes appears necessarily to foil his endeavour. As Kafka neatly put it: 'He has the feeling that by the very act of living he obstructs his path.' But Kafka adds to this gloomy insight the further observation: 'This obstruction gives him the evidence for believing that he lives.'[39], thus revealing his conviction that even despair can yield its opposite, hope. He also believes that, by stating that something is unknowable, we have already admitted the possibility of knowing that which is unknowable. For to limit knowledge is to know something of the limits themselves. It means that we have been able to reconnoitre the boundaries, even the territory beyond, and have thus assimilated it to the pattern of our thinking. Kafka desires to attain that which is philosophically impossible. But to desire this is the imaginative writer's right. He can be ambivalent where the philosopher needs to be clear and unambiguous. For Kafka the artist, the general epistemological problem becomes a literary one.

Kafka was thus haunted by the fear of having to face an unintelligible world and of his own inability even to communicate this experience adequately. He was tormented, too, by a desire to understand this unintelligibility, a desire which at times failed to yield results; if not to the satisfaction of reason, at least to that of feeling. And yet these findings were again and again subjected to scrutiny prompted by apprehension, a perpetual alternation. There seems to be no end to the questioning, but even this supposition seems doubtful. The whole process led only to a form of infinite regress. The light appears to recede, the more closely we approach it. 'Our art is something blinded by truth. The light on the receding, distorted face is true, and nothing else.'[40] If there be truth, it can be represented imaginatively only by distortion which cannot be truth. But distortion can retain an element of truth. 'Right across the words remnants of light come' (K – H., p. 293).

Ambiguity, therefore, appears to be logically necessary. It is appropriate, indeed, essential for Kafka to use it. It necessarily gives rise to a multitude of meanings. Not surprisingly, many interpretations of his work emerge. But need they all, even the more circumspect ones, be totally useless? Kafka, perhaps, anticipates this question. For his radical scepticism about knowledge does not exclude the possibility that a kaleidoscope of views may convey a measure of truth. Although art cannot communicate truth, a host of perspectives – and here Kafka is very close to

Nietzsche[41] – may give us some ground for hoping to say something that is not entirely unsatisfactory and may even contain a measure of truth, though this is incapable of proof.

Confessing and lying is the same. In order to be able to confess we have to lie. We cannot express that which we are; for that we are; we can communicate only that which we are not, thus the lie. Only in the chorus some measure of truth may be found (K-H., p. 343).

8 Bertolt Brecht
(1898—1956)

Brecht's attitude to art differs radically from that of the writers so far discussed. Born in 1898, his formative years did not belong to the pre-1914 period, but rather to the First World War and its immediate aftermath. Outward reality may have made too immediate, too disturbing demands on the sensitive youth, demands which he could neither ignore nor evade by abandoning himself to cultivating his inner life. Nietzsche does not seem to have profoundly inspired him either. Later in life Marx was the lodestar of his thought. At the very beginning of his creative career, from his brief obituary of Frank Wedekind in the *Augsburger Neuesten Nachrichten* (12 March 1918)[1] and, even more strikingly, from his first theatre reviews in another Augsburg newspaper, *Der Volkswille* (from October/November 1919 onward),[2] he declared war on any purely intellectual, let alone spiritual approach to the world; for sensuous, material reality appeared far too real and overpowering to him. Of course, by valuing undifferentiated life above mind he is closer to Nietzsche than he may have surmised, though, of course, like Nietzsche, too, he never ceased to question all phenomena of experience with an acutely searching mind. But it was the outside world and not his inner soul which, despite all sensitivity, mattered to him first and foremost.

Therefore, Brecht had no truck with the artist's exclusive concern with himself, with self-justification and excessive self-reflection. Nor was he afflicted with doubts about the value of the artist's work, or if he was, he kept them to himself. Thus, it mattered to him as much as it did to George, Rilke or Thomas Mann; only it did so in a different way. He sought to discover the precise manner in which the artist could fulfil his social obligations without becoming untrue to his art and to explain his philosophy of art in rational discourse. In short, he also sought to elaborate an aesthetic theory in his discursive writing.

I

Yet, first and foremost, Brecht wanted to be a writer. Not unlike Rilke, he was ruthless in the pursuit of his goal. But he was also a man of deep feeling and not without sensitivity and tenderness. However, the claims of writing and the desire to be independent in mind and body, always reasserted themselves and triumphed over other demands. And these features of character and circumstance made their impact on his discursive prose: for it reveals an independent mind at work, continuously and strenuously seeking to see through convention, to destroy received opinions, to discover a way for himself through the maze of ideas which he encountered. He has no compunction about attacking, with much force, and often unfairly, all *idées reçues* as well as all those views that hindered the development of his own thought. Not for him the niceties of urbane scholarly discourse, but rather the *odium theologicum*. Thus, he showed no mercy to those who were not committed to his creed. But even when he himself was committed to the cause of Marxism he did not follow orthodox paths; he certainly did not toe an official line. His presence with the Communist camp was a discomfiting one, though he never developed a philosophical Marxist position of his own.

For Brecht was a poet and a playwright, and not a theoretician of literature or aesthetics. But it suited his purpose to pronounce upon historical aesthetic or literary matters. He wrote profusely about the theatre and reflected upon the nature of drama. His concern with these problems was almost obsessive. He turned to them again and again, voicing his opposition to conventional opinion and emphasising his own findings. It was obviously a matter that deeply agitated him. Shifts in his opinions can be detected, but once he had embraced Marxism, they do not reveal any profound realignment of thought. In his earlier years he was still groping for a distinct point of view. Much of his writing deals with theatrical practice and does not concern us here. But he did, unlike the other authors discussed above, venture into the field of poetic theory. His contribution, though limited, is interesting for the light it sheds on his own drama, though we must be careful not to interpret his plays too narrowly in the light of his own theories. To do so is, in any case, hazardous and frequently inappropriate. Why did Brecht write on poetics and aesthetic theory? For several reasons: to justify his work, to understand what kind of work he was creating, to confound those who disagreed with him, and to launch, promote and capture an audience for his drama.

Brecht is a very powerful writer. His lucidity is remarkable, a comparatively rare event in German, a language in which opaqueness has too frequently been accounted a virtue. His style is trenchant and chiselled. His argument appears simple, but it must not be adjudged superficial merely because it is clear and straightforward. He enjoyed debunking pretensions. He deprecated the ancient view of the poet as a seer. He did not call himself a *Dichter* (poet), but a *Stückeschreiber* (playwright – the German term sounds much more denigratory than the English one). He gave his most important treatise on aesthetics the apparently modest title *Kleines Organon für das Theater* [*A Minor Organon for the Theatre*] (1948), presumably an allusion to Aristotle's *Organon*, the classic account of science and deductive scientific reason, as well as to Bacon's *Novum Organon*, the first great philosophical work expounding a modern view of science and of inductive reasoning, the starting-point of a whole new important movement of ideas. And like Bacon, Brecht wanted to assail the prevailing conventional 'Aristotelean' wisdom and launch a new way of thinking about his sphere of activity, in his case, the theatre. And to call himself the Einstein of the modern theatre (or stage),[3] as Brecht did, is hardly an act of humility and self-effacement, but confirms that it is best to view his approach with suspicion.

Brecht is never dull; he makes his points forcefully. He shows verve and is often entertaining. When he writes dialogue – and some of his theoretical writings, in particular *Der Messingkauf* [*The Purchase of Brass*] (1937 – 51), are in dialogue – he is masterly. Yet his range is limited. The same questions preoccupy him throughout – and he gives virtually the same answers. He is monotonously repetitive, almost to the point of monomania.

Brecht's impact on the post-1945 German theatre and indeed on European theatre has been profound. What was denied him in his exile during the Nazi period has been given to him manifold since, especially after his death. He has attained virtual apotheosis. He gave international status to German drama as no one, not even Schiller, had ever succeeded in doing before. Because he bestrides the contemporary Western stage like a giant his ideas on drama and on the theatre have had an immense influence. But these ideas were few, and they were, in the end, despite his attempt to compose an aesthetics, primarily concerned with his own dramatic practice. Doubtless he sought to generalise by focusing attention on what he did and wanted to do. Spurred on by moral indignation and the conviction of the need for a better world he set out to present his ideas with vigour and force. But what he had to say is, in the main, neither profound nor original, though it is usually clever, provocative and stimulating.

Brecht's conception of the artist's task sprang from his antagonism to the world as he found it. As a young man the First World War and the sufferings it had caused deeply disturbed him. He learnt to hate the society which created these evils, and he savagely attacked conventional wisdom of any kind which sought to excuse them. Not only militarism, but dominant bourgeois beliefs and customs of all kinds became the target of his criticism. But, in his early days, he was like many a young man a rebel without commitment to any specific cause. Admittedly, his rebellion was more thoroughgoing and radical than that of most others, but he had no coherent philosophy to use as an arsenal for his attack. His early approach was basically negative; rejection was the keynote of his utterances and actions. In his view, the artist had to challenge the prevailing assumptions and ideas. The world had to be changed, and bourgeois complacency ended. He rejected, as radically as Georg Büchner had done almost a century earlier, the ideas of German Classical and Romantic writers, as they had been filtered down through the medium of German nationalist and humanist education. He held nationalism in complete contempt as the source of the war and of the resultant post-war misery. But he also despised humanism, which appeared to him to condone these ills. For him, it was nothing but a hollow creed. Above all bourgeois thought of any kind was his bugbear, though he often, rather wilfully, ignored that not all bourgeois thought was complacent and not all thought deemed to be bourgeois (a term, in any case, only too frequently used in an imprecise manner) was really of bourgeois origin. Brecht was never inhibited by punctiliousness and a desire for scholarly exactitude. However, his criticism was always trenchant, unambiguous, radical. Indeed, he was absolutely opposed to conventional ideas as George had been, but for different reasons. He did not care at all for George,[4] whose work appeared to him empty and pointless. Likewise, he had no use at all for Rilke[5] and Thomas Mann,[6] nor even for the Expressionists,[7] among whom he is sometimes not very suitably placed.[8] But he greatly admired Kafka,[9] whom he considered to be the leading twentieth-century writer on account of his integrity of mind and radical stance. Basically, he had however no truck with anyone who saw reality through a mystical veil which had, in fact, distorted it; Brecht was, so at least he claimed, not at all interested in spiritual values or salvation, but in man's material condition. Appalled by the human suffering caused by the war and its aftermath and by the complacency which official established opinion condoned, he looked for a valid response.

At first his protests and satires were inspired by a rebel – Frank Wedekind (1864–1918), playwright and cabarettist; for Wedekind used unconventional means to castigate the bourgeoisie, and mock pretence and shallowness not by lecturing, but by entertaining. Revolt was made effective through art. Above all, Wedekind's art appeared palatable to Brecht because he laced it with wit and spoke openly and directly. His language, indeed, his whole approach as a performer was appropriate to the task; it was daring, resourceful, full of verve. It pointed to underlying forces within man and society about which convention had remained silent. It was art, and powerful, effective art at that. In this reaction we catch a glimpse of Brecht's early response to the artist's problem, a response that was to deepen in time. For to rebel was not enough; it had to be done effectively, and this meant that all the means at the artist's disposal had to be skilfully and resourcefully used. His art should appear to be as novel, bold and revolutionary as the message which he wished to convey. The form had to be matched to the content.

Brecht's early revolt against bourgeois respectability, mediocrity and shallowness and, in particular, against all the conventions of Wilhelminian Germany, shows him rebelling against the same world against which the German Expressionists writers rebelled, but in fact Brecht was a lone fighter. His first play, *Baal* (1918),[10] was a protest as much against the idealism of all Expressionist writers as against the Naturalists. Above all, it was a protest against the maudlin sentimentality of Hanns Johst, whose drama *Der Einsame* [*The Solitary Man*] (1917) romanticised the nineteenth-century German dramatist Christian Friedrich Grabbe (1801–36), a gifted writer but a victim of alcoholism. (Johst later became established as *the* Nazi playwright.) Like the Expressionists, Brecht had no use for the moral conventions and ideals of the older generation and he was no less a parent-slayer than they were. And he sided with them in so far as they were political rebels. His second play *Trommeln in der Nacht* [*Drums in the Night*] (1919),[11] though by no means a revolutionary drama, tells of his deep interest in politics. And so do many of his early lyrics collected in the *Hauspostille* (1927).

A typical poem of that period 'Vom Geld' [Of Money] sums up his cynical view of the human situation and his belief in the primacy of economics. Three of its stanzas will suffice to convey his attitude.

Ich will dich nicht zur Arbeit verführen.
Der Mensch ist zur Arbeit nicht gemacht.
Aber das Geld, um das sollst du dich rühren!
Das Geld ist gut! Auf das Geld gib acht!

Die Menschen fangen einander mit Schlingen.
Groß ist die Bosheit der Welt.
Darum sollst du dir Geld erringen
Denn größer ist ihre Liebe zum Geld.

Dem Geld erweisen die Menschen Ehren.
Das Geld wird über Gott gestellt.
Willst du deinem Feind die Ruhe im Grab verwehren
Schreibe auf seinen Stein: Hier ruht Geld.[12]

But the man whose work made him fully aware of the possibilities of political theatre was not a writer, but a producer, Erwin Piscator (1893–1966), whose theatre differed from that of Max Reinhardt (1878–1945) and Leopold Jessner (1878–1945), the other two contemporary producers of genius. These three men dominated the Berlin, indeed, the whole German stage; but unlike the theatre of Reinhardt and Jessner, Piscator's aim was, as he claimed himself, essentially political. And political meant for him a fairly extreme left-wing stance. Piscator did, however, not wish to initiate political action. He sought to stage an evening of powerful theatre, a performance well worth remembering that aroused the spectators' emotions against injustice, but did not—here it differs from the later Brecht—appeal specifically to their reason.

Brecht was however not content with his early attitudes. Indeed, as a young man – and probably not only as a young man – he was a soul in travail. Those of his early diaries which have survived (for instance,

Tagebücher 1920–1922) reveal him as a man with a tempestuous inner life   *ihe .*
torn by conflicting desires vigorously exposing the emotional cant of others,
and he was particularly ruthless in his analysis of the feelings and conduct
of those of his own personal life. He felt ill at ease in modern urban life. One
of his early poems portrays this experience succinctly:

ÜBER DIE STÄDTE
Unter ihnen sind Gossen
In ihnen ist nichts, und über ihnen ist Rauch.
Wir waren drinnen. Wir haben nichts genossen.
Wir vergingen rasch. Und langsam vergehen sie auch.[13]

Apart from this early rebellion against the world as he encountered it,
the great intellectual event in his life was undoubtedly Marxism. He
desperately wanted to change the world. For an artist merely to protest
and to point out social and political evils by holding up a mirror to the
world was not enough. Social and political injustice would never be
eradicated by merely following that course. An artist had to do more, and
Marxism extended the promise of creative action. Once he had encountered and learnt about it by way of systematic study, under the
guidance of Karl Korsch (1889–1967), an unorthodox Marxist philosopher, he believed he had found the way in which the ills of society could
be cured.[14] This conviction gave his criticism strength and persuasive
power; for he believed he now knew the laws according to which society
was inevitably changing. Since the world in its imperfection disgusted him
he blamed those who, in this view, had brought about or were condoning
the present state of affairs. After his conversion to Marxism in the late
nineteen-twenties he continued to be a fervent Marxist throughout his life,
but he never abandoned his thoroughgoing individualism. For instance, he
never became a member of any Communist party. Nor did he spend the
years of exile, except for a brief spell, in the Soviet Union, but went first to
Denmark, then to Finland and finally to the United States. And when he
returned to settle in the German Democratic Republic he first took out
Austrian nationality to safeguard his independence.

This independent approach also characterises the way in which he used
Marxism to develop his work. For Brecht, Marxism was not a mere
theoretical structure, something that could safely be left to philosophers or
politicians while he went on writing his plays in his own manner. It was
something vitally alive and all-embracing. Since his major interest was the
drama and the theatre, he had to apply Marxist thought to the writing and
production of his plays. As a playwright he dramatised his experience of
the world's shortcomings and evils interpreting them in the light of Marxist
doctrine, but it was not enough to stage plays written in that spirit. The
theatre itself had to be adapted to this insight, for he found the
conventional theatre wanting. It did not, as it ought to, provide an arena

for revolution, but was a place of pleasure where producers and actors, managers and owners, all connived at the evils of the world. Some writers, such as Ibsen and Zola, Hauptmann and Wedekind, and some of the Expressionists, had attempted to criticise aspects of contemporary political life. But the form in which their works were cast and their plays produced took the sting out of their criticism. Also, their criticism was not thorough enough. It was tepid. The horror unleashed by the war, the misery created by its aftermath, the social and political unrest, and consequent social and economic dislocation caused by runaway inflation – all these evils demanded a much more radical response.

Brecht was a full-blooded writer who wanted to get to the heart of any matter. Although he despised any form of grandiloquence or overstatement he had no compunction in using grand phrases when it suited his purpose, for instance, if he wished to capture attention. Thus, he set himself up against the whole tradition of the theatre since the Greeks by claiming to be the first to establish non-Aristotelean theatre;[15] and by equating his dramatic theory and practice with Einstein's achievement in the realm of physics[16] he implied yet another Copernican revolution – in the realm not of cosmology (nor of philosophy, as Kant had claimed)[17] but of drama.

Yet these claims sprang from a deeply felt conviction: the conviction that the theatre – and, on balance the theatre rather than the drama – had failed. The theatre had become a mere place of entertainment in the bourgeois age; it had become a bourgeois pastime. But his attack was radical and he waged total war on tradition.[18] He asserted that all theatre before him had always been excessively tarnished with the brush of entertainment. No one before him, so he implied, had written genuine theatre, and that meant revolutionary theatre. Thus, the theatre had not lived up to the political challenge of the day to indict, and to convict, the powers that be for crass political and economic failure; for that bourgeois capitalism was bankrupt must be, so Brecht thought, patent to all those who had eyes to see. In fact, the bourgeois world had already been engulfed by the deluge. The theatre had lost the vitality of the great ages; for the bourgeoisie had deprived it of its daemonic character. It had become a cosy affair, a palliative for those who were not only content with the deeply unsatisfactory conditions of the world, but even profited from them. After his conversion to Marxism Brecht thought he knew the root of evil: it was the class division of the world which was, for him, in the wake of Marx, the original fall of man. Hence, the bourgeoisie on which the mantle of the feudal aristocracy had fallen inevitably made use of the theatre as of all other institutions for its own nefarious purposes.[19] Above all it oppressed and exploited the underprivileged, i.e., the proletariat. Not that Brecht would have claimed that the bourgeoisie's worst crime consisted in having rendered the theatre innocuous or perhaps merely having perpetuated an error handed down from the Greeks. The bourgeoisie ignored the fact that a new class, the proletariat, was waiting outside the theatre, ready to enter and take it over.[20] Yet, as a playwright and theatrical producer, it was that crime that mattered most to him.

Brecht's attitude towards the theatre of the past is not without contradictions. On the one hand, he clearly respected, even admired, great writers, such as the Greek and the English Renaissance dramatists[21] – and wanted the theatre to return to those more vital days; on the other hand, he felt – and he said so emphatically, too – that all theatre from the Greeks onward had failed in its task; it had not served the community since it had not been a vehicle for social and political change. He never resolved that contradiction, indeed, he never seemed to have been fully aware of it.

Rather Brecht was always a polemicist, and an extremely clever, skilful and vigorous one at that. He attacked Aristotle, but whether he had studied him as profoundly as Lessing had done, for instance, is more than doubtful. He was no scholar. He also seems to have been quite unfamiliar with the history of dramatic theory and, in particular, with the history of the reception of Aristotle's *Poetics*. Not unlike Lessing, he was often an unfair polemicist.[22] He certainly blamed Aristotle for theories foisted upon him by some (though by no means all) commentators since the Renaissance.[23] Of course, Brecht was not really interested in the exegesis of the *Poetics* nor did he consider or care whether Aristotle gave a fair account of Greek drama;[24] his aim was merely, with much guile and skill, to launch his own drama, to change current theatrical practice and make us see the whole world of drama in a novel manner. The main target of his attack was not even drama, but opera.[25] It constituted the negation of all that the theatre ought to be in the modern age; it existed purely for enjoyment and carried no purpose beyond itself. It revealed the pretensions and dismal failure of bourgeois art most clearly; for it pretended to be representative and profound, but in fact merely appealed to the senses and was, as he remarked in a memorable phrase, 'culinary',[26] i.e. it was on the low level of enjoyment which the eating of a good meal entailed. It did not challenge the mind at all. (Since the pretensions of grand opera were far greater than those of operetta or musical comedy,[27] grand opera was much more insidious.) It was pernicious because it lulled the spectator into accepting the *status quo* by stifling his critical sense and by giving him a false feeling of contentment and a spurious belief in participating in a higher spiritual realm as well as by creating the illusion of understanding reality, whereas the opera-goer was in fact turning his back on reality. Opera thus belonged to a lower unthinking level; for it lacked all that mattered: intelligence, purpose, meaning. It was just another chattel of capitalism, a mere object to be traded and consumed. It was performed in an outmoded institution, as obsolete as the ideals of 1789; for time had moved on and the bourgeoisie was no longer in the vanguard of progress. That place had been taken by the proletariat. The enemy was no longer feudalism, but capitalism and it was thus necessary to attack capitalist theatre, where ownership of the means of production, too, dominated theatrical practice.

Inevitably, the theatre, like all social institutions, had to be understood in the light of history.[28] This view was bound to have a decisive impact on the way in which human existence was represented in literature. For a writer to be unaware of these changes was to fail to master reality and that was the decisive criterion in deciding whether an artist had lived up to the challenge confronting him.

III

In his pre-Marxist period Brecht wrote plays for the reasons most playwrights write plays: because he wanted to, because he had the gift for it and desired success on the stage. Once he had become a Marxist he changed his mode of writing and although the creative impulse was not changed by his theoretical discoveries he found reasons for what he was doing. Just as, according to Nietzsche,[29] Euripides wrote for Socrates and himself alone, Brecht claimed that Marx was the sole spectator of his plays (B, xv, p. 129f). (presumably taking for granted that like all artists he also wrote for himself). Just as Marx had sought to turn social and historical studies into a science, Brecht wanted to create a drama and theatre for a scientific age.[30] Of course, he knew that drama and theatre were not able to be scientific in the strict sense of the word, but he demanded that plays should be written in the spirit of science. But what kind of works would they be? For Brecht, the Marxist playwright, it seemed axiomatic that they should reveal what went on in history and society. Marx had taught him that values and truths were not universal but determined by the social and historical situation. The playwright had not merely to present actions and events, but to uncover the historical conditions determining these actions or events,[31] to reveal 'the contradictions' in society and not to obscure them, as was done in bourgeois theatre.[32] In other words, he had to reveal causes and not merely effects. Also, he had to show that all situations were social and historical situations which did not reveal perennial truths, but intellectual positions and views capable of change. Brecht wished to apply to drama the insight which Marx had taken over from Hegel, who had in turn applied to history Heraclitus's conception of nature, viz. that all history is change. For Brecht the writer's task was therefore to make plain the reasons for any historical situation which he was writing about, to show that this situation was not caused by some blind unintelligible fate beyond the comprehension of man, but by forces that could be isolated, analysed and understood. But the business of art was not merely to depict or understand, but also to foster the spirit of revolution. He sought to apply Marx's dictum (expressed in the eleventh thesis on Feuerbach) that what mattered was not to interpret the world but to change it.[33] Thus, his aim was through his writing to recreate reality in order to change it. He had to emphasise the importance of property relations and the need for the prevailing injustice in these relations to be corrected. This view also refuted the contention that art must be judged on aesthetic grounds alone. Art is never for Brecht an autonomous realm, but must always be judged at the bar of social usefulness. A contemporary audience cannot appreciate the social and political issues depicted in the classics of the theatre. These plays have to be adapted to deal with the issues of the day. A theatre is not a museum. A great play of the past reveals a historical situation which must be shown to be historical. Audiences have to be made aware of the lessons for contemporary society that can be culled from the awareness of historical events related in dramas of the past.

The playwright has to teach us to imbibe the scientific spirit in other ways too. He has to make use of scientific knowledge, be it of biology or psychology, for instance, but he has to transform his knowledge into poetry so that it can please the readers or spectators. But the scientific spirit requires objectivity of which the bourgeois is essentially incapable.[34] The bourgeois, Brecht maintains, does not even crave for objectivity [*Sachlichkeit*], the proletariat alone does that. Drama ought to be written for the proletariat and not for the bourgeoisie, for whom art is a chattel and the theatre a piece of private property, and not what it ought to be, a socially useful public institution. In principle, Brecht excludes the bourgeois from the theatre though in fact the audiences of his plays were mainly bourgeois. An objective approach, according to Brecht, reveals the theme of all art since the Greeks, viz. that the world is out of joint. For instance, Shakespeare saw that the world was rotting away; hence he portrayed rottenness in the kingdom of Denmark by depicting the tragedy of Hamlet;[35] i.e. did so because he was writing in an age of transition and thus of turmoil, portraying the transformation of the feudal into the bourgeois world. Brecht's aim was to uncover the malaise detected by Marx, a malaise, now unmistakably visible, caused by the change from the rule of the bourgeoisie towards that of the proletariat. Until the rule of the proletariat is achieved, the artist's task is to further the inevitable historical progress towards the victory of the proletariat in the class war, the return to harmony of the socially and politically divided world. Whether, once the perfect socialist society had been created, there will still be any need for art, Brecht does not say; for he does not speculate on what the perfect society will be like. Just as he despised metaphysics, he disliked speculations about utopian solutions or further utopias and therefore kept them out of his plays.[36] He was concerned with the here and now. He however believed that it was impossible to write a good play which runs counter to the demands of history. Art could help to foster revolution because it could make people think by arousing criticism. The greatest possible improvement of the human race is brought about by criticism, which is thus the most important human characteristic. Art thus needs criticism.

The didactic task of art is then clearly defined: it is to make people aware that they must not be satisfied with the *status quo*: for however settled social and political conditions are, however long-established a regime may be, change is always intrinsically possible, indeed necessary and realisable. To arouse the desire for change, to make people reflect on the way in which it can be most speedily and most effectively brought about is what art can do as an agent of criticism, thus fulfilling a most valuable and necessary function.

To criticise properly involves using the so-called method of dialectics.[37] The audience has to be confronted with a critical commentary on the dramatic action. In order to produce an effective critical commentary the artist needs to be aware of man's ability to master reality, to control the globe and to change human and social relations. Life can be improved and suffering can be prevented, or at least assuaged, by art. (Brecht even maintains that by criticising, or running counter to, the spirit of the age, art reveals to us which decisions need be taken in time of need.)

Of course, art cannot deal with the whole of life. It is reserved for the borderline areas of social life where change is imperative and possible. Yet the desire to change ought to motivate the artist; for all art is partisan. He who is not for change is against it; to pretend to be impartial is to deceive oneself. It means to be on the side of the ruling class against the oppressed. No one can escape having his various attitudes and his conduct determined by the *Gestus* (a term by which Brecht seeks to denote one's whole way of life as it has become historically conditioned).[38] For any 'gestus' arises from the historical situation to which one belongs. But one can choose the class in history to which one wishes to belong. Brecht himself left the bourgeoisie, because it repelled him, and joined the proletariat. (At least so he claimed. Whether he really did is another question.) A writer ought then to espouse the right kind of 'gestus'. To be a genuine writer alive to the needs of the age he has to adopt a socialist 'gestus'. Otherwise he will not be able to write the right kind of plays, plays capable of changing human nature. Brecht is here again close to the Expressionists; for they demanded a regeneration of man,[39] a new man altogether. Brecht also calls for a new man to create or ensure the emergence and continuity of a truly socialist society, a society characterised by the resolution of social conflict, a progressive science and a realistic art, but he never portrays that new man. Genuine realist art does not merely entail fidelity to historical facts, a (so-called) 'social realism'; it needs also to arouse the desire for a knowledge and by virtue of that knowledge it is able to transmute reality.

In short, Brecht's conviction is plain: culture and politics cannot be divorced. Any attempt to do so is futile. It springs from a delusion and spreads deceit. Art has to tell the truth. But it is not enough merely to do that. Truth has to be made acceptable to those who are able to hear it. The artist needs the right means for that purpose. The conventional way of writing is not enough. Like all great writers Brecht wanted to speak with a voice of his own. He felt the need to have his own style. To understand and to vindicate his attempt to do so entailed formulating a new aesthetic.

IV

What manner of aesthetics was this to be? There were five requirements for the artist if he set out to tell the truth and make it palatable to others: courage, intelligence, skill, judgement and cunning.[40] They are needed to fight and overcome untruth and ignorance. Firstly, courage is needed (B, xviii, pp. 222f.); for while it is natural to tell the truth and not to tell an untruth it is not easy to do so in practice; for this means not giving way to flattering the powers that be; it means risking the loss of property and payment for work. Above all, it means telling unpalatable, indeed dangerous truths to pierce through the veil of high-sounding, generalised metaphysical speech and to speak to the lower social classes whom art would otherwise not reach. It means speaking about things that matter, food and work for the workers. It means saying that the good are not vanquished because they are good, but because they are weak. Courage is needed to expose particular abuses. For there is no merit in complaining about the evil in the world and the ruthlessness of men in general terms. To inveigh against the *status quo* in general is easy and does not require courage.

But it is not easy to discover the truth; for there are many obstacles. Nor is it easy to find out what truth is worth saying. The second quality needed is therefore intelligence (B, xviii, pp. 224ff.). For the truth cannot be discerned without a knowledge of materialist dialectics. It requires intelligence to acquire that knowledge. However, courage and intelligence are still not enough. We need, thirdly, skill (B, xviii, pp. 226ff.) so as to be able to use truth as an effective weapon. Only if all barbarous actions are seen as consequences of capitalism, only if the evils of capitalism are exposed, only if the real social, economic and historical causes of suffering and ruthlessness are revealed can truth be conveyed effectively. Yet more is necessary to utilise truth. We need, fourthly, judgement (B, xviii, pp. 229ff.) to choose those who can profit from the knowledge that can thus be gained. Truth has therefore to be written with a view to one's audience and the appropriate form of truth has to be found to make it acceptable. Furthermore, truth has to be conveyed by selecting the right words and the right example. To achieve this, a fifth quality is needed – cunning (B, xviii, pp. 231ff.), of which there are many forms; for only with the help of cunning can the rulers and oppressors be hoodwinked so that they are prevented from suppressing the artist's expression of truth and his discussion of the issues at hand. Cunning, too, alone makes it possible for truth to reach the oppressed who have to be roused from their uncritical slumber.

These views, expressed in a brief essay *Fünf Schwierigkeiten über das Schreiben der Wahrheit* [*Five difficulties in writing truth*] (1935) are not specifically related to art, but apply to all writing in the service of truth or of Marxist doctrine, which, in Brecht's view, are for practical purposes synonymous terms.

For Brecht art is only a specific instance of writing. Yet even if he appears to cast his net wide, his main concern, under the guise of a concern with broader issues, is with his own *métier* with 'art'. He is setting out the programme for the artist; he is laying down the plan of action for the man of the theatre to attract and capture the right kind of audience and to convey to it the right kind of view.

Brecht's programme had to be radically different from the theory and practice of the contemporary conventional theatre. Half-measures would never do for him. Thus, with a grand gesture of flamboyance and exaggeration no one less than Aristotle, the father of all poetics, had to be his adversary who had to be tumbled down for his pre-eminence. But however sweeping Brecht's condemnation of Aristotle's view, his attack on Aristotle's thought is not at all comprehensive. He fastens on one point in the *Poetics* only, on the famous definition of tragedy 'as a representation of action, which, by way of arousing pity and fear, brings about a *catharsis* [purgation] of emotion.'[41] Indeed, even here Brecht concentrates on catharsis. He does not interpret that controversy, but blandly assumes that it entails an act of empathy [*Einfühlung*] or identification with the characters of the play which, by arousing pity and fear, allows the spectator to have an experience of emotional excess and thus makes him content with things as they are. Whether this is correct is another matter. Indeed, there is every reason to believe that it does not tally with what Aristotle, or the Greeks in general, thought. (Whether Aristotle interpreted Greek tragedy correctly[42] is another matter not discussed by Brecht.) For Aristotle catharsis may well have meant (there is of course no consensus of opinion on this controversial subject) that to be purged of emotional excess made the spectator more suited to be a citizen of the *polis*. Presumably the individualist interpretation of catharsis attributed by Brecht to Aristotle would have made no sense to a Greek of antiquity who could not have conceived of life other than as a citizen of a *polis*. Theatre was for the Greeks part of a religious ritual; it was a public occasion, and it certainly was not a 'culinary' experience. Of all these questions Brecht shows no awareness whatsoever.

The Greek theatre was not a cosy affair; it was not a place of entertainment. Brecht turned to Aristotle not merely because the *Poetics* served as a useful stratagem to hoist his own flag as a dramatist, but he did so because he believed that Aristotle in proclaiming the doctrine of empathy had put the theatre on a wrong course. Empathy with the tragic hero or indeed with any character was dangerous. It deflected men from their appointed task of changing the world; for it stifled criticism.

However, the strictness which Brecht applies to the Aristotelean theory and practice is not directed against the Greeks; they are attacks upon the nineteenth-and early twentieth-century theatre or at best upon interpretations of Aristotle by superficial critics. Brecht inveighs against the practice and theory advanced by the great theatre producers of his era, whose aim was solely to make great theatre and who did not set out to foster revolution. To produce theatre for theatre's sake meant to blind men to the necessity of bringing about a revolution; for it made the spell-bound spectator suspend his critical judgement. Distancing was therefore necessary. Brecht, in an allusion to *Entfremdung* [alienation], a term used by Marx (and Hegel before him) to denote man's estrangement from work through the division of labour and a class, uses the word *Verfremdung* [distancing] (or *V-Effekt*)[43] to convey an impression of kinship with Marx, but also to communicate a different meaning. (Ironically, the origin of the term goes back to Aristotle's *Poetics* where the term ξενικόν is used[44] in the discussion of a similar problem.

Brecht's theory and practice are well-known. There is no need to elaborate. Suffice it to say that the spectator should continuously be reminded that he is seeing a representation of an imaginary action only, and that he should continuously be exhorted to regard what is happening with a sense of critical awareness so that he does not become absorbed in the performance of the play. Brecht therefore propagated the 'epic' theatre[45] (later changed to 'theatre in the scientific age'[46] and sometimes even called 'dialectical theatre'),[47] a term coined to denote discontinuous action, i.e. action interrupted by commentary on the action, which, so Brecht believed, is more easily capable of arousing the spirit of criticism. By modelling characters and situations on patterns of human behaviour in the light of behaviourist psychology[48] he thought to emphasise the scientific nature of his work and make plain his anti-metaphysical stance. Similarly, the actor's comments on the plot and on the part which he is playing are to prevent the spectator from wallowing in the pleasure of having his emotions aroused and satisfied. The actors – and thus the author – have to address the audience directly.[49] The spectator must be instructed about the real, i.e. the social and historical, causes of the events which he is seeing. Above all, he must be stirred to action.

Yet Brecht knew that drama was bound to arouse emotion.[50] He was therefore not arguing against emotion, only against empathy. Emotion should not drown the intellect; it had to be harnessed to the didactic and political needs of art. This was not easy. Brecht was aware of the perpetual tension between satisfying the emotions and using emotions to arouse criticism; he hoped that the dramatic devices of his epic theatre would succeed in resolving this problem, but whether they were able to do so or have done so is, to say the least, doubtful.

Brecht was, in the last resort, a descendant of the German Enlightenment, a moralist for whom the stage replaced the pulpit (or, indeed, the podium). He wanted to teach, if not to preach, in the theatre. Or at least he wanted to do so for some years after his conversion to Marxism. The pleasure aroused by theatre was either ignored or subordinated to the didactic purpose of the play. But not for long. Whether it was the (relative) failure of his *Lehrstücke* [*Didactic Plays*][51] to appeal to the public at large and repeat the success of the *Dreigroschenoper* [*Threepenny Opera*] (1928) or whether Brecht's own aesthetic instincts prevailed over abstract dogma, he soon realised that art cannot succeed in appealing to an audience without giving pleasure, and without keeping the audience's attention unflagging. Otherwise the teaching will not be conveyed; indeed, the spectator will be put off instead of being convinced. More important still, it may not even attract him to go to the play. To act to an empty theatre is as pointless as to preach to an empty church. But Brecht was too creative a mind to succumb for long to a line of thought arrived at by abstract reflection. Thus, when Brecht was asked whether he wanted to have the spectators enjoy themselves his reply was unambiguous and lapidary: 'What else?'[52] And he spoke of the spectator delighting in the (so-called) changeability of the world.[53] In *Kleines Organon für das Theater* Brecht claimed that pleasure is and has always been the business of art (B, xvi, 663); indeed, with apparent unconcern he abandons his earlier position.[54] For him art cannot achieve its end without pleasure. But his moralism does not rest with aesthetic pleasure as an aim in itself. Although he refers to Schiller's aesthetic theory,[55] he never seems to have properly appreciated the distinction drawn by Schiller and before him by Kant in the *Critique of Judgement* between sensuous pleasure and the aesthetic experience where the senses and the moral or intellectual faculty coalesce. It is as if Brecht was plagued by a guilty conscience; art had always to justify itself at the bar of reason, and for him reason, in the last resort, was wedded to social and political awareness and action. As a theorist Brecht remains didactic, indeed, there is an element of the schoolmaster about his theorising (though as a man he was certainly totally unlike a conventional schoolmaster and of course he was untainted by any kind of pedantry). He was too good a poet for that. He is indeed didactic when he postulates that it was the business of the theatre in the scientific age to make men enjoy dialectics. But, in his dramatic work, at its best, his natural playfulness and imaginative powers render didacticism powerless to disturb the aesthetic experience.

Brecht's reflections on the role of art and the artist are both rationalist and down to earth; their debt to historical materialism is obvious. So is his conviction that the artist ought to help suffering mankind. Yet however strong these convictions and desires were he was again brought up against the intractable nature of art. For art makes its own demands on the artist, however much he may wish to subordinate it to extraneous aims and ideals. In fact, Brecht did not solve the particular problem of the tension between pleasure and morality, between the need to entertain and the desire to instruct that confronted so highly moralistic a writer as himself. A century and a half earlier Schiller faced the same problem, even if he saw it in terms of a very different philosophy. But Schiller's aesthetics, far subtler and more complex than that of Brecht, is consequently also more comprehensive and satisfactory. Brecht as a theorist of aesthetics does not attain the stature of Schiller; like popularisers of the Enlightenment he takes too rationalistic a stance to do justice to the complexity of art. He is in fact closer to Lessing than to Schiller and he savoured polemics as much as Lessing did. Yet he became aware of the affinity of his own position to that of Schiller whose emphasis on the moral nature of art and of the need to combine morality with sensuous pleasure appeared to him sensible. Also, Brecht's attempt to place aesthetics in a cultural perspective recalls Schiller. But Brecht is basically a man of the Enlightenment looking for general rules under which to subsume art. Like Lessing, but unlike Schiller, he did not leave a comprehensive treatise that defines the function of art, although, again like Lessing, he composed several important pieces of writing dealing with aesthetic problems. But whether his theoretical writings, however influential they have been in his own day, will stand the test of time as Lessing's have still remains to be seen.

Lessing, while desiring social change, did not demand revolution.[56] Like many eighteenth-century thinkers, he believed that the growth and spread of enlightenment would necessarily secure social and political progress.[57] For Lessing, unlike Brecht, literature and the theatre are not judged by their social utility. Like all rational activities they need only further understanding which, if properly developed, will generate an improvement in the human condition.

Unlike Lessing, but perhaps much more like Schiller, Brecht wrote essentially on theory because he was hoping to discover the truth about his work. Yet unlike either of them he devoted much of his theory to propaganda designed to explain his work to the public, to woo the public and to establish his work as a major literary force. It is impossible to know precisely to what extent his own personal wish to succeed, as well as to understand himself, and to what extent his Marxist ideology determined his thought. Obviously, both impulses were at work, though often it seems as if the desire for personal acclaim was paramount, despite all apparent submission to ideology.

Yet Brecht was always skilful, if not cunning, true to his own injunction. He would invest personal desires with the aura of impersonal, objective aims. Doubtless he wanted to understand and explain to the world what he was doing, but it was only natural that he also wanted to have his ideas discussed and accepted. Hence he had no compunction either about using propaganda or attacking those who held different views. It was not merely a matter of disseminating his ideas. He also – and probably much more so – wished to have his plays performed and acclaimed; for that was, after all, the most powerful means of communicating ideas known to and mastered by him. Brecht, even if he was Teutonic enough to feel the need to vindicate his work, was artist enough to make sure, as much as he could, that his working would succeed. His theory was an auxiliary weapon in that task, conditioning the climate of opinion for the reception of his plays.

For he grasped that the world was becoming increasingly attuned to scientific discourse and thus he wanted to make men believe that his plays fell within that orbit.

V

For that purpose, Brecht set out to create a new drama and theatre; after a time-lag, partly caused by the rise of the Nazi regime, during which his plays were banned, he became famous. Indeed, for many he is *the* leading playwright of the twentieth century, though, indeed, his reign over the Western stage may be drawing to its close more quickly than most of his admirers are likely to suspect. While the novelty of his dramatic technique had much to do with his success it did not ensure that audiences reacted to his plays in the expected manner. On the contrary, they remained remarkably obstinate in seeing his works from their own point of view. It is easy to blame the public for their cussedness, but the fault is not necessarily always theirs. Intention and execution do not always match. Literary history affords many instances of this fact, and Brecht's drama is but another example. The spectator often does precisely the opposite of what Brecht demanded. (And not necessarily so on account of some innate perverseness, generated by his social origin.) He feels himself carried away by the plot and has empathy for the character[58] when, according to Brecht, this should not be so. This is, to some extent at least, inevitable since Brecht's own subconscious wishes often overrode or negated his conscious intentions. *Dreigroschenoper* was to be a revolutionary work but audiences from its first performances onward have almost invariably enjoyed it in the 'culinary' manner so detested by Brecht. This was not because 'bourgeois' audiences are ineradicably perverse, but because there is a deep-seated ambiguity in Brecht's plays, an ambiguity[59] which arises from the conflict between Brecht the poet and Brecht the theoretician but which is also the source of their artistic power. Like many artists, he became too involved in his stories and characters, an involvement that necessarily infected his audience. It has frequently been remarked that spectators, instead of becoming critical of many of the characters and of their actions and attitudes, find Mother Courage and Puntila, the protagonists respectively of *Mutter Courage und ihre Kinder* [*Mother Courage and her Children*] (1939) and *Herr Puntila und sein Knecht Matti* [*Puntila and his Servant Matti*] (1940/41), appealing and thus do not draw the right critical (socialist) conclusions. Of course, Brecht did not want to make Mother Courage an evil person, there would not have been enough dramatic conflict in merely depicting the failure of an evil person. He found it much more rewarding to show the failure of a misguided, all-to-human woman. Yet there is always sufficient ambiguity in character and situation for the spectator to draw different conclusions from the ones (officially) advocated by Brecht.

Or consider Shen-te in *Der gute Mensch von Sezuan* [*The Good Woman of Sezuan*] (1938/39). The desire for goodness and the need for self-preservation are locked in irreconcilable conflict because the action takes place in a capitalist world, but the helplessness of the Gods and their questions to the spectators as to how this state of affairs could be remedied might – and just as easily do – meet with the response that life is essentially unjust, that high ideals cannot consistently be followed and that compromise is the order of the day. Even a specifically didactic play like *Die Maßnahme* [*The (disciplinary) Measure*] (1930) did not win men over to Communism, but struck most observers as a dire warning against its ideology even more than its practice. No wonder that it was not welcomed by Communist parties themselves. There is no need to document or argue this view of his drama in detail; it has been put forward by almost all Western critics, and the official Communist suspicion of Brecht's work only corroborates it.

For Brecht, then, the role of art and the artist is not a central theme. He was, in the last resort, a more outward-looking author than the other six authors discussed in this volume; or rather in so far as he wrote about his own problems he tackled the question of survival, i.e. he explored the means of survival frequently needed by a sensitive man in a hostile environment where the impulse to do good or to act morally only exacerbates the perils facing him. Only once did Brecht expressly depict the problem of the artist's survival in the modern world, in *Baal*, his first play. In Hans Johst's drama *Der Einsame*, Grabbe had been portrayed as a misunderstood genius, a man of great spiritual power who came to an unhappy end. Baal is a totally different character. He is deeply rooted in the earth; he has no use for high-sounding phraseology; he is ruthless and egocentric in a powerful way. Poetry is not a sacred task, not a spiritual activity; it springs from the life of the senses, from the earth, indeed, from an all-too-earthy view of life where man is seen in all his crudity and where moments of high emotion are debunked. Indeed, the various revisions of the play over the years (from 1918 to 1926)[60] only made the play even less romantic, however, Baal does not survive; he perishes because he lives by instinct and for the immediate gratification of his desires only. He lives for the moment, a moment that may embrace, a poetry often designed merely *pour épater les bourgeois*. He fails because his reaction to life is one-sided; he lacks sufficient cunning and resilience, skill and prudence, wisdom and luck. His instinct serves him badly and sensual satisfaction quickly palls.

Only one other major figure in Brecht's drama could be seen as a symbol of a poet. It is Azdak, the down-and-out scoundrel who, by accident, becomes a judge in *Der Kaukasische Kreidekreis* [*The Caucasian Chalk Circle*] (1944/45). He acts in a manner befitting a poet by not taking a conventional view of life, but by allowing his imagination to dominate events and master reality. Azdak is consistent in applying his imagination to life; he is a jester who applies cunning and skill, but also a surprising verve, to any problem that confronts him. He succeeds, much to the spectator's delight, in dispensing justice in a totally unorthodox manner, for the time being. However, it would be foolish to press the argument too far. Suffice it to say that Azdak reveals something of the freedom which a poet might like to have in life and which he can apply to his work. Puntila acts somewhat like a poet by giving free rein to his imagination when he is drunk (which he is often), but he is a ruthless rationalist when he is sober.

Neither instance gainsays Brecht's approach to art and the artist, but it does not corroborate it either. The basic problem remains: the theatre stubbornly insists on being a place of entertainment; it cannot be restored to its religious origins in a secular society. In the modern world, men and women flock to the theatre for entertainment, and not for instruction or edification. In the last resort, then, it will always remain a question to what extent, if at all, Brecht's dramatic practice confirms his theoretical pronouncements; for, despite the ideological mask which he donned, his primary commitment remained the theatre and poetry. Still, both his theory and his practice had the same roots: they sprang from a poet's desire to impose his imaginative view of life on his work and make the world accept it.

Brecht wanted to change the world. The world has certainly changed since he started writing more than half a century ago, but that was hardly his doing. But he also wanted to change the theatre, and he did so – and not only in Germany. Changing the theatre indeed means changing an important sector of cultural life. But to believe that to change the theatre could entail changing the world is a very German belief, going back to the days of the rise of the German national theatre,[61] where culture, in the absence of a nation state, seemed to matter more than politics and economics – a mistaken attitude of mind castigated by Lessing, in his *Hamburgische Dramaturgie* (1767–68) when he became aware of the illusion (to which he had himself succumbed) fostered by a group of Germans who had the ingenuous plan of founding a national theatre before Germany had become a nation.[62]

In his lyric poetry, Brecht's approach is no different. He protested and wanted his protest to make an impact on the world. The theme of injustice is writ large across the pages of his lyric poetry. He inveighs against the injustice wrought upon man by man. In particular, he attacks the injustice of poverty, of political and economic exploitation and any other injustice brought about by capitalism which has turned human relations into commodities dealt with in the market place. Above all, he slates the injustice of human enslavement and degradation caused by Hitler. The poet, as Brecht explicitly says, must keep his independence of mind – François Villon is an example (B, VIII, pp. 38f.) – and enjoy doing so whatever the consequences so that he can give vent to his indignation and criticise abuses. But Brecht is no puritan. He knows that the artist must not be hostile to sense-experience in which all art is rooted; for the artist has to be aware of the tangible world as it is (cf. B, VIII, p, 45f.). Above all, the poet has to search for truth and tell the truth. But it is not easy. The poet

can, through his structures and images, only too easily create an order that
is inherently defective, an order that has left out something of significance.
This order, perhaps useful for a time, then quickly dates. The poet must
therefore be always on the lookout for new structures and new images to
correct those that have outlived their usefulness. (B, x, pp. 902f.) Also, the
poet ought not merely to voice generalities or truisms. He has to recognise
that to have the truth is not enough. He needs to have a home, an
environment to which he belongs, symbolised in Brecht's case by his house
and car.[63] Deprived of them by exile, he has lost touch with truth, too. For
the poet has always to speak about particulars if he is to be effective.

In fighting injustice Brecht, in the main, attacks political and social
injustice, and his tone is, understandably, strident, but in his last years, as
his physical powers were (probably) waning with the approach of death,
his tone changes. It becomes almost elegiac. The poetry of Horace appears
to inspire him with hope, but with not too much hope; for while the deluge
will pass, in the end only a few will survive:

> BEIM LESEN des HORAZ
>
> Selbst die Sintflut
> Dauerte nicht ewig.
> Einmal verrannen
> Die schwarzen Gewässer.
> Freilich, wie wenige
> Dauerten länger![64]

Hope may also be mistaken. The Trojans hoped, according to a late Greek
poet, even when their fates were sealed (B, x, p. 1016). But we must beware
of rushing to simple conclusions on reading Brecht's poems. They are often
more complex than they seem at first sight. We are apparently told in a late
poem that the poet rates the emotions expressed on the faces of workers
higher than the poetry of his contemporary Gottfried Benn (who is
yearning for death) and the smile of Mona Lisa:

> Beim Anhören von Versen
> Des todessüchtigen Benn
> Habe ich auf Arbeitergesichtern einen Ausdruck gesehen
> Der nicht dem Versbau galt und kostbarer war
> Als das Lächeln der Mona Lisa .[65]

But, on more careful analysis, we discover that what is stated is merely that
the workers' emotions are not directed to the verse structure of Benn's
poetry and that they are more valuable than the smile on the face of
Leonardo's masterpiece (a reference to an expression that has become a
cliché in any case). The poem might thus even speak of the power of poetry

and does not necessarily contain social criticism, though that interpretation, too, cannot be excluded. We cannot be sure.[66] Brecht's poetry remains, like so much fine poetry, elusive at times. He did not always make apodictic statements, as he recognised in a poem that he wanted to stand in lieu of an epitaph. Here his hopes are modest: all that he could wish for is that he will be seen to have made proposals which were accepted. His poetry does then confirm the general direction of his thought, but it also shows that his creative mind was at times more complex than his theory suggests. He may have realised that the obsessive repetition of his discursive writings was a sign that he was protesting too much to reassure himself of the rightness of his point of view. He may have had more doubts than he admitted. But here we reach the frontiers of speculation.

Brecht was too complex a mind for his imaginative conclusions concerning the writer's task to be summed up in any unambiguous manner, however much he himself desired to find simple answers to the complex questions which he encountered. To have communicated a more complex work than is dreamt of in his own philosophy is a sign of Brecht's greatness as a poet. Nor is it a mean thing for a poet to qualify his theories by the creations of his imaginative faculty. Thus, Brecht emerges a subtler and more profound mind than his theory sometimes leads us to believe. His artistic achievement widens the scope which he allotted to the writer in theory. His plays and poetry are none the worse for that.

9 *Conclusion*

Almost a century elapsed between Nietzsche's first steps in classical studies at school in Pforta and the deaths of Thomas Mann and of Brecht, which followed one another within a year. During these hundred years the history of Europe, indeed of the whole world, was radically changed, and Germany itself was for much of the time in the centre of these changes. But it was not only political and social life that underwent profound upheavals; the realm of ideas was also full of turbulence. Nietzsche was certainly fighting different battles from those fought by Brecht or the later Thomas Mann. Yet there is also a marked continuity. Nietzsche's cultural criticism reconnoitred much of the terrain upon which subsequent generations of writers campaigned. Though the work of the seven writers of this study is so varied that any attempt to put them into common (superficially defined) categories is mistaken, yet they were facing common problems, and, in one respect at least, their work reveals a similarity of outlook; all of them – and many other writers of the period, too – treated art and the artist with the utmost seriousness, even to the point of placing this concern in the centre of their work.

The emphasis varied. For poets like George and Rilke it seemed to be the central question around which all others revolved; for Hofmannsthal, Thomas Mann and Kafka, on the other hand, this concern arose from their questioning the validity of their own writing. For Brecht it was the starting-point rather than the end of his enquiry. Yet all of them were concerned to know what the artist could do, and all of them had doubts. The task of the writer, however important, was not certain. This uncertainty reflects the writer's own uncertainty concerning man's role in society, indeed, in the world itself – and though Brecht at least claimed to have a solution to these ills, he had arrived at it only after much questioning and, on closer analysis, the solution is not as unambiguous as he pretended it was. Indeed, whatever individual answers are revealed by the attitudes of these writers, no uniform body of thought, let alone doctrine, emerges. Rather, a wide spectrum of opinion can be perceived. Each writer is presenting his individual answer and yet all their answers are linked to the need to explain and vindicate the writer's task. In so doing they revealed a deep-seated need to understand themselves and their work and see it in relation to the world around them.

But this quest to understand and to explain is not concealed by strident assertions, even when they come from the pen of such apparently self-confident writers as George or Brecht; for their self-confidence itself is the result of the reaction to much inner struggle, doubt and self-analysis. Whence comes this uncertainty and what manner of uncertainty is it? It is spiritual uncertainty born of social and intellectual change, a change exacerbated by its speed, force and profundity. It was a revolution in values – a revolution which seemed for the writer all the more powerful since apparently, in the age of German classicism, great writers had succeeded in achieving a sense of harmony and stability that had been widely proclaimed as a model for all literary and cultural endeavours. Doubtless the great classical writers, Goethe and Schiller, were often misinterpreted, and it was forgotten how much they had criticised their own age and how much their critical diagnosis of the flaws in the whole structure of modern Western culture could also be applied to later periods. Yet in comparison with the achievement of Weimar classicism and even more with their Greek models, what art and artists could achieve in the modern world seemed of doubtful quality. Values appeared uncertain. Modern writers were concerned that man was no longer able to respond to life as a whole man and that culture lacked unity. Of course, they conveniently forgot that in earlier periods, even in the heyday of Weimar classicism, there had not been that sense of unity whose absence they now complained about. But the classical writer still believed that whatever was wrong could be put right without a profound upheaval.

Not so the modern writers. They threw the gauntlet down to their age because, in the main, they felt profoundly alienated from the conventional ideas of the time, and most of them were convinced of the need for radical change.

The reasons for this estrangement from the predominant culture are only in part intellectual. There is no need to repeat what has been said above (p. 7f.) about the social reasons influencing attitudes of mind. The writers' response inevitably varied; but it had one feature in common. For all writers, to a greater or lesser degree, the nature of this response mattered; it was a problem with which they took issue in their work. Or, in other words, they desired to understand why they wrote and what art could achieve. Unless they began to understand this they felt they had no business to write.

The understanding of their own task entailed radical self-criticism. Nietzsche led the way in exploring skilfully and persistently the psychological presuppositions of human actions. The artist was not sacred for him; on the contrary, he questioned with relentless vigour the artist's claim to reveal the truth cherished by the classicists and hallowed by the Romantics. He found all their claims without substance and he was never content to live with mere shadows. In his view, the artist was unable to tell the truth because truth was unattainable. The task of art was different: it was to make life bearable by concealing its horror. Of course, George was unable to accept that view; his opinion of the intrinsic importance of art was too great for him: it brought out the significance of life, if it did not give it meaning. Nor was Hofmannsthal able to hold it. Yet both poets had to grapple with the problem raised by Nietzsche and their answer did not come to them easily; they reached it only after a severe spiritual crisis. For George the artist established truth but he never provided any objective criteria by which the validity of this assertion could be tested. Here he is also close to Rilke, for whom the poet transmuted reality into his poetry so that it appeared true by virtue of its magic. Hofmannsthal, although assailed by doubt, believed that the poet could communicate truth; but, in his case, this view was supported by religious faith. So did Brecht once he had embraced Marxism, but his own view of truth was entirely historical. He believed that it sufficed to lay bare the historical conditions of all statements and events. That was all the truth that could be known. For Thomas Mann the artist's ability to know was a dubious quality, like all the artist's faculties subject to error, ambiguity and uncertainty. For Kafka, the most extreme radical questioning of all the artist's claims to knowledge and an exploration of his ignorance alone seemed appropriate.

This uncertain attitude to truth was closely related to the writer's response to science. For many writers of the period technology – and they more often than not failed to distinguish clearly between science and technology – seemed a threat to individual existence. Either ignorant of science or at least not practising scientists themselves, only too often did they fail to grasp the imaginative and intellectual adventure which it represents. Understandably repelled by the misuse of technology, they condemned it in its entirety. They protested against a disenchanted world, to use Max Weber's[1] (and Schiller's[2]) phrase, and wished to promote a more humane one. The quest for a new humanism was, in the main, anti-scientific. But not entirely: two writers – Mann and Brecht – differed. Mann wished to embody scientific knowledge in his work in order to humanise it; for he realised that unless a place was found for science in the imaginative life of the sensitive individual, and even in the work of the artist, a major segment of experience was ignored, giving rise to an impaired vision. Brecht felt that science, like history, had to be encompassed by the artist; his grasp of science was, however, naive. (When he wished to write a drama about Einstein it was, not surprisingly, about Einstein's politics, not his physics.) He appears to have believed that this dramatic method corresponded to modern scientific developments, such as those achieved in the realm of physics by Planck, Einstein and their successors, but his understanding of science seems to have been inadequate. Thus, his claims do not carry conviction. Still, at least neither Mann nor Brecht, otherwise antipodes, viewed science with the hostility of a George, Rilke or Hofmannsthal.

Nor did some other imaginative writers – Robert Musil,[3] Hermann Broch and Gottfried Benn, for instance – each of whom, doubtless influenced by their own scientific training,[4] attempted to strike the right balance between the imagination and science, and each of whom portrayed the difficulties in doing so. Indeed, they sought to defend art against neglect in a world dominated by science and technology; for art, in their view, has something of great interest to say about the world. Rooted in the imagination it can provide a necessary corrective to the scientist's (necessarily) limited view of the world;[5] for there are areas of experience which elude scientific analysis since science is concerned only with recurrent events which can be quantitatively measured. Science presupposes uniformity of nature, but there are aspects of life – and important ones at that – where other forms of understanding are required. Both Hofmannsthal and Rilke – and even Thomas Mann – urged men to discover relations in society and nature that cannot be discerned by scientists. Yet they claimed that their discoveries, too, gained objective validity through poetry. For their work contained associations which, though subjective in origin, acquired the power of objectivity through the magic of their art.

Because imaginative literature was able to depict the irrational elements in life the emphasis, so to speak, was on the exception rather than on the rule, and yet it was the task of the imaginative writer to endow the exceptional or individual instance with a general significance. For only thus can it point to knowledge. In the last resort, imaginative literature carries conviction only if it conveys thought.

The search for an answer to the problem posed for the imaginative writer by the rise and predominance of science and technology and their social, cultural and spiritual consequences was genuine. The scientific view of the world, especially if accepted and propounded by non-scientists, appeared to lead to fragmentation of experience. Certainly this charge was, by imaginative writers and critics of culture, frequently levelled against the age. Of course, it was only too often inspired by a jaundiced view of science, which is after all a magnificent intellectual adventure. This hostility is an easy dogmatic way out. But the experience of the power of science and technology was real and the threat to artistic creativity appeared unmistakable. In order to deal with this predicament a quest for wholeness was mounted by many.[6] An integrated personality was the ideal, and that ideal could be attained only if one was able to respond to life both with reason and emotion. But that was not easy. To experience and to understand merely particular events, and not life as a whole (whatever that phrase may mean), a sense of the unity of culture appeared necessary. Yet that sense seemed only too frequently incapable of realisation. Writers found it difficult to accept a pluralism of values and of cultural interest. They opposed to this pluralism demands for wholeness of personality and culture, couching them in an impressive, though often obscure, terminology stemming from the Romantic heritage. These ideas were taken up by men who were not rigorous thinkers, and even Nietzsche was not free from striking Romantic attitudes, among which hostility to science is one, though he, at least in contrast to others, is not consistent here either.

The rise of science and technology was paralleled at the end of the nineteenth century by the assertion of the value of life. This assertion was both an attempt to issue a counterblast against the inhumanity of science and a consequence of the new biology. Nietzsche's influence on these ideas was profound and explains, to some extent at least, the frequent attempts to develop a *Lebensphilosophie* which was one of the catchwords of the age[7] as writers sought to develop their own conception of what life might be if it were to comprehend the whole of existence. Inevitably, this conception gave rise to much vague speculation. Equally important – and, in some ways Nietzsche only propagated these ideas – was the rise of biological science; for the impact of the 'scandal' of the Darwinian theory of evolution and of Darwin's popularisers, such as Ernst Haeckel (1834–1919), must not be underrated.

Still, Nietzsche's ideas were all-pervasive. There is no need here to prove this in detail. T. J. Reed, in an illuminating essay, has shown how one set of imagery, that of animal imagery,[8] and the themes associated with it, affected the thought of some writers – Thomas Mann, Rilke, Gottfried Benn and Kafka; he also shows that what matters is not the imagery or the themes themselves but each author's response to them. Indeed, it can be argued that the whole theme of the status of art and the artist is a Nietzschean theme, not in the sense that it was invented by him, but in that he made it very much his own. So too did the writers discussed in this study as well as for a host of others. They wrestled with this problem; for they felt that it laid bare the very nature of their own experience of life as writers. And they saw it, more or less, in Nietzsche's terms, even if each time the response was predictably different. Nietzsche had radically questioned the place of art; he had, within his metaphysical system, assigned it a central place, but any one who would not accept his peculiar philosophical premises might well have doubts whether that centrality could be justified. Hence the continuous endeavour to vindicate the philosophical status of art, to answer the epistemological problem of knowledge entailed by the dichotomy between art and intellect, poetry and science or scholarship, brought to the fore by Nietzsche. And, similarly, his radical linguistic scepticism made its impact. George and Rilke, for instance, sought to justify poetry by assertion, dogmatic and uncompromising in the case of George, more subtle and arcane in the case of Rilke, and they buttressed their claims by striking out on new paths of linguistic creation. Hofmannsthal was likewise perturbed by the uncertainty of linguistic discourse in a universe which had become bereft of magic. Again, the sense of a world disenchanted by criticism, as analysed by Nietzsche, and the reduction of man's spiritual claim to its animal origin was seen as a threat. Hofmannsthal sought to find his way back to magic just as George and Rilke had done. Thomas Mann's and Kafka's uncertainty in their approach to writing, their doubts as to the meaning of life, again present variations on the same theme, as do other writers of that generation, such as Musil, Broch, Hesse and Sternheim. Even Brecht did not escape dealing with this issue. For *Baal* is an attempt of this kind. It explores the artistic life outside the Romantic spiritual setting criticised by Nietzsche.

Baal is a paean to life in which the hero asserts his right to live regardless of social convention and responsibility. Nietzsche's influence is unmistakable, though Brecht did not take over Nietzsche's ideas uncritically; for Baal comes to grief and the play is thus also a criticism of the unbounded worship of life. This criticism was not uncommon and reflects the belief, again held by Nietzsche, in the decadence of the age, an age that lacked strength, vigour and unity of culture. Alerted by Nietzsche, many writers perceived a host of threats to life, Max Nordau's *Entartung* and Oswald Spengler's *Der Untergang des Abendlandes* [*The Decline of the West*] (1918–23) are the most striking and popular works on that theme. The decay of culture which Nietzsche had diagnosed and attacked was believed to amount to the decline of the West – a far cry from the optimism of the *Aufklärung*. Many of these beliefs were myths, and dangerous myths at that. Yet the rapid technological change, the sweeping political and economic upheaval as well as the consequent social disturbance presented a realignment which made individuals feel vulnerable. And secularism made it difficult for most thinkers to fall back on the comfort of religion and on the experience of stability conveyed by a theocentric universe. The sense of the individual's vulnerability was heightened as the new secular God, progress, appeared dethroned. Even Brecht, who as a good Marxist believed in the inevitability of progress, took a poor view of the human race. Like orthodox Christian theologians he believed in the prevalence of original sin – although he would of course not have called it that – but not for him the redemption by grace, only by history (though we may wonder whether he really conquered his doubts).

Brecht blamed man's alienation and the writer's estrangement from others on the bourgeois capitalism which he abhorred. His conclusion seems unambiguous. Yet his late poems reveal a sense of strain, even though he was living in a socialist state which, in principle, was supposed to have successfully solved the problem of the writer's alienation. Perhaps he realised that the strain of civilisation is not so easily overcome, and, despite his own political commitment, he, too, may have felt that the writer was after all not without his share of social irresponsibility. For fundamentally writers were not prepared to accept the prevailing conventions of thought – they refused to glorify mediocrity, to pay lip-service to tradition which had, so they believed, been emasculated by worship of Mammon. To put material success above spiritual awareness was not good enough. Yet we must not attribute to all the writers the belief that bourgeoisie was always hostile to art. Of course, many bourgeois critics failed to distinguish genuine talent, or even genius, from second-or third-rate stuff, even from

Kitsch. But not only bourgeois critics commit these errors. Critics from other classes do so too. Of course, the operations of the marketplace, and the conventions of the materialistically-minded society are discouraging to artists; for quality cannot be quantified. Many writers therefore attacked the bourgeoisie, at that time economically – and not only economically – the dominant class, in their polemical writings.[9] But we must not be taken in by all these stances. For not all writers clung to that attitude consistently. Thomas Mann and Hofmannsthal even defended bourgeois existence on occasion, although they severely criticised its shortcomings. In any case, the term 'bourgeois' is rather vague, and some of the most striking features of so-called 'bourgeois' conduct are not necessarily 'bourgeois' at all. The dance round the golden calf had after all taken place in a much earlier, non-bourgeois civilisation. Display of wealth is as much an aristocratic characteristic as thrift is a peasant one. The term 'bourgeois' in fact represents a target of abuse denoting all those who raised obstacles to artistic freedom and creativity. They were the philistines of the day and represented a mode of living which earlier writers, the Romantics, for instance, had ruthlessly satirised.

There is however no doubt that all of these writers, in some way or other, felt that they were outsiders. This is true even of Mann and Hofmannsthal. Yet there was no escape from the demands which bourgeois society imposed on writers; for they had to deal with publishers, theatre agents, producers and managers to have their books sold or plays produced. And they had to pay attention to their reading public which was overwhelmingly bourgeois. None led a completely bohemian life, in any case inimical to consistent artistic production. The accident of birth made a genuine artistocratic life impossible. For that the company of the nobility or the assumption of an aristocratic pose can be no substitute. Nor did they lead working-class lives: not even Brecht, for all his alleged espousal of a proletarian ethos.

Yet the hostility to prevailing social conventions was genuine and deeply felt. It sprang from the conviction that the imagination was imperilled in modern 'bourgeois' society. It was the protest of the individual against the coercive powers of a society that allegedly did not cater for sensitivity and individuality; for it applied the wrong criteria and made demands on writers which they could fulfil only at the peril of stunting their creativity.

The starting-point of this protest was not, even in the case of Brecht, a criticism of social conditions, but a revulsion at a narrow vision of the world. This is why none of these writers would have any truck with Naturalism, which appeared to them too narrow, and why even the most gifted German Naturalist writer, Gerhart Hauptmann, turned away from Naturalism to symbolism. The artist had, so all of them said, to do more than just reproduce reality; he had to transmute it. Art was an independent power. Even Brecht, who refused to accept that it constituted an autonomous realm, was convinced of its power. If art was a power to reckon with, what was its scope? The answer to that question, as we have seen, necessarily differed. Yet the underlying tendency was unmistakable. Kafka apart, all these writers believed that the artist had a distinct social and cultural function to fulfil, but one fraught with difficulties – indeed, that the prevailing conventions frequently prevented him from carrying out this task. Even Kafka would have liked to believe in the writer's cultural task, but he despaired of his ability to define it, a theme which he relentlessly explored in his writings.

The work of these seven writers reveals much poetic or literary power; it reflects sensitivity of mind and force of the imagination, but none of these writers possessed the intellectual power of a Lessing or Herder, Goethe or Schiller. Even Nietzsche did not have it, for however impressive his mind, his lack of consistency and rigour of thought is disturbing. Yet even if their non-imaginative writings do not always appear succinct or convincing they must still be taken seriously for two reasons: firstly, they express the strain of cultural change experienced by men of imaginative power; secondly, these great writers impregnated the intellectual and spiritual climate of the day. We do not really know too much about the cultural world as a whole. Like all historical analysis, cultural history has to be selective, but culture is even more difficult of access than politics or social life. Also, we know so little about what goes on in the minds of most men that it is difficult to generalise about the state of sensibility or imaginative life in any era. We have to content ourselves with those few records which we have, and the evidence is scant at the best of times. Inevitably, the more powerful a writer, the more profound his impact on the age, and the more prominent his work will appear in the cultural landscape, especially in retrospect (for the immediate impact is often made by the lesser writer or by the feuilletonist.)

None of these writers studied here, however, with the exception of Nietzsche, was a major cultural critic. And Nietzsche's cultural criticism is only in part concerned with art. Some of the writers, like George and Kafka, never attempted extensive cultural criticism. Brecht is too limited, his perspective is too one-sided to carry conviction. He is also too sure of himself and not always sufficiently aware of the complexities of cultural life. His lack of knowledge is also disturbing; for he was not a learned man. Basically, his concern was with one cultural institution only, the theatre, traditionally in Germany a major cultural force. Here he has something of interest to say, but otherwise his social and cultural criticism runs along well-established Marxist lines and hardly reveals the originality which stamps his work as a poet and dramatist. Hofmannsthal is not a major critic of culture either. His essays are too impressionistic, too poetic in manner, to stand up well to careful analytical scrutiny. More serious claims could be advanced for Thomas Mann, but his criticism of culture is not comprehensive and penetrating enough either. Although interested in ideas he is not a sufficiently philosophical writer. He is also too much concerned with his own personal position. So much for the non-imaginative work of these writers. But Mann's imaginative writing is another matter. Here European culture is explored, portrayed and summed up with remarkable skill. We are given a lively and vivid picture of what civilised life was like in the period which he describes with much insight and great narrative skill. And he – like the other writers – gives us glimpses of the life of the emotions and imagination from which the philosopher or historian, by the nature of logical argument and concern with evidence, is, in principle, barred.

Nietzsche was perceptive in singling out as target some of the main flaws in German, indeed, European civilisation. However unfair he was to Wagner, he acutely perceived Wagner's frequently unfortunate impact on the German mind. Yet his main onslaught was directed against Christianity and Western rationalism and, more specifically, against German chauvinism and militarism. His campaign was for awareness, for recognition of the vitality of Darwinian selectivism and had little to do with his enquiry into art beyond the general postulate that the true artist must be aware of the primordial, vital basis of all art and culture. And, of course, art provides the criteria by which to judge a culture. Homer and Aeschylus were proof of a great culture, and by comparison the Germany of his day was a cultural desert. However, his psychological exploration was, in the main, directed to other areas, the unmasking of convention, of false attitudes of mind and of self-deception.

Yet Nietzsche, however powerful a critic of culture – and he is never dull, though often infuriating – had a limited range of themes. He also lacked awareness of the consequences of his thought, and though a highly sensitive man in personal life, was not conscious of the brutality entailed by his thought both implicitly and at times explicitly. On the one occasion – in his attempt to revitalise German tragedy – where he actively seeks to promote culture, his ideas are interesting, even if they are mistaken. And his criticism of German educational institutions is significant since he goes to the heart of the matter, seeking to correct major abuses. He knew that institutions are important, but that they cannot alone guarantee the survival or health of a culture. Great works are needed too – and he is seeking to pave the way for them in the *Geburt der Tragödie*. For great works set the standard by which achievement can be judged and provide an example for others to emulate. Nietzsche's strategy in each case was to discern the conditions which he believed to be necessary for his own development and for his own work to flourish and which he, with his remarkable tendency to self-assertion, assumed to be the right ones for general cultural prosperity. Nietzsche, then, as a writer, was necessarily concerned with his own work. Likewise, those writers who followed him also wanted to defend their work before the world at large and win a public by making it understand the aims and nature of their work – how they saw their own status, that of their art. In the last resort, their non-imaginative writings were placed in the service of their art, a natural decision for a writer to take since for him writing is necessarily the pivot of his existence. Their approach did not necessarily lead to a profound philosophy of culture, but it does throw light on their work. The writings of George, Rilke, Hofmannsthal, Mann, Kafka, and Brecht prove the vitality of culture to which they belonged, however much they themselves rightly criticised its shortcomings.

Cultural criticism is, if not overtly, a latently political activity, but this does not necessarily turn an imaginative writer concerned with cultural criticism into a political thinker, let alone a politician. None of these writers, in fact, was politically active, nor were they closely associated with political life and institutions. Some of them had political interests and convictions, but they were not friends, companions or counsellors of rulers and statesmen. For the politicians of the day were not in the habit of consulting writers, or even spending their leisure hours with them. But this is no exception. On the contrary, the poet who holds public office or is even the counsellor of rulers has always been rare. Yet while, in the past, in the age of princely patronage, writers might grace a court, in the late nineteenth and early twentieth century, specialisation has, in the main, succeeded in separating politicians and imaginative writers from one another.

Although some of them, notably Nietzsche, Thomas Mann and Brecht, wrote on political questions, and although both Thomas Mann and Brecht made political themes the centre of some of their work, they were not political theorists. Nor was Nietzsche, though he held outspoken and insidious views on the need of the strong, of an elite to rule over the mass of weak and unproven men. He did not develop a political theory properly speaking; for his political thought is not comprehensive and takes adequate account neither of history nor institutions. Mann, who wrote a lengthy tract in the field of political theory in which he maintained the apparently contradictory view that a writer should not meddle with politics, was not an important political thinker either. His later courageous attacks on Hitler, however praiseworthy, belong to the realm of political polemics (in this case amply justified) and not political theory. Nietzsche and the early Mann were concerned with culture. When Mann defended republicanism and democracy, he is of course not original, though what he said was timely. Lack of originality does not mean that ideas which he expressed were shallow or unimportant. But, however commendable, they lack the logical rigour of Kant's argument for political freedom guaranteed by law. Mann as well as Hofmannsthal and even George recognised that the writer has not merely to develop personal responsibility towards himself and his work, but also a social one towards others. The concern for culture, indeed, even the preoccupation with the writer's own imaginative experience, can have political significance. Since the artist says how he sees and experiences the world, he is likely, sooner or later, to be forced to come to terms with social and political problems. But if his response is inadequate from the point of view of political theory or political practice it is wiser not to censure him too harshly and to eschew the stance of sanctimonious self-righteousness. Not that flirtation with or surrender to evil movements, such as Nazism, should be condoned. It is not surprising that Rilke and Kafka are not overtly political in their work; for they came from a German-speaking minority group in Prague with which they never identified themselves; nor did they find a home in another national or political group. And it is in no way an accident that those imaginative writers who wrote more extensively on political issues, such as Mann and Hofmannsthal, felt that they were speaking for the culture of the German or Austrian nation respectively. Yet to have done so did not make them, not even Thomas Mann, political writers. Politics might, at some stage or other, matter to them, but it never absorbed the whole of their imaginative powers. Even Brecht, as political a writer as any, soon discovered that the imaginative writer's concern is wider than that of political issues.

Hermann Hesse, a lifelong enemy of narrow and extremist politics, summed up the task of art succinctly: it was to be the perennial unmistakable voice of humanity![10] Although each writer has his own view of humanity the thought of radical thinkers, even of Nietzsche and Brecht, was not determined by a political programme or by political opportunism, but by their conception of humanity. But their concern too, was primarily with culture, that is with the creative powers of mankind or humanity. Still, their reflections on the cultural implications of politics never have sufficient weight to rank as major philosophical writings on politics. They were, after all, imaginative thinkers who were not deeply concerned to explore political life. It would be easy to reproach these writers, even Brecht at times, for lack of commitment to politics. But it would be mistaken to do so. Political practice inevitably demands simplification of issue. A politician can ill afford to ponder on the niceties of political thought before dealing with the issues of the day. But, in Thomas Mann's view,[11] the creative artist must suspect, indeed abhor, simplification, though he recognised that in face of *terribles simplificateurs*, such as the Nazis, it was necessary to speak out in a simple straightforward manner so as to make an unambiguous and trenchant attack on evil. Nothing less would have done. And it might even lead to a rejuvenation of intellect. But to ask an imaginative writer to guide men in times of peace was, as Hesse perceptively remarked, to ask for too much; for a writer does not reveal superior unassailable knowledge; he is only someone groping for truth.

Writers must not expect, as Hesse observed,[12] to be interested in day-to-day politics. If they are it is likely that their art will suffer. And if they believe that their work will affect contemporary political events they deceive themselves. Yet, in the long run, their work will have political consequences. It will wield power over the minds of men when the political leaders of the day are long forgotten. Still, this does not mean, Hesse avers,[13] that a writer should not speak out. He is the conscience of the world who recalls those spiritual rules and values that matter.[14] He represents a nerve in the body politic that arouses attention to problems or issues warnings about the course of events.[15] Admittedly, of late German writers, such as Günther Grass and Siegfried Lenz, have actively campaigned for the West German Social Democratic party and a Swiss writer, Max Frisch, has accompanied a West German Chancellor, Helmut Schmidt, on a diplomatic mission to China. Still, it must be doubted whether, welcome as they may have been as political allies, they were genuinely able to exercise power and determine political decisions of substance.

The writer's task is indeed different. Whatever his political convictions or indeed whatever his opinions on any issue, his primary business is to write and therefore his first concern must necessarily be with his medium, language – the main means of communication. The writer has to avoid slogans and combat the misuse of language. This need to be the custodian of language and therefore of writing was emphasised again and again by the controversial Viennese satirist, polemicist and poet, Karl Kraus, for whom the proper use of language was the very criterion by which a culture ought to be judged.[16] For if language is abused, if words no longer correspond to things, events or situation, language no longer to ideas, the whole social edifice is, in his view, undermined, a view shared by other Viennese writers, in particular by Musil. Those who neglected or brutalised language reflected, in Kraus's view, spiritual confusion and poverty, but Kraus did not abandon hope, rather he believed that it was possible to purify language. To do so was not to cure a symptom but to tackle the disease itself. Kraus's concern for language is an extreme case, but it goes back to Nietzsche. It was shared by many writers who, like Nietzsche and George, attacked the abuse of words. Yet this reverence for language is closely connected with the writer's sense of inadequacy in the face of language which deeply disturbed Nietzsche, Hofmannsthal and Kafka.[17] Kraus's passionate interest in language was also, just as Hofmannsthal's, rooted in Viennese intellectual life which was influenced by Nietzsche and by Franz Mauthner's sceptical philosophy of language and which has received wide currency among philosophers through the later Wittgenstein's attempt to base philosophy on an analysis of language.[18]

Whatever a writer's political conviction may be, he can, however, hardly afford, in the modern world, to be purely didactic; for the writer needs an audience. Preaching to an empty church has always been a pointless exercise. To write books that will not reach a public and, worse still, do not even find a publisher is at least equally frustrating, especially since writers, unlike most parsons, do not receive stipends (however meagre). The modern writer, unlike the medieval one, is uncertain of his public. He must discover what public he can appeal to – and the public which he may find may not tally with his expectations and surmises, let alone with his hopes and dreams. And he may even have to create a public, a most hazardous undertaking. Consequently, the situation in which he finds himself may not at all be to his liking. He who feels that he is telling the truth is not valued for what he says, but for how he says it. His ability to entertain matters more than his insight. For without this ability to entertain he will not have a public at all. The dramatist Frank Wedekind felt this predicament most acutely. This is not surprising, since he actually sang in a cabaret where he had literally to entertain night after night. He resented this dependence and the audience's misunderstanding, as his play *König Nicolo* (1901–2) reveals. Others, like Thomas Mann, were afraid that the entertainer lurked behind the façade of respectability which the success of their work had bestowed on them. Others again, like Brecht, and Nietzsche before him, felt the need to debunk high-sounding claims to spiritual or intellectual superiority though they were not averse to making equally high-sounding claims on other accounts. But they felt it important to emphasise that the power to entertain constituted the proper sphere of the artist; and Brecht knew well that entertainment can only too easily interfere with a political purpose, making the artist an uncertain ally for the political revolutionary or rulers.

This question of whether art should be praised or debunked is of course closely related to another question, that of the contrast between the poet [*Dichter*] and the writer [*Schriftsteller*], a contrast expressed by the dichotomy of the two terms in German. Since *Dichtung* connotes not only poetry, but all kinds of imaginative writing and since the word, in the era of German Classicism and Romanticism, was invested with an aura of near sanctity, reaction against exaggerated claims was as inevitable as were the protests of those who felt they ought to be ranked as *Dichter*, and not as *Schriftsteller*, but were frequently denied their wish. The question worried Thomas Mann,[19] perhaps particularly since he was not a lyric poet. Since he felt, in principle, never entirely sure whether his work attained sufficiently high standing, or rather because his defence against undue praise or self-doubts contained a good dose of irony, he felt the need both to justify his place in German literary history and to direct his irony against himself for making such claims until he became convinced of the futility of making the distinction at all. George, Rilke and, to a lesser extent, Hofmannsthal always believed in belonging to the elect, and all of them asserted that a gulf separated the poetic elite from the rest of mankind. Brecht, on the other hand, deliberately debunked such claims, which he detested, and he pretended, both in dress, conduct and literary style, to be one of the people. But, in fact, he too, with great cunning, took all kinds of steps to safeguard his individuality and to prevent his becoming submerged in the common crowd. For after all he was as different from the overwhelming majority of mankind as only a genius can be, and he knew it. Indeed, he too struck a pose and his attack on convention resembles, for all their differences, that of Nietzsche. He wanted to establish a new drama, even if under a different banner. Like Nietzsche, he rebelled against the view that art was mere entertainment; this was to trivialise it, and he, too, despite all disclaimers, held art in high esteem.

Fundamentally all these writers were preoccupied with the need to clarify the artist's status as well as with their fear of being mere entertainers or adventurers. This concern springs, on the one hand, from their fear of not finding a place within culture, of becoming or staying a social outcast, of being a mere adventurer without home or purpose, and, on the other hand, from their innate desire to escape from the strait-jacket of convention, social and literary, governing society.

The desire and the need to enjoy adventure and the awareness of its dangers is but another aspect of the writer's predicament, revealing that his freedom is curtailed by his very ambiguous existence in society where he can be both fêted and despised. The struggle to survive and to succeed is a real question, but in the modern world, dominated by science and rationality, and yet prone to irrational forces more than ever, this problem of the artist's survival is allied to the more general human one of finding a way of reconciling the intellectual and emotional impulses within man, of harmonising thought and feeling. To portray the struggle or the failure to cope with this problem is necessarily a central theme of modern imaginative writing that is alert to the genuine problems of our culture.

The status or function of art and the artist is then a question that preoccupied German and Austrian writers of the late nineteenth and early twentieth century, far more than those in other European countries. Writers such as Mallarmé, Valéry, Gide, Proust, Eliot, Pound, Joyce and Yeats were certainly concerned with art and with poetic tradition. Indeed, in many of their works the fate of the artist is of central significance. Stephen Dedalus in Joyce's *The Portrait of the Artist as a Young Man* and *Ulysses*, Edouard in Gide's *Les Faux Monnayeurs* and Elstir in Proust's *A la Recherche du Temps Perdu* are proof of these writers' concern with this theme. But this concern never became a focus of interest for them in the same (almost metaphysical) way in which it did for German writers. The reasons for this difference are obscure; many hypotheses can be advanced, none of them satisfactory. The different social, political and economic development in Germany and Austria may be an important factor: so may be the long-established tendency of German thinkers and writers to treat most problems in a metaphysical manner, but that would explain German, and not Austrian, attitudes only; for in Austria a different, much more down-to-earth philosophical approach has always prevailed: there Bolzano, and not Kant or Fichte, Schelling or Hegel, has been *the* representative philosopher![20] Doubtless the character and influence of German Romanticism has played a major role; after all it created a gulf between German and Western thought. Undoubtedly the German metaphysical tradition, reinforced by the secularised theologising of so many writers whose home had been the Protestant parsonage and interlaced as it so frequently is with Romanticism, has conditioned much of German thought. Certainly, the intellectual – and therefore also the writer – held a different position in German social life and in England, for instance. Much more was expected of him, and he himself expected that he would be held in high esteem, but at the same time – and this was the reverse of the same basic situation – he was likely to be much more savagely attacked when not complying with the community's expectations. Tensions resulted, inducing him to theorise about his position, and often to make utopian demands incapable of practical realisation. Germans are perhaps particularly inclined to those often fruitless theoretical speculations because the lack of metropolitan culture and the centuries-long exclusion of the intellectual, indeed, even the whole bourgeoisie, from political power, produced a climate of opinion propitious to this kind of activity, a state of affairs which had not materially changed by the beginning of the twentieth century.[21]

The whole tone of German writing on this subject – and not only on this subject – is of course different from English and French literature, for instance. Germans, as Goethe perceptively remarked – and he did so in the last decade of the Holy Roman Empire of which Austria was still an integral part – 'like to give an account of everything they do'.[22] In the English-speaking world it is different. Poets like T. S. Eliot or Ezra Pound certainly took ideas seriously and poetry mattered to them greatly. And Pound believed that great literature, or, presumably, his own, could herald a new Renaissance and that, since civilisation had broken down, only a few individual scattered survivors, such as T. S. Eliot or James Joyce, carried on its lamp and therefore needed encouragement and help.[23] In answer to the challenge presented by this fragmentation of culture he did, in the main, turn his mind to practical issues – how to help fellow-writers (which Thomas Mann did, too, during his exile under the pressure of Nazi persecution) and to tackle, rather unsuccessfully (to put it mildly) economic theory, an aberration which had most dire consequences: he became a supporter of Italian fascism. His concern was not with the status of the artist as such. Nor was that of T. S. Eliot, although he was aware of the poet's interest in the social 'uses' of poetry and in his own place in society, a problem which 'is now perhaps more importunately pressed upon his conscious attention than at any previous time'.[24] For Eliot, every poet would like to be able to think he has some direct utility, but this does not mean 'that he should meddle with the tasks of the theologian, the preacher, the economist, the sociologist or anybody else; that he should do anything but write poetry, poetry not defined in terms of something else'.[25] Eliot rejects the notion that poets should either be saviours or handmaidens to some social or political programme or revolution.[26] And he accepts that poets cannot expect to live by their craft, and, 'as things are, and fundamentally they must always be, poetry is not a career, but a mug's game.'[27] He advises poets to be interested in other activities and spheres of life so that they have something to write about. His claims for poetry are, then, limited, far more so than those of many of his

German counterparts. His humility springs from the essential doubts which any honest poet should always entertain about the quality of his work; he can never 'feel quite sure of the permanent value of what he has written'.[28] And he advises the poet to turn to the theatre so that he can have 'at least the satisfaction of having a part to play in society as worthy as that of the music-hall comedian'.[29] These remarks represent of course a deliberate understatement, but they also reflect a much more pragmatic attitude of mind, a conviction that social change and the rescue of culture are best left to those whose primary concern it is, and not to poetry. Not that he was not aware of the problems facing our culture, of the destruction of its unity – a unity which, in his view, needs always to be balanced by diversity. But his counsels, like those of Pound, are practical; they aim at problems of education, at the restoration of the teaching of Latin for instance, a language which it is necessary for any aspiring poet to know and which forms the basis of European culture. His concern, just like that of Pound or of the great French poets, such as Mallarmé and Valéry, is with the writing of poetry, and the whole thrust of his highly influential criticism – and it has been the most influential in the English language in this century – is devoted to creating a climate favourable to the writing of good poetry. For the practical consequences of poetry Eliot's claim is modest, sensible and, fundamentally, incontrovertible: 'While the practice of poetry need not in itself confer wisdom or accumulate knowledge, it ought at least to train the mind in one habit of universal value: that of analysing the meanings of words: of those that one employs onself, as well as the words of others.'[30]

Or, to take D. H. Lawrence, a writer fundamentally different in approach and outlook from Eliot and Pound, Mallarmé and Valéry, he too, was convinced that our civilisation was diseased because of the 'diseased atrophied condition of the intuitive faculties'.[31] He knew that great social changes were afoot, but he did not think it his business to bring about or promote that change. His concern was with 'the change inside the individual'.[32] His task was 'to know the feelings inside a man, and to make new feelings conscious'.[33] In his view, modern society was at fault because man was not responding as a whole man; for unless he did this creativity was not possible,[34] and without it health could not be restored to a civilisation.

For French symbolist and poet-symbolist writers literature was all-important. To write the perfect poem or novel, to create the perfect work of art, was all that mattered to them. That desire excluded preoccupation with the status of art in society or the cosmos. In its extreme form, this belief was expressed in Mallarmé's celebrated phrase: 'Au fond . . . le monde est fait pour aboutir à un beau livre.'

Whatever differences there are in the attitude evinced by writers from the different Western nations, almost all of them were critical of their age and, at some time or other at least, of themselves. One of the consequences of that temper of mind was a heightened self-awareness, though that tendency need not necessarily be metaphysical or Romantic in origin. But in Germany and, to a lesser degree in Austria (but hardly ever in Switzerland), it has had Romantic overtones. It has often taken the form of a strong self-regard, if not egocentricity, which insisted on self-vindication and self-explanation. George Santayana, somewhat unduly influenced by anti-German feeling during the First World War, spoke of egotism in German philosophy,[35] and made this telling phrase the title of a book. More soberly it may be argued that the innate tendency of all writers to be concerned with their own experience from which they draw the sap to make their works live has both dangers and advantages; it may breed narcissism or even solipsism, but it may also unearth problems that would otherwise be concealed. It can also tell us something not merely about German culture, but European, indeed Western culture; for imaginative writers also tell us something about the emotional response to the impact of a changing world on a sensitive and gifted man; their concern with their trade – art – and with their status as artists is not some recondite, abstruse enterprise, but an important activity. Without art life would not only be substantially different, but also far poorer. Art also reminds us that there are things which can only be dreamt of, or, rather, it suggests to us that not all knowledge can be made explicit, and that scientific knowledge is not the whole of knowledge. It was not an imaginative artist, but Einstein, one of the greatest scientists of all time, who expressed its significance in a few well-chosen words when he wrote to his friend,   /hi Hermann Broch, on reading his *Der Tod des Vergil* [*Death of Vergil*] (1945), a novel about a dying poet and the meaning of poetry:

> That which is truly essential remains mysterious and will always remain so: it can only be apprehended by intuition, but never be grasped by knowledge.[36]

Apart from works of art themselves art cannot have a better defence. We should be content to leave our enquiry here.

Notes

EPIGRAPHS

1. Quoted as a proverb by Aristotle, τὰ μετὰ τὰ φυσικά; *Opera*, II, Berlin-Academy edition, ed. I. Becker, p. 983a. ('Poets lie much'.)
2. Goethe to Carl Friedrich von Reinhard, 31 December 1809; W. A. IV, 21, p. 153.
3. Saul Bellow, interview with Melvyn Bragg, 15 November 1975; *Radio Times*, 209, No. 2714, p. 15.

CHAPTER 1 INTRODUCTION

1. Richard Alewyn, *Johann Beer. Studien zum Roman des 17. Jahrhunderts*, Leipzig, 1932, pp. 129f.
2. Paul Kluckhohn, *Dichterberuf und bürgerliche Existenz*, Tübingen/Stuttgart n.d. [1949], p. 15.
3. This reference is Elizabeth M. Wilkinson's seminal article, '*Torquato Tasso*. The Tragedy of a Creative Artist', *Publications of the English Goethe Society*, N.S., XV, 1946; reprinted in *Goethe. Poet and Thinker*, London, 1962, pp. 75–92. For an account of Goethe's view of art and the artist cf. Georg Gerster, *Die leidigen Dichter, Goethes Auseinandersetzung mit dem Künstler*, Zürich, 1954, a most interesting work so far inexplicably ignored by Goethe scholars.
4. Cf. my book *Goethe's Novels*, London, 1969, (Miami, 1971) pp. 52ff., for a fuller discussion of this point (cf. also the German version *Goethes Romane*, Berne/Munich, 1963, pp. 58 ff.).
5. Novalis, *Briefe und Werke* (ed. Ewald Wasmuth), III, Berlin, 1943, p. 330; cf. also H. S. Reiss (ed.), *The Political Thought of the German Romantics 1795–1815*, Oxford, 1965, pp. 6 ff., for a fuller discussion of this aspect of Romantic thought; and my *Politisches Denken in der deutschen Romantik*, Berne and Munich, 1963, pp. 12 ff.
6. Cf. Friedrich Sengle, *Biedermeierzeit. Deutsche Literatur im Spannungsfeld zwischen Restauration und Revolution 1815–1848*, I, Stuttgart, 1971, pp. 83–100, an outstanding work, for a discussion of this aspect.
7. The full title is *Die Weise von Liebe und Tod des Cornet Christoph Rilke* (1906).
8. Cf. F. A. Hayek, *The Counter-Revolution of Science, Studies on the Abuse of Reason* (paperback edition), New York and Toronto, 1964, pp. 13 ff., for an account of the widespread misunderstanding of the methods and nature of science.
9. In his first *Unzeitgemäße Betrachtung: David Friedrich Strauss. Der Schriftsteller und Bekenner* (1873): N, I, pp. 135–207.

CHAPTER 2 NIETZSCHE

1. Cf. A. H. J. Knight, *Some Aspects of the Life and Work of Nietzsche*, Cambridge, 1933, pp. 4 f.
2. Byron, *Letters and Journal*, ed. R. E. Protheroe, London and New York, 1904,

v, p. 191, Diary of 28 and 29 January 1821.

3. Cf. Paul Böckmann, 'Die Bedeutung Nietzsches für die Situation der modernen Literatur', *Dt. Vjs*, XXVII, 1953, pp. 77–101.

4. Cf. Walter H. Sokel, *The Writer in Extremis, Expressionism in Twentieth-Century German Literature*, Stanford, Calif., 1959, a most stimulating study; and Armin Arnold, *Die Literatur des Expressionismus. Sprachliche und thematische Quellen*, Stuttgart, 1966, both of whom make this point.

5. Cf. René Wellek, *A History of Modern Criticism*, IV, London, 1966, who makes this observation (p. 356), and Elrud Kunne-Ibsch, *Die Stellung Nietzsches in der Entwicklung der modernen Literaturwissenschaft*, Tübingen, 1972, for a full-length study of Nietzsche's place in German literary history and criticism.

6. This aspect of Nietzsche's thought is stressed by Peter Pütz, *Nietzsche*, Stuttgart, 1967.

7. A study of his letters, a most interesting exercise, clearly reveals the development of his ideas on the subject of his studies. He gave the first comprehensive public expression of his unease in *Über die Zukunft unserer Bildungsanstalten* [*On the Future of our Educational Institutions*] (1872), and he wrote on it at his most militant in *Unzeitgemäße Betrachtungen*, particularly in the second essay, *Vom Nutzen und Nachteil der Historie für das Leben* [*Of the Use and Abuse of History for Life*] (1873).

8. 'Versuch einer Selbstkritik' ['Attempt of Self-Criticism'] second Preface [of 1886] to *Geburt der Tragödie*; N, I, p. 12.

9. The relationship between Wagner and Nietzsche has been most perceptively analysed by Ernest Newman in his standard work, *Richard Wagner. His Life and Work*, IV, London, 1947, pp. 475–520. Newman's account is masterly. Cf. also Dietrich Fischer-Dieskau *Wagner und Nietzsche*, 1974 (English trs., New York, 1976)

10. Cf. to Hans von Bülow, 20 July 1872; N-Br., III, p. 263f.

11. Cf. to Nietzsche, 24 July 1872; N-Ges. Br., III, pp. 249ff.

12. Cf. his letter to Hans von Bülow, 22 October 1887; N-Ges. Br. III, p. 367. and my 'Nietzsche's *Geburt der Tragödie*', p. 505ff. For a thorough account of the character of Nietzsche's music, cf. Martin Vogel, *Apollinisch und Dionysisch Geschichte eines genialen Irrtums*, Regensburg, 1966, pp. 219–45.

13. *Versuch einer Selbstkritik*; N, I, p. 11.

14. *Versuch einer Selbstkritik*; N, I, p. 11.

15. Cf. Vogel; also Anni Carlsson, 'Der Mythos als Maske Friedrich Nietzsches', *Germanisch-Romanische Monatsschrift* (XXXIV [N. F. VIII], 1968, and Max Baeumer, 'Das Dionysische-Entwicklung eines literarischen Klischees', *Colloquia Germanica*, 1967, pp. 253–62, for a discussion of this question. The suggestive power of Nietzsche's work is stressed by H. A. Reyburn (in collaboration with H. E. Hinderks and J. G. Taylor), *Nietzsche. The Story of a Human Philosopher*, London, 1949, p. 119.

16. J. J. Winckelmann, *Sämtliche Werke*, I, Osnabrück, 1965 (photographic reprint of the 1825 edition), p. 30; for the importance of this view for German thought cf. E. M. Butler, *The Tyranny of Greece over Germany*, Cambridge, 1935, who also emphasises Nietzsche's important role in reversing this intellectual trend. Of course, Winckelmann's view was criticised from the outset – from Christoph Martin Wieland to Heinrich Heine. (I owe this observation to Friedrich Sengle.)

17. Cf. Erwin Rohde's letter to Nietzsche of 22 April 1871 (N-Ges. Br. ii, p. 236) in which Rohde attacks the concept of Greek serenity and appears to expect Nietzsche's assent. Cf. also *Götzen-Dämmerung* [*The Twilight of Idols*], N, ii, p. 1031; and N-Gr. xvi, p. 252; N, Gr. ix, p. 80; *Geburt der Tragödie*, N, i, p. 111; cf. also Hans Eberhard Gerber, *Nietzsche und Goethe. Studien zu einem Vergleich*, Berne, 1933, who discusses this problem (p. 1 and p. 24).

18. Hugh Lloyd-Jones, 'Nietzsche and the Ancient World', *Studies in Nietzsche and the Classical Tradition*, ed. James C. O'Flaherty *et al.*, Chapel Hill, 1976, pp. 9 f., maintains that this insight, in the long run, made a decisive impact on classical scholarship. His view is in some ways similar to that of Charles Andler in his monumental six-volume work, *Nietzsche. Sa Vie et sa Pensée*, Paris, 1920–31 (cf. particularly vol. iii, p. 245–65).

19. For a fuller analysis of this problem cf. my article 'Nietzsche's *Geburt der Tragödie* . . . ', and Reyburn, p. 132.

20. For a discussion of this aspect of Nietzsche's work cf. Maria Bindschedler, *Nietzsche und die poetische Lüge*, 2nd ed., Bâle, 1966, who argues that Nietzsche sought to vindicate poetic fiction in the *Geburt der Tragödie* (p. 38).

21. *Über Wahrheit und Lüge im außermoralischen Sinn* [*On Truth and Lying in the extramoral sense*] (1873; published posthumously, N, iii, p. 314).

22. The connection between Euripides and Socrates is of course false as Ulrich von Wilamowitz-Moellendorff was quick to point out in *Zukunftsphilologie* i, Berlin, 1872, pp. 24ff. (reprinted Gründer, pp. 47f.) Cf. also Ernst Howald's important book on Nietzsche and classical studies (*Nietzsche und die klassische Philologie*, Gotha, 1920, p. 43).

23. To Nietzsche, 14 February 1872; N-Br. iii, p. 141.

24. Diary entry of 2 February 1872; N-Br. iii, p. 461.

25. To Friedrich Wilhelm Ritschl, 30 January 1872; N-Br. iii, pp. 201f.

26. Rohde's published review is printed in Gründer pp. 15–26; Friedrich Zarncke, a distinguished medieval German scholar, had refused to let Rohde review the *Geburt der Tragödie* in the *Literarische Zentralblatt*, a renowned scholarly journal. Rohde's review for that journal is reprinted in Gründer, pp. 1–14.

27. Reprinted Gründer, pp. 27–55.

28. Reprinted Gründer, pp. 57–64.

29. Reprinted Gründer, pp. 65–111.

30. Wilamowitz published a second *Zukunftsphilologie II*, Berlin, 1873 [Reprinted Gründer, pp. 113–35] which had no further reply cf. Howald, and my article 'Nietzsche's *Geburt der Tragödie*', for a fuller discussion of the whole episode. Cf. also Lloyd-Jones, pp. 5–10.

31. *Der Fall Wagner* [*The Case of Wagner*] N, ii, p. 913.

32. *Nietzsche contra Wagner*, N, ii, p. 1042.

33. *Der Fall Wagner*, N, ii, p. 912.

34. *Ecce Homo*, N, ii, p. 1119.

35. Cf. Andler, iii, pp. 77–107; and W. M. Salter, *Nietzsche the Thinker*, London, 1917, pp. 72–7 and pp. 129–147 for a succinct account of his political thought. For a concise account of his view of culture which mattered far more to him cf. Frederick J. Copleston, S.J., *Friedrich Nietzsche. Philosopher of Culture*, London, 1942.

36. Cf. Reed, 'Nietzsche's Animals, Image, Ideas and Influence' *Nietzsche:*

Imagery and Thought, (ed. Malcolm Pasley), who makes this point.

37. Nietzsche's attitude to the intellect is as ambivalent as his view of Socrates. Walter Kaufmann, in his influential book, *Nietzsche. Philosopher, Psychologist. Antichrist*, Princeton, N. J., 1950, makes the point that Nietzsche was, in principle, not an enemy of Socrates. This view is attacked by Georg A. Wells, 'The Birth of Tragedy. An Analysis and Assessment of Nietzsche's essay', *Trivium*, III, 1968, p. 73. It must however be doubted whether Nietzsche really hated Socrates as much as Wells claims (ibid., p. 66). His attitude was ambivalent, as is shown by his remark: 'Socrates . . . is so close to me that I am always fighting a battle with him' (N, III, p. 333). For a full discussion of Nietzsche's attitude to Socrates cf. Hermann Josef Schmidt, *Nietzsche und Sokrates. Philosophische Untersuchungen zu Nietzsches Sokratesbild*, Meisenheim/Glan, 1969.

38. The obvious stages are well charted by Helge Hultberg, *Die Kunstauffassung Nietzsches*, Bergen and Oslo, 1964, p. 23. Hultberg's account of the later Nietzsche's conception of art is particularly useful. Cf. also Peter Pütz, *Friedrich Nietzsche* and his *Kunst und Künstlerexistenz bei Nietzsche und Thomas Mann*, Bonn, 1963, for a most helpful analysis of the same problem.

39. Cf. Pütz, *Friedrich Nietzsche*, p. 32f.

CHAPTER 3 GEORGE

1. Cf. Michael Winkler, *George Kreis*, Stuttgart, 1972, for a good survey; cf. also *Stefan George und sein Kreis, Eine Bibliographie*, ed. G. P. Landmann, Hamburg, 1960.

2. For a representative work of that kind cf. Gerd Mattenklott, *Bilderdienst, Ästhetische Opposition bei Beardsley und Stefan George*, 1970. The criticism of George on political grounds is however of long standing. He was seen as a precursor of Nazism, for instance, by R. O. D. Butler, *The Roots of National Socialism, 1789–1933*, p. 200, who cites an appalling statement by George in which he applauds the German soldiers who had destroyed Rheims and Ypres. A similar view is expressed by Aurel Kolnai, *The War against the West*, London, 1938, for instance. But these views are one-sided; cf. his letters to Gundolf of 5 October 1914 in which he severely castigates the German government of the day and criticises Gundolf's enthusiasm for the war. (SG-FG Br., p. 263f.)

3. For a perceptive consideration of their relationship cf. Th. Weevers, 'Albert Verwey and Stefan George. Their Conflicting Affinities', *GLL*, XXII, 1968, pp. 79–89.

4. The George-Hofmannsthal correspondence gives an outline of the story of the two poets' relationship (Br. SG-H).

5. For a thorough appraisal of this journal cf. Karlhans Kluncker, *Blätter für die Kunst. Zeitschrift der Dichterschule Stefan Georges*, Frankfurt/Main, 1974. There were 12 volumes altogether, which appeared between 1892–1919.

6. Cf. Eudo C. Mason, 'Rilke und Stefan George', *Rilke in neuer Sicht* ed. Käte Hamburger, Cologne/Mayence/Stuttgart/Berlin, 1971, for an analysis of their relationship.

7. Cf. A. Mockel, 'Quelques Souvenirs sur Stefan George', *Revue d'Allemagne*, II, 1928, p. 391 also quoted by Hans Wendt, *Stefan Georges Gespräche* (Lubeck,

1970, unpublished MS, Stefan George Archiv, Württembergische Landesbibliothek, Stuttgart) p. 16, a most informative work that merits publication.

8. Cf. to Arthur Stahl, 15 July 1888, quoted by Robert Boehringer, *Mein Bild von
Stefan George*, Munich and Düsseldorf 1951, pp. 28f., where George states that
he is becoming more cosmopolitan in England; cf. also his remark, 'Germany
is unbearable', made to Ernst Robert Curtius ('Stefan George im Gespräch',
Kritische Schriften, Berne, 1950, p. 153).

9. Cf. Paul Gerhard Klussmann, *Stefan George. Zum Selbstverständnis der Kunst und
des Dichters der Moderne*, Bonn, 1961, who emphasises this desire (pp. 13 ff.).
Klussmann's book is an excellent monograph from which I have learnt much.

10. The word 'Mache' (Bl. 1, p. 1) (literally meaning 'to make' or 'making') is
here used. It usually denotes cheap, inferior production but here it is intended
to evoke the etymological root of poetry which derives from ποιεῖν (to make).

11. Kurt Hildebrandt, *Erinnerung an Stefan George und seinen Kreis*, Bonn, 1965, p.
108.

12. Mockel, p. 393.

13. G. I. p. 159.

14.   AUGURY

    Once I saw the swallows winging,
    Swallows snow-and silver-white,
    In the wind I saw them clinging,
    Windy weathers, hot and bright.

    Saw the jays alight and glimmer,
    Parakeet and colibri
    Through the trees of wonder shimmer
    In the wood of Thusferi.

    Saw the ravens flap and slacken,
    Daws of black and sombre grey
    Over adders, near the bracken
    Where the magic forest lay.

    Now again I see the winging
    Snow and silver swallows veer,
    In the wind I see them clinging,
    Windy weathers, cold and clear.

[*The Works of Stefan George*, trs. Olga Marx and Ernst Morwitz, Chapel Hill, N. C.,
1949, p. 38.)

15. Ludwig Klages, 'Aus einer Seelenlehre des Künstlers', Bl. 11, p. 138. Cf. B.A.
Rowley, 'The Ages of Man in Goethe and George', *Modern Language Quarterly*,
XVII, 1956, for instance, who interprets the poem as a *Lebenslied* symbolising
the three stages of man's life.

16. Jethro Bithell, 'Stefan George and Ida Coblenz', *German Studies presented to
Leonard Ashley Willoughby*, Oxford, 1952, particularly pp. 5f. for an account of
George's attitude to Dehmel who married Ida Coblenz, the only woman in
whom George ever showed any interest. But George's contempt for Dehmel

antedates that marriage and was based not on personal grounds but sprang
from his conception of poetry.

17. Cf. Klussmann, *passim*.
18. Cf. Klussmann, p. 9; cf. also Mockel p. 393 who quotes George's demand: 'il
    nous faut développer d'abord la plastique du langage.'
19. Cf. Manfred Durzak, *Der junge Stefan George, Kunsttheorie und Dichtung*,
    Munich, 1968, p. 110. Durzak's book is most interesting as is also his *Stefan
    George. Zwischen Symbolismus und Expressionismus*, Stuttgart/Berlin/Cologne/
    Mayence, 1974, p. 138.
20. Cf. Paul Gerardy, 'Geistige Kunst', Bl. II, p. 111ff..
21. Cf. Carl August Klein, 'Unterhaltungen im grünen Salon', III, 'Das doch
    nicht Äußerliche', Bl. I, p. 144; cf. also his article 'Über Stefan George', Bl.I,
    pp. 45–50, which was obviously meant to be authoritative.
22. Cf. Claude David, *Stefan George. Sein dichterisches Werk* (trs. Alexa Remmen
    and Karl Thiemer), Munich, 1967, p. 38.
23. G, I, p. 10.

> The poet also hears the lure of sound,
> And yet today he must not yield to spells,
> Because his speech with spirits, holds him bound.
>
> His hand must goad the pen – though it rebels.
> *(The Works of Stefan George*, p. 4)

24. Cf. David, *Stefan George*, p. 66.
25. G, I, p. 40.

THE CLASP

> I planned it as an iron band,
> As something cool and smooth and plain,
> But not a mine in all the land
> Had metal of the wanted grain.
>
> So now it shall be otherwise:
> A rare and lavish cluster tooled
> Of gold as red as flame, and jewelled
> With precious stones in flashing dyes.
>
> *(The Works of Stefan George*, p. 26).

26. Cf. the account given by Marianne Weber of the relationship between the
    two men in *Max Weber. Ein Lebensbild*, Tübingen, 1926, pp. 462–72.
27. Cf. Hildebrandt, p. 125.
28. Cf. for instance the essays in the *Jahrbücher für die geistige Bewegung*, ed.
    Friedrich Gundolf and Friedrich Wolters, 3 vols, 1910–12, a journal which
    was closely supervised by George. Cf. Winkler, *George Kreis*, pp. 65–77, who
    calls George its 'real editor' (p. 67); cf. also Frank Jolles, 'Die Entwicklungen
    der wissenschaftlichen Grundsätze des George Kreises', *Etudes Germaniques*,
    XXII, 1967, pp. 346–58 for a good account of the aims of the 'Kreis' which

amounts to a conception of 'Wissenschaft' diametrically opposed to that based on natural science (p. 358) and indeed on traditional scholarship. Cf. also Claude David, 'Jahrbuch für die geistige Bewegung (1910–11), *Études Germaniques*, x, 1955, pp. 276–97 for another discussion of the ideas pervading this journal. David argues convincingly that its emphasis on the deeds of heroes and creative artists were the main tenets of the essays.

29. For a discussion of Gundolf's work cf. Lothar Helbing and C. V. Bock, 'Friedrich Gundolf', Arthur R. Evans, Jr., *On Four Modern Humanists*, Princeton, N. J., 1970, pp. 54–84.

30. For a discussion of Kantorowicz's (1895–1963) work cf. Yakov Malkeil, 'Ernst Kantorowicz', ibid., pp. 146–219.

31. Cf. Hildebrandt, p. 211.

32. Cf. Kurt Breysig, *Aus meinen Tagen und Träumen. Memoiren, Aufzeichnungen, Briefe, Gespräche* ed. Gertrud Breysig and Michael Landmann, Berlin, 1962, pp. 26ff..

33. Cf. David, *Stefan George*, p. 193.

34. Cf. to Hugo von Hofmannsthal, 4 December 1905; Br. SG-H, pp. 226f.

35. Cf. to Stefan George, 1 December 1905; Br. SG-H, pp. 223f.

36. Cf. David, *Stefan George, p. 193.*

37. *Cf. David, Stefan George*, p. 198.

38. Cf. David, *Stefan George*, p. 192.

39. Cf. Michael M. Metzger and Erika A. Metzger, *Stefan George*, New York, 1972, p. 104.

40. Cf. Metzger, p. 106.

41. Walter Müller-Seidel, ' "Diskussion" zu Vincent J. Günther, "Der ewige Augenblick" ', *Stefan George Kolloquium*, ed. Eckhard Heftrich et al, Cologne, 1969, p. 206. George never fully disclosed his own thoughts. According to Henry Benrath (quoted by Wendt, p. 171), he intimated that not all could and should be revealed.

42. Cf. David, *Stefan George*, p. 225.

43. Cf. David, *Stefan George*, p. 223.

44. Cf. David, *Stefan George*, p. 252.

45. Cf. David, *Stefan George*, p. 273, who speaks of George returning once more to solipsism.

46. G, I, p. 280.

> Now the miracle befalls:
> dream is blended into dreaming.

(*The Works of Stefan George*, p. 195.)

47. G, I, p. 350.

> Then you, our own from native stock, appeared
> Before us in the naked glow of godhood.
> No statue was so fair, no dream so real.
> Then out of hallowed hands fulfilment flooded,
> And there was light, and all desire died.

(*The Works of Stefan George*, p. 244.)

48. G, I, p. 416.

> When all are blinded he, the only seer,
> Unveils the coming doom in vain, but though
> The cries of a Cassandra fill the house,
> The frantic rabble sees one thing alone:
> The horse, the horse, and rushes to its death.

(The Works of Stefan George, p. 295.)

49. G, I, p. 418.

> And when the final hope has almost perished
> In sternest grief, his eyes already see
> A coming light.

(The Works of Stefan George, p. 296.)

50. Cf. Donald G. MacRae, *Max Weber*, London, 1974, p. 88.

51. G, I, p. 121.

> Come to the park they say is dead, and you
> Will see the glint of smiling shores beyond,
> Pure clouds with rifts of unexpected blue
> Diffuse a light on patterned path and pond.
>
> Take the grey tinge of boxwood and the charm
> Of burning-yellow birch. The wind is warm.
> Late roses still have traces of their hue,
> So kiss, and gather them, and wreathe them too.
>
> Do not forget the asters – last of all –
> And not the scarlet on the twists of vine,
> And what is left of living green, combine
> To shape a weightless image of the fall.

(The Works of Stefan George, p. 81.)

CHAPTER 4   VON HOFMANNSTHAL

1. Cf. Ludwig Rohner, *Der Deutsche Essay. Materialien und Ästhetik einer literarischen Gattung*, Neuwied and Berlin, 1967, a comprehensive study of the literary genre, in which this point is made convincingly.

2. This view is confirmed by the observation made by Leopold von Andrian, one of his closest friends of his youth, who states that his fine intellect lacked the fullest of systematic thought ('Erinnerungen an meinen Freund Hugo von Hofmannsthal', *Hugo von Hofmannsthal. Der Dichter im Spiegel der Freunde*, ed. Helmut A. Fiechner, Berne, 1963, p. 80), a remark quoted with approval by Marcel Reich-Ranicki, 'Hofmannsthal in seinen Briefen', *Neue Rundschau*, LXXXV, 1974, p. 146.

3. Cf. Mary E. Gilbert, Introduction to *Hofmannsthal's Selected Essays*, Oxford, 1955, p. XVII ff.; 'Essays 1900–1908' 'A poet in transition', *Hofmannsthal:*

Studies in Commemoration, (ed. F. Norman), London, 1963, pp. 30ff., who makes this point in both studies.

4. Cf. *Hofmannsthal – Carl J. Burckhardt. Briefwechsel* (Br. H-CJB).

5. Cf. Carl J. Burckhardt, *Erinnerungen an Hofmannsthal*, Munich, 1964 (first published *Neue Rundschau*, LXV, 1954), who attests to this experience (pp. 7f.)

6. Cf. Burckhardt, who quotes Hofmannsthal's own words used in a letter *(p. 21)* to Carl J. Burckhardt, 28 October 1922; Br. H-CJB, p. 105.

7. *Richard Strauss-Hugo von Hofmannsthal. Briefwechsel*, ed. Willi Schuh, 3rd ed., Zurich, 1964.

8. Cf. Reich-Ranicki who, in his perceptive essay, states that while Rilke in his letters spoke to posterity Hofmannsthal always wanted to achieve something concrete (p. 139).

9. Cf. Walter Jens, *Hugo von Hofmannsthal und die Griechen*, Tübingen, 1955, who draws this conclusion.

10. Cf. H. Jürgen Meyer-Wendt, *Der frühe Hofmannsthal und die Gedankenwelt Nietzsches*, Heidelberg, 1973, who discusses Nietzsche's impact on Hofmannsthal fully; cf. particularly p. 14.

11. The significance of Hofmannsthal's mixed heritage is emphasised by Hermann Broch in his stimulating essay: 'Hugo von Hofmannsthal und seine Zeit' (1951) *Gesammelte Werke*; *Essays* I, 1953, pp. 106–10.

12. To Rudolf Borchardt, 3 August 1912; *JDS6*, VIII, 1964, p. 23.

13. For a discussion of this important matter cf. Karl Pestalozzi, *Sprachskepsis und Sprachmagie im Werk des jungen Hofmannsthal*, Zürich, 1958; cf. also Richard Brinkmann, 'Hugo von Hofmannsthal und die Sprache', *Dt. Vjs*, XXXV, 1961; cf. Rolf Tarot, *Hugo von Hofmannsthal, Daseinsformen und dichterische Struktur*, Tübingen, 1970, an important book to which I am much indebted; and Lothar Wittmann, *Sprachthematik und dramatische Form im Werke Hofmannsthals*, Stuttgart/Berlin/Cologne/Mayence, 1966, particularly pp. 60–6.

14. To Edgar Karg von Bebenburg, 18 June 1895; Br-H-EKG, p. 82.

15. To Edgar Karg von Bebenburg, 18 June 1895; Br. H-EKG, p. 81.

16. This point has been frequently made in Hofmannsthal's criticism, cf. Gilbert, 'Essays 1900–1908 . . .', p. 45.

17. Cf. Tarot, pp.380ff., cf. also pp. 364ff. The reference to Bacon's writings, *De augmentis scientarum* and *The Advancement of Learning*, is particularly valuable in this context.

18. For a discussion of Hofmannsthal's debt to Bacon cf. H. Stefan Schultz 'Hofmannsthal and Bacon. The Sources of the Chandos Letter', *Comparative Literature* XIII, 1961. Hofmannsthal's emotional disturbance is compared by Franz Kuna, 'The Expense of Silence. Sincerity and Strategy in Hofmannsthal's *Chandos Letters*', *PEGS* XL, 1970, pp. 76–85, with a similar experience of Hume's who after all maintained that it was impossible to vindicate induction philosophically. Cf. Karl R. Popper, 'Conjectural Knowledge', *Objective Knowledge. An Evolutionary Approach*, Oxford, 1972, who argues that the whole problem of induction is a pseudo-problem capable of a logical solution.

19. This point is convincingly made by Tarot, pp. 360ff.

20. I owe this observation to Achim Wierzejewski.

21. *Poesie und Leben*; H-Pr, I, p. 305.

22. *Algernon Charles Swinburne*; H-Pr. I, p. 113.

23. *Eine Monographie. Friedrich Mitterwurzer von Eugen Guglio*, H-Pr. I, p. 268.
24. *Poesie und Leben*; H-Pr. I, p. 307.
25. Hofmannsthal quotes the sentence twice in English (*Briefe des Zurück-gekehrten*, H-Pr. II, p. 323; and as the motto of a letter to Eberhard von Bodenhausen, 7 June 1906; Br. H-EB, p. 78). Cf. also the use in German translation, for instance in *Das Schrifttum als geistiger Raum der Nation*, H-Pr. IV, p. 409. Hofmannsthal actually misquoted the passage by substituting 'at once' for 'together' and mistakenly attributed the authorship to Addison; cf. motto to letter to Eberhard von Bodenhausen 7 June 1906; cf. Elizabeth M. Wilkinson and L. A. Willoughby, 'The "Whole Man" in Schiller's Theory of Culture and Society', *Essays in German Language, Culture and Society*, (ed. S. S. Prawer *et al.*), London, 1969, p. 184ff. and p. 208, who discuss Steele's original use of the model and his desire 'to shew up the essential one-sidedness of the man of fine parts'. They also point out (p. 186) how Hofmannsthal's appropriation of the model is a far cry from the spirit of the *Spectator*, from that of the *Aufklärung* or from 'what Lichtenberg actually wrote' since Hofmannsthal welcomed an endeavour 'whose watchword was not . . . liberty but community, not "Freiheit" but "Bindung" ' (p. 186).
26. These experiences are well analysed by David H. Miles, *Hofmannsthal's Novel Andreas, Memory and Self*, Princeton, N. J., 1972, pp. 50–9, who includes the Chandos letter as another example of an 'epiphany'. He also draws intention to Theodore Ziolkowski's seminal study *Dimensions of the Modern Novel*, Princeton, 1969, who discusses the general significance of these monuments for European literature: 'The great monuments of modern literature are' instants of a sudden, intense, almost blindingly vivid perception: what Virginia Woolf in *The Waves* called "rings of light", wherever we look, we are confronted with these moments of revelation. Joyce called them epiphanies, and his works are in one sense a catalogue of these moments of Thomist *claritas* . . . (p. 212).
27. To Edgar Karg von Bebenburg, 18 June 1895; Br-H-EKG, p. 82.
28. *Eine Monographie* . . . ; H-Pr. I, 26ff.
29. To Stefan George, 1 December 1905, Br. SG-H., p. 223f.
30. To Hugo von Hofmannsthal [not sent], 4 December 1905; Br. SG-H, pp. 226f.
31. This aspect is well discussed by Brian Coghlan, *Hofmannsthal's Festival Dramas*, Cambridge and Melbourne, 1964, who examines 'three historical studies', pp. 83–113 – *Grillparzers politisches Vermächtnis* [*Grillparzer's Political Legacy*] (1915), *Prinz Eugen* (1914) and *Maria Theresa* (1917) – and three cultural-political studies (pp. 114–49) – *Oesterreichische Bibliothek* [*Austrian Library*] (1915), *Oesterreich im Spiegel seiner Dichtung* [*Austria in the Mirror of its Literature*] (1916), *Die oesterreichische Idee* [*the Austrian Idea*] (1917); cf. also Egon Schwarz, 'Hugo von Hofmannsthal as a critic', *On Four Modern Humanists*, in Arthur R. Evans, Jr., ed.), who stresses Hofmannsthal's opposition to bigotry and chauvinism and his genuine Europeanism (p. 47).
32. Cf. Claude David 'Hofmannsthal und die Deutschen', *Hofmannsthal-Forschungen*, III, *Referate und Diskussionen der dritten Tagung der Hofmannsthal-Gesellschaft* (1974), pp. 102–14, in which this view is developed.
33. To Edgar Karg von Bebenburg, 5 September 1895; Br. H-EKG, pp. 98f.
34. Cf. the Introduction by Elizabeth M. Wilkinson and L. A. Willoughby (eds) to their *Schiller: In a Series of Letters, On the Aesthetic Education of Man*, Oxford,

1966, for a profound account of Schiller's analysis of culture and society. H-Pr., IV, p. 394. The reference is of course to Nietzsche.

35. Cf. *Unzeitgemäße Betrachtungen*, I: *David Friedrich Strauss. Der Schriftsteller und Bekenner* (1873); N, I, pp. 135f.

36. Cf. the books quoted above in note 5 to the Introduction for an analysis of Romantic political thought in Germany and further bibliography on this subject. The influence on Josef Nadler, the Austrian literary historian, on Hofmannsthal's thought is also bound to arouse concern; for some of Nadler's ideas were highly dubious: cf. Werner Volke, 'Hugo von Hofmannsthal – Josef Nadler in Briefen', *JDSG*, XVIII, 1974, pp. 46f. Still, as Volke points out, Nadler's writings had their positive aspects; cf. Robert Pick, 'Professor Nadler thinks again', *GLL*, VI, 1953, pp. 132–5 for a very just reappraisal of Nadler's importance as a literary historian. For a criticism of Hofmannsthal's attitude cf. for instance Egon Schwarz, 'Hofmannsthal as a Critic', p. 34, who accuses him of identifying himself with a part of the extreme right-wing movements.

37. Cf. note 25.

38. Wilkinson and Willoughby 'The "Whole Man" in Schiller's Theory . . .' (cf. note 25), p. 187.

39. Cf. *Aufzeichnungen zu Reden in Skandinavien* (1916) [*Notes for Lectures in Scandinavia*]; *Die Idee Europa* [*The Idea of Europe*] (1915).

40. H-G, p. 198.
'But he has always seen beauty,/And each moment was fulfilment for him,/While we do not know how to create/and must wait helplessly for revelation . . . / And our present is dark and empty/If our inspiration does not come from without . . .

'We lived on without purpose in the halflight/And our life would have no sense . . ./But those who are like the master,/they move on purposefully,/But there will be beauty and meaning wherever they cast their eyes.'

41. H-G, p. 476.
'Blazing with destruction/Shining with death/Burning life itself/Where is within us glowing a gleaming genius.'

42. To Stephan Gruss, 23 January 1907; H-Br. II, p. 254.

43. Cf. Richard Alewyn, 'Der Tod des Aestheten', *Über Hugo von Hofmannsthal*, Göttingen, 1963, pp. 14–77, a sensitive study which, like all of Alewyn's work on Hofmannsthal, is seminal. The Nietzschean influence in Hofmannsthal's conception of life is analysed by Meyer-Wendt (cf. for instance p. 41). (Cf. note 10.)

44. This play has been frequently analysed. Cf. for instance Emil Staiger, 'Hofmannsthal, Der Schwierige', *Meisterwerke deutscher Sprache des neunzehnten Jahrhunderts*, 2nd ed., Zurich, 1948, pp. 225–59; cf. also W. E. Yates's Introduction to *Hugo von Hofmannsthal: Der Schwierige*, Cambridge, 1966.

45. The threat of petrifaction is important in Hofmannsthal's work. It forms the major theme for instance in *Der Kaiser und die Hexe* (1897), *Das Bergwerk zu Falun* (1899) and *Die Frau ohne Schatten* (1913).

46. Cf. also Ewald Grether, 'Die Abenteurergestalt bei Hugo von Hofmannsthal', *Euphorion*, XLVIII, 1954, pp. 169–209, who however identifies the adventurer and the poet far too closely. This William H. Rey, 'Dichter und

Abenteurer bei Hugo von Hofmannsthal', *Euphorion*, XLIX, 1955, pp. 56–69, rightly criticises. Rey's analysis of this aspect carries conviction.

47. Cf. Peter Christian Kern, *Zur Gedankenwelt des späten Hofmannsthal. Die Idee einer schöpferischen Restauration*, Heidelberg, 1969, pp. 87ff., who discusses Hofmannsthal's concern with order as an aesthetic and spiritual criterion.

CHAPTER 5 RILKE

1. Cf. Mason's various works on this subject, above all his pioneering *Lebenshaltung und Symbolik bei Rilke*, Weimar, 1939; cf. also *Rilke*, Edinburgh, 1963, and the enlarged German version of this book, *Rilke. Sein Leben und Werk*, Göttingen, 1964; cf. also E. M. Butler, *R. M. Rilke* Cambridge, 1941, for a critical biography.

2. Cf. Käte Hamburger, 'Die phänomenologische Struktur der Dichtung Rilkes', *Rilke in Neuer Sicht*, p. 84. Only in this sense can Käte Hamburger's statement, influential in present-day Rilke scholarship, that Rilke wrote 'lyric poetry in lieu of an epistemology', be accepted; for to suggest that Rilke deliberately wrote lyric poetry in lieu of grappling with epistemological theory would be misleading; either this statement is so general as to amount to very little, or if specific, as Miss Hamburger's analogy of Rilke's poetry with Husserl's phenomenology might suggest, it does not tally with Rilke's poetic impulse. He did not primarily raise epistemological questions, though the epistemological problem of what kind of objective statements we can make about the world and our experiences plays a central part in some, but by no means in all, of his poetry.

3. Cf. Mason, *Rilke*, p. 11, who discusses this aspect at length. For a detailed critical account of Rilke's early years cf. Peter Demetz, *René Rilkes Prager Jahre*, Düsseldorf, 1953.

4. Pindar, Pythian Ode II, line 72: γένοι' οἶος ἐσσὶ μαθών ('Learn what sort of person you are, and be such').

5. Cf. Rilke's own comments in the *Geburt der Tragödie*, [Marginalien] zu Friedrich Nietzsches 'Geburt der Tragödie'; (R, VI, pp. 1163–1177), cf. also Fritz Dehn, *Rilke und Nietzsche. Ein Vergleich*, Dichtung und Volkstum (= *Euphorion*), XXXVII, 1936; Erich Heller, 'Nietzsche and Rilke, with a discourse on Nietzsche's belief in Poetry', *The Disinherited Mind: Essays on Modern Literature and Thought*, 7th ed., 1975, pp. 123–77; and Walter Kaufmann, 'Nietzsche and Rilke', *From Shakespeare to Existentialism*, New York, 1960, pp. 200–18.

6. To a young woman friend, 17 March 1920; R-Br. II, p. 517.

7. To Robert Heinz Heygrodt, 24 December 1921; R-Br. II, p. 277.

8. Cf. also to Friedrich von Oppeln-Brownikowski, 29 May 1907; R-Br. 1906–7, p. 255f., According to Eudo C. Mason, 'Rilke and Stefan George', (see Chapter 3, note 6), p. 35, Hermann Kasack informed Mason that George had deeply hurt Rilke by saying 'You are too facile in rhyming'. Rilke had been present when George had read poetry at the house of Reinhold Lepsius, the painter, and there had been correspondence but they never talked alone to one another.

9. R-Tb, pp. 13–120.

10. Cf. Hamburger, pp. 85ff. and 96ff., who stresses this aspect of his thought.

11. Anthony Stephens, *Rainer Maria Rilkes 'Gedichte an die Nacht'. An Essay in*

Interpretation Cambridge, *1972*; cf. also Mason, *Rilke*, p. 29.

12. Cf. the works by Mason quoted above, as well as the bibliography of his writings on Rilke in his *Rainer Maria Rilke. Leben und Werk*, pp. 149–52; cf. also Stephens; Jacob Steiner, *Rilkes Duineser Elegien*, Berne and Munich, 1962; Hans Egon Holthusen, *Rainer Maria Rilke in Selbstzeugnissen und Bilddokumenten*, Reinbek bei Hamburg, 1952; *Rilke. A Study of his later Poetry*, New Haven, Conn., 1952; and Judith Ryan, *Umschlag und Verwandlung, Poetische Struktur und Dichtungstheorie in R. M. Rilkes Lyrik der mittleren Periode* (1907–14), Munich, 1972.

13. Rilke, on the whole, used more frequently the terms art (*Kunst*) and the artist (*Künstler*) than poet (*Dichter*) and poetry (*Dichtung*). In the main I have followed his usage, but throughout both terms are usually, though by no means always, interchangeable.

14. Cf. Joachim W. Storck's invaluable study *Rainer Maria Rilke als Briefschreiber*, an unpublished dissertation, Freiburg i. Br., 1957, a work which merits publication.

15. To Ludwig Ganghofer, 16 April 1897; R-Br. 1897–1904, p. 40.

16. *Demnächst und Gestern*; R, v, pp. 346f.

17. Cf. *Moderne Lyrik*; R, v, p. 362.

18. *Moderne Lyrik*; R, v, p. 363.

19. Cf. *Münchener Kunstbrief*; R, v, p. 322.

20. Cf. *Wilhelm von Scholz, Hohenklingen*; R, v, p. 397.

21. Cf. *Moderne Lyrik*; R, v, p. 368.

22. *Moderne Lyrik*; R, v, p. 365.

23. Cf. *Moderne Lyrik*; R, v, p. 361.

24. *Moderne Lyrik*; R, v, p. 360.

25. *Moderne Lyrik*; R, v, p. 361.

26. *Moderne Lyrik*, R, v, p. 366.

27. Cf. *Moderne Lyrik*, R, v, p. 379.

28. Cf. *Moderne Lyrik*, R, v, pp. 361f.

29. *Moderne Lyrik*, R, v, p. 365.

30. Cf. Mason, 'Rilke und Stefan George' (cf. Chapter 3, note 6), p. 18, who argues that the entries made after 17 May 1898 sound like a unilateral account of the conversation with George and represent a defence of his approach to poetry and of his conception of art.

31. R-Tb., p. 46. Cf. also the remarks in *Zur Melodie der Dinge* (presumably written in the summer or autumn 1898), particularly R, v pp. 415f.

32. R, v, pp. 426–34 (first published 1898/99).

33. Cf. Mason, *Lebenshaltung und Symbolik bei Rilke*, p. 8, who stresses how important this belief was for Rilke and quotes a conversation; cf. also *Über Kunst*, R, v, p. 429; cf. R, v, p. 584–92, a review of Ellen Key's *Das Jahrhundert des Kindes* [*The Century of the Child*].

34. Cf. *Mauriel Maeterlinck*; R, v, p. 527.

35. *Heinrich Vogeler*; R, v, p. 554.

36. *Heinrich Vogeler*; R, v, p. 555.

37. Cf. Michael Oakeshott, *Poetry in the Conversation of Mankind*, London, 1959, for a persuasive statement of this point of view.

38. Cf. *Über Kunst*; R, v, p. 428.

39. *Auguste Rodin* i; R, v, p. 141.

40. Cf. R, v, p. 588; Rilke emphasies in his review of Ellen Key's *Das Jahrhundert des Kindes* how much a child's development to an independent personality is impaired in school and how all great ideas have lost their vitality and have become abstruse and boring because they are used with a view to education, expressing a criticism also voiced by many other writers of this period, e.g. Heinrich and Thomas Mann, Hermann Hesse and Robert Musil.

41. Cf. Mason, *Rilke*, p. 29, who argues that one should be on one's guard against 'the common error', that of interpreting the *Stundenbuch* 'as evidence that Rilke "believed" in a personal transcendental God'.

42. Cf. Eudo C. Mason, 'Zur Entstehung und Deutung von Rilkes Stundenbuch', *Exzentrische Bahnen*, Göttingen, 1963, p. 199.

43. Cf. Mason 'Zur Entstehung und Deutung von Rilkes Stundenbuch', who quotes the phrase p. 199.

44. R, I, p. 259:

'I believe in all that's unuttered still.
My devoutest feelings shall have their say.
What no one as yet has dared to will,
I shall involuntarily one day.'

Rainer Maria Rilke, *Selected Works*, II (*poetry*), trs. J. B. Leishman, London, 1960, p. 32.

45. R, vi, p. 863.

46. Cf. Mason, *Rilke*, p. 48.

47. To Clara Rilke, 26 September 1902; R-Br. 1899–1902, p. 44.

48. Cf. to Lou Andreas-Salomé, 8 August 1903, Br. R–LAS, p. 87; 10 August 1903, Br. R–LAS, p. 95; cf. also to Clara Rilke, 5 September 1902, R–Br. 1902–06, p. 36.

49. Cf. to Lou Andreas-Salomé, 10 August 1903, Br. R–LAS, p. 98; cf. also to Lou Andreas-Salomé, 12 May 1904, R–Br. R–LAS, p. 161.

50. Cf. Storck, pp. 346ff. (cf. note 14); cf. also to Lisa Heise, 19 May 1922, R – Br. II, p. 357.

51. Cf. *Auguste Rodin* I, R, v, p. 147; cf. also to F. X. Kappus, 23 April 1923; R – Br. j. D., p. 19.

52. Cf. to Lou Andreas-Salomé, 8 August 1903, Br. R–LAS, p. 83; to Clara Rilke, 5 September 1902, R–Br. 1902–06, p. 36f.

53. Cf. to Lou Andreas-Salomé, 11 August 1903, Br. R–LAS, p. 101.

54. Cf. to Clara Rilke, 24 June, 1907, R – Br. I, p. 171; cf. also to Countess Manon zu Solms-Laubach, 12 January 1912; R–Br. I, p. 339.

55. To Lou Andreas-Salomé, 8 August 1903, Br. R–LAS, p. 84. Rilke is of course close to Nietzsche in expressing this view.

56. Cf. to Lou Andreas-Salomé, 8 August 1903, Br. R–LAS, p. 88.

57. To Lou Andreas-Salomé, 8 August 1903, Br. R – LAS, p. 83; cf. also *Auguste Rodin* II R, v, p. 282, and R, v, p. 260 (posthumously published notes for *Auguste Rodin*, where the close relationship with nature is emphasised).

58. Cf. *Auguste Rodin* I, R, v, p. 81.

59. Cf. to Marie von Thurn und Taxis, 14 May 1914, Br. R–TT, p. 147.

60. Cf. to NN, 26 December 1911, R–Br. 1907–14, p. 154.

61. Cf. to Lou Andreas-Salomé, 11 August 1903, Br. R–LAS, p. 101.

62. Cf to Lou Andreas-Salomé, 11 August 1903, Br. R–LAS, pp. 101f.

63. Cf. *Briefe über Cézanne* (to Clara Rilke), ed. Clara Rilke, Leipzig, n.d.; cf. also Herman Meyer, 'Rilkes Cézanne-Erlebnis', *Zarte Empire. Studien zur Literaturgeschichte*, Stuttgart, 1963.

64. Cf. the letter to Elisabeth Taubmann, 18 May 1907, R – Br. 1914–21, p. 138; to Clara Rilke, 19 October 1907, R – Br. II, pp. 207f.

65. Cf. to Clara Rilke, 9 October 1907, R – Br. I, p. 191

66. Cf. to Clara Rilke, 21 October 1907, R – Br. I, p. 214.

67. Cf. to Clara Rilke, 22 October 1907, R – Br. I, p. 217; cf. also to F. X. Kappus, 23 April 1903, R – Br. j. D, p. 19.

68. Cf. Mason, *Rilke*, p. 5. 'On closer examination, it emerges that, extraordinary and many-sided as his developments were as an artist, he went through no fundamental developments as a thinker and prophet after 1899 or even earlier, but merely amplified, subtilised and played variations upon the body of ideas at which he had arrived when he was little more than twenty-two. There is, however, really only a development of the ideas expressed, or at least implicit, in the *Florentine Journal*.'

69. Cf. Ryan, who discusses this aspect fully.

70. Cf. Ryan, particularly pp. 11–17, for whom it is, in the main, a poetic principle; cf. also Mason, *Rilke*, p. 77, who related it to his personal background and states that Rilke saw it to be universal law; cf. also Idris Parry, 'Rilke and the Idea of *Umschlag*', *Modern Languages*, XXXIX, 1958, pp. 136–40, who relates this principle to Rilke's attitude to life.

71. Cf. my article, 'Tradition in Modern Poetry. T. S. Eliot and Rainer Maria Rilke. A Comparison', *Proceedings of the IVth Congress of the International Comparative Literature Association*, The Hague and Paris, 1966.

72. R, I, p. 759:

BLUE HYDRANGEA

These leaves are like green paint's last persistence
in colour-pans, harsh, lustreless and dried,
behind the umbelled blooms, whose blue's not dyed
into themselves but mirrored from a distance.

Mirrored in some tear-dimmed, uncertain way,
as though they wanted it to leave their faces,
and, as in old blue note-paper, ther're traces
of yellow in them, violet, and grey;

the washed-out look of many a childish dress,
the no-more-worn no more can happen to:
how much you feel a small life's fleetingness!

But suddenly the blue appears more keen
within one umbel, and there's shown to you
a moving blue's delight in front of green.

(Paris, mid-July 1906), Rainer Maria Rilke, *New Poems*, trs. J. B. Leishman, London, 1964, p. 109.

73. Cf. Herman Uyttersprot, 'Rainer Maria Rilke – Der Turm', *Neophilologus*, XXXIX, 1955, pp. 262–75.

74. Cf. also Ryan, pp. 28ff.

75. Cf. Ryan, pp. 52ff., and also the pioneering study by Herman Uyttersprot, 'Rilkes Gedichte Die Gazelle', *Deutschunterricht*, LXIV, 1962, pp. 20–9.

76. Cf. for a study of these poems Manfred Hausmann, *Rilkes Apollosonette* and H. J. Weigand, 'Rilkes Archäischer Torso Apollos', *Monatshefte für den Deutschen Unterricht, deutsche Sprache und Literatur*, LI, 1959. Cf. also Jacob Steiner, 'Kunst und Literatur. Zu Rilkes Kathedralengedichten', *Wissen und Erfahrungen. Werkbegriff und Interpretation heute, Festschrift für Herman Meyer zum 65. Geburtstag*, ed. Alexander von Bormann, Tübingen, 1976.

77. Cf. Parry, 'The Idea of Umschlag; pp. 138f.

78. To Lou Andreas-Salomé, 8 August 1903, Br. R – LAS, pp. 89f.

79. Ryan, p. 16.

80. R, I, p. 557;

ARCHAIC TORSO OF APOLLO

Though we've not known his unimagined head
and what divinity his eyes were showing,
his torso like a branching street-lamp's glowing,
wherein his gaze, only turned down, can shed

light still. Or else the breast's insurgency
could not be dazzling you, or you discerning
in that slight twist of loins a smile returning
to where was centred his virility.

Or else this stone would not stand so intact
beneath the shoulders' through-seen cataract
and would not glisten like a wild beast's skin;

and would not keep from all its contours giving
light like a star; for there's no place therein
that does not see you. You must change your living.

Paris, early summer 1908). *New Poems*, pp. 165–9.

81. Mason, *Rilke*, stresses this aspect of Rilke's thought quoting a letter to F. X. Kappus, 16 April 1903; *R – Br.j. D.* 1929, p. 20, and pointing out how close it is to sexual experience.

82. Mason, *Rilke*, p. 54; cf. to Baron von Uexküll, 19 August 1909, R – Br. 1907–14, p. 74.

83. R – Br. 1906–07, p. 214. I am here using Eudo C. Mason's translation (*Rilke*, pp. 54f.).

84. Cf. to Lou Andreas-Salomé, 28 December 1912, R – Br. LAS, p. 246.

85. To Lou Andreas-Salomé, 19 December 1912, Br. R – LAS, pp. 284f.

86. Cf. to Lou Andreas-Salomé, 28 December 1912, Br. R – LAS, p. 248.

87. Cf. to Princess Marie von Thurn und Taxis-Hohenlohe, 31 May 1911, R – Br. II, p. 42.

88. Quoted by Katharina Kippenberg, *R. M. Rilke. Ein Beitrag*, Leipzig, 1935, p. 143. The translation is Mason's (*Rilke*, p. 72).

89. Mason, *Rilke*, p. 72.

90. Br. R – TT, i, p. 27. The translation is Mason's (*Rilke*, p. 73).

91. Cf. to Lou Andreas-Salomé, 26 June 1914, Br. R – LAS, p. 349.

92. Cf. to Karl und Elisabeth von der Heydt, 6 November 1914, R – Br. 1914–1921, pp. 25f.

93. Cf. to Ellen Delp, 10 October 1915, R – Br. 1914–21.

94. Cf. to Bernhard von der Marwitz, 12 February 1918, R – Br. 1914–21, p. 175.

95. To Clara Rilke, 4 November 1917, R – Br. 1914–21, p. 165.

96. Cf. Egon Schwarz, *Das Verschluckte Schluchzen. Poesie und Politik bei Rainer Maria Rilke*, Frankfurt/Main, 1972, a well-written book which however overrates the significance of Rilke's political stance.

97. Cf. Joachim W. Storck (ed.), *Rainer Maria Rilke 1875–1975* (Catalogue of an Exhibition under the Auspices of the Deutsche Literaturarchiv, Schiller-Nationalmuseum, Marbach a. N.), Stuttgart, 1975, p. 190.

98. I owe this observation to Dr Joachim W. Storck, whose knowledge of Rilke's letters is profound.

99. Cf. Storck, *Rainer Maria Rilke 1875–1975*, pp. 286ff., who prints letters by Alexander Prince von Hohenlohe to Rilke (pp. 288–91) and by Walther Rathenau (p. 292) and comments by Rilke on Rathenau's murder in a letter to Nanny Wunderly-Volkart of 28 June 1922. For a diametrically opposite view cf. Schwarz, for whom Rilke's fascist tendencies are unmistakable.

100. Schwarz (p. 52) quite rightly points out the dangers inherent in Rilke's criticism of the industrial world and in his longing for a preindustrial one which Mason had detected (cf. his *Rilke, Europe and the English-Speaking World*, Cambridge, 1961) as a major aspect of his thought.

101. Cf. the important essay by William Rose, 'Rilke and the Conception of Death', W. Rose and G. Craig-Houston, *R. M. Rilke: Aspects of his Mind and Thought*, London, 1938, pp. 41–84, for a penetrating discussion of the whole subject.

102. There is a not surprisingly rather difficult, if not obscure, book, on this Rilke by Werner Günther with the title *Weltinnenraum* (Berne, 1946).

103. *Duineser Elegien* I: 'Aber Lebendige machen alle den Fehler, daß sie zu stark unterscheiden', (R, i, p. 688), which J. B. Leishman and Stephan Spender (eds and trs), *Rainer Maria Rilke: Duino Elegies*, London, 1939, p. 29, translate as:

> 'Yes, but all of the living
> make the mistake of drawing too many distinctions.'

104. Cf. Idris Parry, 'Rilke and Orpheus', *Times Literary Supplement*, No. 3848, 12 December 1975, who develops this theme.

105. Cf. Eudo C. Mason, *Rilke und Goethe*, Cologne and Graz, 1958 for an analysis of Rilke's attitude to Goethe.

106. To Benvenuta [Magda von Hattingberg], 13 February 1914, Br. R – B., p. 66.

107. Mason, *Rilke, Europe and the English-Speaking World*, pp. 184ff., for a thorough discussion of this aspect of his thought.

108. Cf. to Countess Sizzo, 19 February 1922, Br. R – Gr. S., p. 15; and cf. also to Countess Sizzo, 12 April 1923, Br. R – Gr. S., pp. 40f.
109. Cf. to Lou Andreas-Salomé, 26 June 1914; Br. R – LAS, pp. 352f.
110. Cf. to Lou Andreas-Salomé, 26 June 1914; Br. R – LAS, pp. 349f.
111. Cf. to Lisa Heise, 2 August 1919; R – Br. II, p. 135.
112. Cf. Mason, *Rilke*, p. 82f., who examines Rilke's dissatisfaction with his Narcissism very carefully; cf. also Frank Wood, *The Ring of Forms*, Minneapolis, 1958, pp. 140–3, who discusses this aspect of Rilke's thought with great discrimination and draws attention to the approving and critical views of this aspect of experience by S. S. Prawer in *German Lyrical Poetry. A Critical Analysis of Selected Poems from Klopstock to Rilke*, London, 1952, p. 218, and Holthusen, p. 28.
113. Cf. to Ilse Erdmann, 9 October 1916, R – Br. II, pp. 68f.
114. Cf. Mason, *Rilke*, pp. 108ff.
115. Cf. to Pfarrer Friedrich, 31 October 1915, R – Br. 1914–21, p. 52.
116. Cf. *Über den jungen Dichter [On the Young Poet]*, R, VI, pp. 1052f.
117. Cf. *Worpswede*, R, V, p. 66.
118. Cf. *Worpswede*, R, V, p. 87.
119. This point is made by Mason, *Rilke* as well as by T. J. Casey, *Rainer Maria Rilke. A Centenary Essay*, London, 1976.
120. Cf. Otto Friedrich Bollnow, *R. M. Rilke*, 2nd ed., Stuttgart, 1951, p. 16, who stresses the importance of this world.
121. R, I, p. 737:

Knowing it or not, friends – which is our case? –
Both alike has the lingering hour
graved in the human face.

Rainer Maria Rilke; *Sonnets to Orpheus*, trs. J. B. Leishman, London, 1946, 53.

122. R, I, p. 685:

Who, if I cried, would hear me among the angelic
orders? And even if one of them suddenly
pressed me against his heart, I should fade in the strength of his
stronger existence. For Beauty's nothing
but beginning of Terror we're still just able to bear,
and why we adore it so is because it serenely
disdains to destroy us. Each single angel is terrible.

Duino Elegies p. 30.

123. Mason, *Rilke*, p. 79, who maintains that the cycle, in its entirety, does not, as is mostly assumed, turn on the universal question 'What is man?', but almost exclusively on the virtually anti-human or extra-human lot of the poet; cf. also Mason, 'Problems of the Duinese Credo', *Rilke, Europe and the English-Speaking World*, pp. 179–86.
124. Cf. also Steiner, *Rilkes Duineser Elegien*, for a detailed analysis of the work.
125. Cf. Idris Parry 'Space and Time': 'Rilke's Sonnets to Orpheus', *MLR*, LXVIII, 1963, for an imaginative account of the main problems of the cycle. Cf. also Hans Egon Wolthusen, *Rilkes Sonette an Orpheus Versuch einer Interpretation*, Munich, 1937; Hermann Mörchen, *Rilkes Sonette an Orpheus*, Stuttgart, 1958, for detailed accounts of this cycle.

126. *Die Sonette an Orpheus*, I, 3; R, I, p. 732:

> A God can do it. But can a man expect
> to penetrate the narrow lyre and follow?
> His sense is discord. Temples for Apollo
> are not found where two heart-ways intersect.
> For song, as taught by you, is not desire,
> not wooing of something finally attained;
> song is existence . . .
>
> *Sonnets to Orpheus*, p. 132.

127.
> Praising, that's it! As a praiser and blesser
> he came like the ore from the taciturn mine.
> Came with his heart, oh, transient presser,
> for men, of a never-exhaustible wine.
>
> Voice never fails him for things lacking lustre,
> sacred example will open his mouth.
> All becomes vineyard, all becomes cluster,
> warmed by his sympathy's ripening south.
>
> *Sonnets to Orpheus*, p. 47.

128. January 1913; Br. R – TT, I, p. 254:
   No, Dottore Serafico, you are not a saint, and even if you were on your knees
   (spiritual knees, bien entendu), all day and all night. And it is right like that.
   A saint would never have written the Elegies.

129. To Katharina Kippenberg, 15 September 1919, Br. R – KK, p. 376.

130.   MAGIC

> From indescribable transforming flashes
> such figuration – : Feel and trust!
> We know too well how flames can turn to ashes:
> in art, though, flame is kindled out of dust.
>
> Here's magic. To the realm of conjuration
> the common word seems lifted from above . . .
> and yet it's really like the invitation
> of cock-bird calling to the hidden dove.
>
> (Muzot, 7–11 August 1924)

Rainer Maria Rilke; *Poems 1906 to 1926*, J. B. Leishman (trs.) London, 1968,
   p. 321.

131. To Rilke, 25 May 1953; printed in *Merkur*, IX, 1955, p. 969. Rilke himself used
   this image in a letter to Countess Sizzo, 1 June 1923, Br. – R – Gr, S 47,
   soon afterwards, showing a similar element of caution. Cf. also Storck, p. 170,
   who draws attention to this parallel (cf. note 14).

CHAPTER 6 MANN

1. Cf. R. A. Nichols, *Nietzsche and the Early Work of Thomas Mann*, Berkeley and
   Los Angeles 1955, and H. Peter Pütz, *Kunst und Künstlerexistenz bei Nietzsche und
   Thomas Mann*, Bonn, 1963, for a discussion of Nietzsche's influence on

Thomas Mann; cf. also T. J. Reed, *Thomas Mann: The Uses of Tradition*, Oxford, 1974, *passim*.

2. *Im Spiegel [In the Mirror]* (1967), TM, XI, pp. 332f. Cf. Chapter 4, note 1.
3. Rohner cites Bacon and Montaigne as the founders of the essay as a genre. In a sense their achievement remains unsurpassed.
4. Ernst Nündel, *Thomas Manns Kunsttheorie*, Bonn, 1972, takes the view that Mann's conception of art is based on a series of antitheses of that kind and is best understood in these terms. I prefer not to follow this approach as I do not find it fruitful although Nündel's treatise is otherwise helpful in many ways.
5. *Im Spiegel*, TM, XI, p. 332.
6. Mann's preoccupation with this theme is demonstrated by the fact that he underlined in his edition of Nietzsche's works some of the passages relating to the corruptibility of the artist (*Jenseits von Gut und Böse*, N – 6., VII, p. 473 and p. 478, for instance).
7. 'Notebook No. 9 p. 42', published in Thomas Mann, *Notizen*, ed. Hans Wysling, Heidelberg, 1973, p. 40.
8. *Kultur und Sozialismus [Culture and Socialism]* (1928), TM, XII, p. 640.
9. Cf. Reed, *Thomas Mann*, pp. 105ff., for an illuminating discussion of this problem.
10. Cf. Reed, *Thomas Mann*, p. 92.
11. I am greatly indebted to the perceptive analysis by Elizabeth M. Wilkinson (ed.) in the Introduction to *Thomas Mann: Tonio Kröger*, Oxford, 1943.
12. TM, VIII, p. 330.
13. Reed, *Thomas Mann*, p. 93.
14. Cf. Reed, *Thomas Mann*, p. 10ff., who discusses this question.
15. Quoted by Paul Scherrer in 'Vornehmheit, Illusion und Wirklichkeit', *Blätter der Thomas Mann – Gesellschaft*, I, Zurich, 1958, p. 5.
16. I owe this formulation to Albrecht Schöne, who used it in an as yet unpublished lecture 'Der Hochstapler und der Blechtrommler, Die Wiederkehr der Schelme im Deutschen Roman', given at the University of Bristol on 8 November 1976.
17. Hans Wysling, *Thomas Mann heute*, Berne and Munich, 1976, pp. 21ff.
18. Ibid., pp. 16ff. cf. also *Vorwort zu dem Roman eines Jungverstorbenen*, [Erich von Mendelsohn] (*Preface to the Novel of one who died at an early age*) (1913); TM, X, p. 559.
19. Hans Wysling 'Die Fragmente zur Fürstennovelle', Paul Scherrer and Hans Wysling, *Thomas Mann Studien*, I, Berne and Munich, 1967, pp. 99f.
20. To Wilhelm von Humboldt, 17 March 1832, W. A., IV, 49, p. 283.
21. *Einführung in den Zauberberg [Introduction to the Magic Mountain]* (1939); TM, XI, p. 608. It also occurs in a letter to Hermann Hesse, 25 November 1947; *Thomas Mann-Hermann Hesse Briefwechsel*, ed. Anni Carlson, Frankfurt/Main, 1968, pp. 141f.
22. Cf. Reinhard Baumgart *Das Ironische und die Ironie in den Werken Thomas Manns*, Munich, 1961.
23. This is the title of Erich Heller's book, *The Ironic German*, 4th ed., London, 1975.
24. *Die Kunst des Romans [The Art of the Novel]* (1940); TM, X, pp. 353f.
25. *Versuch Über Tschekow [Essay on Checkhov]* (1954); TM, IX, pp. 857f.
26. To Samuel Lublinski, 23 May 1904; TM – Br., III, p. 450.

27. *Die Kunst des Romans*; TM, x, p. 354.

28. Cf. Reed, *Thomas Mann*, pp. 100–8 makes this important point.

29. For an illuminating analysis of the story cf. the Introduction by T. J. Reed (ed.) to *Thomas Mann: Der Tod in Venedig*, Oxford, 1971, to which I am greatly indebted.

30. Cf. Erwin Rohde, *Psyche, Seelencult und Unsterblichkeitsglaube der Griechen*, 2 vols Freiburg i. Br., 1890–4 a seminal work about Greek religion; TM., viii, p. 447.

31. The combination is Thomas Mann's own, who juxtaposes 'mythology' and 'psychology', cf. for instance in a letter to Karl Kerényi, 20 February 1941, TM – KK, p. 42. Cf. also the important essay by Hans Wysling, 'Mythus und Psychologie bei Thomas Mann', *Dokumente und Untersuchungen, Thomas Mann Studien III*, Berne and Munich, 1974, pp. 167 – 80; cf. also André von Gronicka, 'Myth plus Psychology. A Style Analysis of *Death in Venice*', *Germanic Review*, xxxi, 1956.

32. This is discussed by Reed, *Thomas Mann*, pp. 156–63; cf. also Herman Meyer, *Das Zitat in der Erzählkunst*, Stuttgart, 2nd ed., 1967, pp. 207 – 45 for an account of the function of quotations in Thomas Mann's work.

33. Cf. the excellent chapter in Reed, *Thomas Mann*, pp. 144 – 78, who stresses the fundamental ambivalence of the story and argues that Mann was experimenting 'with the condition and the risks of being a "Master"', basing his argument (p. 177) on Mann's own statement that he saw himself as one of those European writers who grew up in the age of decadence but are now at least experimenting with ways to overcome it (*Betrachtungen eines Unpolitischen*; TM, xii, p. 201).

34. Reed, *Thomas Mann*, p. 163.

35. Cf. Reed, *Thomas Mann*, p. 167, who speaks of 'sordidness as one aspect of the story'.

36. In an unpublished letter to the present author (26 February 1955), for instance, Mann emphasised his profound concern with tradition. It is of course the central theme of Reed's *Thomas Mann*. Cf. also Peter Pütz (ed.) *Thomas Mann und die Tradition*, Frankfurt/Main, 1972.

37. *Joseph und seine Brüder* [*Joseph and his Brethren*] [Ein Vortrag] [A lecture] (1942); TM, xi, p. 658. Cf. also *Freud und die Zukunft* [*Freud and the Future*], TM, ix, pp. 478f.

38. Cf. H. Stefan Schultz, 'Thomas Mann und Goethe', *Thomas Mann und die Tradition*, p. 171, and Katharina Mommsen, *Gesellschaftskritik bei Fontane und Thomas Mann*, p, 74, both of whom make that point.

39. *Joseph und seine Brüder*, [*Ein Vortrag*]; TM, xi, p. 656.

40. Cf. Hans Wysling, 'Thomas Manns Verhältnis zu den Quellen', Scherrer and Wysling, p. 291. Hans Wysling refers to a note found among Mann's posthumous papers.

41. Cf. my article 'Style and Structure in Modern Experimental Fiction', *Stil- und Formprobleme in der Literatur* (*Vorträge des VII Kongresses der Internationalen Vereinigung für moderne Sprachen und Literaturen*), ed. Paul Böckmann, pp. 419–26, for a discussion of some of the problems facing the modern novelist and for further bibliography.

42. *Goethe und Tolstoi* is the title of a long essay (first published 1922, in an enlarged form 1925; first given as a lecture in 1921).

43. Michael Mann 'Rechenschaft, Rekapitulation. Bewussthaltung. Über Thomas Manns Tagebücher', *Neue Zürcher Zeitung*, 7/8 August 1976, No. 183, p. 37.
44. Diary of 10 January 1919 published in Michael Mann, 'Rechenschaft, Rekapitulation, Bewussthaltung'.
45. Cf. Hans Wysling, 'Thomas Manns Verhältnis zu den Quellen', Scherrer and Wysling, pp. 258–322.
46. Cf. ibid., p. 281.
47. T. J. Reed, 'Thomas Mann: The Writer as Historian of his Time', *Modern Language Review*, LXXI, 1976, p. 82 who also writes: 'Its prime purpose was not to judge, but to state a truth which he had first experienced and slowly came to understand' (ibid., p. 94).
48. Cf. for instance Hermann J. Weigand, *Thomas Mann's Novel. Der Zauberberg*, New York, 1933, and E. Hefftrich, *Zauberbergmusik*, Frankfurt/Main, 1976, for a full discussion of the novel.
49. Cf. Gunilla Bergsten, *Thomas Manns 'Doktor Faustus' Untersuchungen zu den Quellen und zur Struktur*, Lund, 1963.
50. Hermann, J. Weigand, 'Thomas Mann's *Gregorius*', *Germanic Review*, XXVII, 1952.
51. Hans Wysling, 'Thomas Manns Verhältnis zu den Quellen', in Scherrer and Wysling.
52. Hans Wysling, 'Wer ist Professor Kuckuck? Zu einem der letzten "großen Gespräche" Thomas Manns', *Thomas Mann Heute*, pp. 48ff.
53. Cf. Bernhard Blume, *Thomas Mann und Goethe*, Berne, 1949, for a perceptive analysis of Thomas Mann's view of, and indebtedness to Goethe; cf. also H. Stefan Schultz, 'Thomas Mann und Goethe', *Thomas Mann und die Tradition*.
54. Cf. Bruford, for a discussion of this whole question.
55. 'Tradition and the Individual Talent', *Selected Essays*, 2nd ed., London, 1954, p. 14.
56. Wysling's essay on this subject 'Thomas Manns Verhältnis zu den Quellen', is the most authoritative account. It would be tedious to list all the other critics who have, frequently in a most interesting manner, examined this problem.
57. 27 February 1904, TM – HM Br., 27.
58. *Die geistige Situation des Schriftstellers in unserer Zeit [The Writer's intellectual situation in his own age]* (1930), TM, x, p. 299.
59. TM, x, p. 299.
60. TM, x, p. 299.
61. *Betrachtungen eines Unpolitischen*, TM, x, p. 147.
62. Reed, *Thomas Mann*, p. 200.
63. Cf. Ernst Troeltsch, *Humanität und Naturrecht in der Weltpolitik*, Berlin, 1923, reprinted in *Deutscher Geist und Westeuropa*, Tübingen, 1925, who contrasted German culture permeated with Romantic thought with the Western intellectual tradition. Thomas Mann reviewed Troeltsch's lecture in *Frankfurter Zeitung*, 25 December 1923; TM XII, pp. 627–9.
64. Bruford, p. 227.
65. Burke's essay had been translated as *Betrachtungen über die französische Revolution*, (2 vols., Berlin, 1793) by Friedrich von Gentz, whom Mann quotes towards the end of his own treatise (TM, XII, p. 582). Mann does not quote Burke as he mistakenly claimed many years later (1952) in *Der Künstler und die*

Gesellschaft (TM, x, 395), but is likely to have been aware of Burke's work when composing his own *Betrachtungen*. I owe this information to his son, Professor Golo Mann, who told me in a letter of 1 March 1976 that Thomas Mann probably used an edition of a selection from Gentz's letters. (*Briefe von und an Friedrich von Gentz*, ed. F. C. Wittichen and E. Saenger, 3 vols, Berlin 1909–) in which Burke is referred to in the preface. Professor Mann also suggests that if Thomas Mann had read Burke at the time of his writing of the *Betrachtungen* he would almost certainly have quoted from Burke's work.

66. I owe this suggestion to Mr T. J. Reed.

67. There are many books and articles on this subject. An interesting account is given by Kurt Sontheimer, *Thomas Mann und die Deutschen*, Munich, 1961.

68. Cf. Reed, *Thomas Mann*, pp. 304f. For an account of how powerfully Rathenau affected many minds cf. Ernst von Salomon's remarkable novel *Die Geächteten* which portrays the fate of his murderers. Cf. also Musil's portrait of him (a vitriolic attack) in the person of Dr Paul Arnheim in his novel *Der Mann ohne Eigenschaflec* [*The Man without Qualities*], (1933ff.)

69. Theodore Ziolkowski; 'Thomas Mann as a Critic of Germany', *Thomas Mann 1875–1955*, Princeton, N. J., 1975.

70. TM, xi, pp. 788–93, in an Open Letter to Eduard von Korrodi, the literary editor of the *Neue Zürcher Zeitung* (*Ein Brief von Thomas Mann*), 3 February 1936.

71. To Karl Kerényi, 20 February 1934, TM – KK, p. 42.

72. Naphta's model was Georg Lukácz, a brilliant Hungarian thinker. In *Der Zauberberg* Mann made use of some of the ideas which Lukácz developed in his *Die Seele und die Formen*, Berlin, 1911. Lukácz later on became a leading Marxist theorist. For a general account of some of the ideologies portrayed in Mann's novels cf. Pierre Paul Sagave, *Realité Sociale et Idéologie Religieuse dans les Romans de Thomas Mann*, Paris, 1954.

73. Reed, *Thomas Mann*, p. 300.

74. To Josef Ponten, 5 February 1925, TM – Br. i, p. 232.

75. Cf. the account by T. J. Reed in his *Thomas Mann*, pp. 360–402, and in his 'The Writer as a Historian of his Time', to which I am greatly indebted.

76. Reed, *Thomas Mann*, p. 363.

77. Cf. Bergsten, *Doktor Faustus*, for instance; E. M. Butler, *The Fortunes of Faust*, Cambridge, 1952; or Patrick Carnegy, *Faust as a Musician*, London, 1973; but there are many other accounts.

78. Cf. Reed, 'The Writer as a Historian of his Time', pp. 93f., who elaborates his view.

79. TM, iii. 686: '*Man shall for the sake of goodness and love, not grant death dominion over his thoughts.*'

80. Michael Mann, Thomas Mann's youngest son stressed this point in conversation; cf. also to Ferdinand Lion, 28 August 1954, TM – Br. iii, p. 251.

81. But cf. to Friedrich H. Weber, 18 July 1954; TM – Br. iii, p. 349, but he also admitted that Muschg is not entirely wrong in stating that he delights a lost world without giving it a trace of saving truth; for he too believed that the world of the declining bourgeoisie was doomed, but that it is also difficult to find the saving word, and Muschg does not know that word either. Mann continues to say that like Chekov he often wonders whether he does not deceive the world with his talent since he does not know the answer to the

ultimate question.

82. TM, IX, p. 869. The confessional nature of the essay is also reflected in the
    , passage in *Versuch über Tschechow* where Mann maintains that art is a quest
    for a better world, a quest which the writer expresses by seeking to perfect
    his writing (TM, IX, p. 850)

83. Cf. for instance to Otto Grauhoff, 25 October 1898; *Briefe an Otto Grauhoff
    1894–1928 und Ida Boyd-Ed 1903–1928*, ed. Peter de Mendelssohn, Frankfurt/
    Main, 1975, p. 106. Cf. also to Irita von Dorn (draft of 28 August 1951): 'In
    fact I feel first of all to be a humorist. Humour is an expression of . . .
    sympathy which has the intention of doing men some good, to teach them a
    sense of grace and spread liberating serenity.' TM – Br. III, p. 220.

84. *Einführung in den Zauberberg*; TM, XI, p. 610.

85. To Siegfried Marck, 23 May 1954; TM – Br. III, p. 342.

CHAPTER 7 KAFKA

1. Cf. for instance, my article 'Kafka Criticism: A Survey', *GLL*, IX, 1956, pp.
   294–305; reprinted in *Franz Kafka*, ed. Ronald Gray, Englewood Cliffs, New
   Jersey, 1962, pp. 163–77. Cf. also the most comprehensive and penetrating
   survey of writing on Kafka by Peter U. Beicken, *Franz Kafka. Eine kritische
   Einführung in die Forschung*, Frankfurt/Main, 1974; cf. my review of this book,
   MLR, XX, 1975, pp. 951–3. The unsatisfactory state of Kafka criticism has
   however not substantially changed in the past decades (cf. also my essay 'Der
   Gang der Kafka-Forschung', *Franz Kafka. Eine Bibliographie*, ed. Rudolf
   Hemmerle, Munich, 1957, pp. 13–18). For a scathing comment on the lack
   of progress by Kafka scholarship on account of its failure to eliminate
   improbable solutions cf. Ulrich Gaier, 'Chorus of Lies – On Interpreting
   Kafka', *GLL*, XXII, 1969, pp. 283–96.

2. I owe this observation to Dr John Hibberd whose book *Franz Kafka*, London,
   1974, is an excellent succinct introduction.

3. For studies discussing Kafka's view of the function of art cf. Heinz Hillman,
   Franz Kafka: Dichtungstheorie und Dichtungsgestalt, Bonn, 1964, particularly pp.
   5–50. Hillmann does not, however, emphasise Kafka's basic ambivalence
   sufficiently. Cf. also Jürgen Demmer, *Franz Kafka. Der Dichter der
   Selbstreflexion*, Munich, 1973, who also discusses this question (pp. 31–99.)
   (Cf. my review of this book in *Erasmus*, XXVI, 1974, pp. 348–50.)

4. For a fuller account of this aspect cf. my *Franz Kafka. Eine Betrachtung seines
   Werkes*, Heidelberg, 1952; 2nd ed., 1956, pp. 148 ff.

5. For Selmak, 1900, K-Br., p. 9.

6. I am using these terms in the sense defined by C.M. Bowra, *The Heritage of
   Symbolism*, London, 1942.

7. Cf. James Joyce, *Finnegan's Wake*, London, 1939, p. 489, who writes 'That
   letter selfpenned to one's other, that neverperfect ever-planned?'

8. To Milena Jesenská; R – Br.M, p. 244.

9. To Robert Klopstock, March 1923, K – Br., p. 431.

10. K – H., p. 348.

11. Diary of 25 September 1917, K – Tb., p. 554.

12. To Grete Bloch, 6 June 1914, K – Br.F., p. 595.

13. Diary of 21 July 1913; K – Tb., p. 311 and p. 320.

14. Max Brod, *Franz Kafka. Eine Biographie*, 3rd ed., Frankfurt/Main, 1954, p. 98.

15. 19 January 1922, K – Tb., p. 555.
16. Diary of 6 August 1914, K – Tb., p. 420.
17. Cf. to Felice Bauer, 30 September or 1 October 1917, K – Br. F., p. 755.
18. Cf. diary of 1910, K – Tb., p. 12.
19. To Max Brod, 17 July 1912, K – Br., p. 98.
20. Cf. diary of 18 September 1917, K – Tb., p. 529.
21. To Max Brod, 5 July 1922, K – Br., p. 384.
22. To Max Brod, 22 July 1912, K – Br., p. 100.
23. To Max Brod, 5 July 1922, K – Br., p. 384.
24. Journal of 23 October 1917, K – H., p. 80.
25. Diary of 16 January 1922, K – Tb., p. 553.
26. Journal of 17 December 1917, K – H., p. 95.
27. Diary of 4 August 1917, K – Tb., p. 523.
28. 27 December 1911, K – Tb., p. 216.
29. Journal of 19 October 1917, K – H., p. 72.
30. Diary of 15 December 1910, K – Tb., pp. 27 f.
31. Diary of 12 June 1923, K – Tb., p. 585.
32. Cf. my analysis of the moods in Kafka's work, 'Zwei Erzählungen Franz Kafkas. Eine Betrachtung', *Trivium*, VIII, Zurich, 1950.
33. To Max Brod, 5 July 1922, K – Br., p. 386.
34. Cf. Heinz Politzer, *Franz Kafka: Parable and Paradox*, Ithaca, New York, 1962, who skilfully explores this question of the parabolic and paradoxical nature of Kafka's work.
35. Diary of 6 August 1914, K – Tb., p. 420.
36. Cf. Malcolm Pasley, 'Two Kafka Enigmas', *MLR*, LIX, 1964, pp. 73–81, and 'Drei literarische Mystifikationen Kafkas', *Kafka Symposium*, Berlin, 1965, 21–37, who discusses the important question of Kafka's use of mystification.
37. 'Betrachtungen über Sünde, Leid, Hoffnung und den wahren Weg' [Reflections on Sin, Suffering, Hope and the true Path], No. 80, K – H., p. 48.
38. 'Betrachtungen . . .', No. 60, K – H., p. 53.
39. *Er (He)*; K – Beschr., p. 292.
40. 'Betrachtungen . . .', No. 46, K – H., p. 46.
41. The relationship between Nietzsche and Kafka is analysed by Patrick Bridgwater in his *Kafka and Nietzsche*, Bonn, 1974. I have serious reservations about his method of dealing with this question. Cf. my forthcoming review to appear in *MLR*, LXXII, 1977.

CHAPTER 8 BRECHT

1. B, XV, pp. 3 f.
2. [*Augsburger Theaterkritiken*]; B, XV, pp. 4–39.
3. Brecht's actual phrase was the 'Einstein der neuen Bühnenform'; cf. Mordecai Gorelik, 'Brecht: "I am the Einstein of the new stage form . . ."', *Theatre Arts*, New York, March, 1957, p. 73. Cf. also Klaus Völker, *Bertolt Brecht. Eine Biographie*, Munich, 1976, p. 241, and Ernst Schuhmacher, *Drama und Geschichte. Bertolt Brechts Leben des Galileo Galilei und andere Stücke*, p. 320. Not surprisingly Brecht's projected drama about Einstein was not concerned with Einstein the scientist, but with Einstein's place in politics. (Cf. Helmut Winter, 'Brecht und Einstein, Anmerkungen zu Skizzen im Nachlaß', *Neue Zürcher Zeitung*, 26 November 1967, No. 5072, 'Literatur und Kunst', p. 6, for

a discussion of Brecht's notes on this play.) Brecht's knowledge of science was not profound. This is borne out by 'Brecht und die Naturwissenschaften. Ein Vortrag' (by Werner Mittenwei) and subsequent 'Diskussion', *Brecht '73, Brecht Woche der DDR. Dokumentation*, ed. Werner Hecht, Berlin, 1973. The remark which Brecht made to Günther Anders that the difference between the conventional theatre and his theatre corresponded to that between descriptive and experimental physics should also corroborate my contention. (Cf. Günther Anders, *Bert Brecht. Gespräche und Erinnerungen*, Zurich, 1962, p. 16.)

4. B, x, xviii, p. 57 f.; pp. 60 f.
5. B, xviii, p. 60.
6. The usually malicious attacks on Thomas Mann are many: cf. *Wenn der Vater mit dem Sohne mit dem Uhu*; B, xviii, p. 40–2; [Unterschied der Generationen], B, xviii, pp. 43–4. Cf. also the phrase 'the encyclopaedia of the *babbit of culture* [*Bildungsspiesser*]' coined by him or by his friend Hanns Eisler about the 'Joseph novels'. Diary of 19 October 1944; B – A, p. 694. The whole relationship is analysed with great skill by Hans Mayer, 'Mann and Brecht: Anatomy of an Antagonism', *New German Critique*, vi, 1975, pp. 101 – 15.
7. B, xviii, p. 55; pp. 57–8.
8. This is done for instance by Sokel in his *The Writer in Extremis*, otherwise a remarkable book.
9. Cf. B, xviii, p. 61; B, xix, p. 447.
10. There were at least four versions (1918–26). Cf. Dieter E. Schmidt, *Baal und der junge Brecht. Eine textkritische Untersuchung zur Entwicklung des Frühwerks*, Stuttgart, 1960.
11. For a perceptive analysis of this play cf. Konrad Feilchenfeldt, *Bertolt Brecht, 'Trommeln in der Nacht'; Materialien, Abbildungen, Kommentar*, Munich and Vienna, 1976.
12. B. G. viii, p. 303 (*Gedichte 1926–1933*).

OF MONEY

I do not wish to seduce you to work. /Man is not born to work. But money that is what you should be after./ Money is good! Do pay attention to money.

Men catch each other with snares. /The wickedness of the world is great. That is why you should acquire money./ For their love of money is greater.

. . . .

Men pay homage to money. /Money is placed above God./ If you want to deny your enemy peace in his grave!/ Do write on his tombstone: here lies money.

13. B, viii, p. 215 (*Hauspostille*).

ON THE CITIES

Below them are drains. /In them is nothing and above them is smoke. We were inside. We consumed nothing./ We withered away quickly. And slowly they wither away too.

14. Cf. Wolfdietrich Rasch, 'Brechts Marxistischer Lehrer'. Zum ungedruckten Briefwechsel zwischen Bertold Brecht und Karl Korsch', *Zur deutschen Literatur der Jahrhundertwende*, Gesammelte Aufsätze, Stuttgart, 1967, pp. 243–73.

15. Cf. the writings collected under the title [*Über eine nicht-aristotelische Dramatik*] (1933–41); B, xv, 227–336.

16. Cf. note 3.

17. Cf. the preface of the second edition of the *Critik der Reinen Vernunft*, Riga, 1787, pp. xvif.

18. *Bei Durchsicht meiner ersten Stücke*; B, xvii, p. 445.

19. Cf. for instance *Weniger Gips!!!*; B, xv, p. 108ff.

20. Cf. *Kleines Privatissimum für meinen Freund Max Gorelik* (1935), B, xv, p. 468.

21. Cf. Paul Kussmaul, *Bertolt Brecht und das Englische Drama der Renaissance*, Berne and Frankfurt/Main, 1974.

22. Cf. Peter Michelsen, 'Der Kritiker des Details. Lessing in den Briefen die Neueste Literatur betreffend', *Wolffenbütteler Studien zur Aufklärung*, ed. Günter Schulz, ii, Wolffenbüttel 1975, pp. 151 ff., who demonstrates this aspect clearly without in any way detracting from Lessing's greatness. Cf. also, for a comparison between Brecht and Lessing, Paolo Chiarini, 'Lessing und Brecht', *Sinn und Form*, Zweites Sonderheft, 1955, pp. 188–203; H. J. Schrimpf, *Lessing und Brecht. Von der Aufklärung auf dem Theater*, Pfullingen, 1965; and also Reinhold Grimm, 'Lessing – ein Vorläufer Brechts I', *Lessing Year Book*, i, 1974, pp. 36–59.

23. The literature on Aristotle's *Poetics* is of course so enormous as to daunt any scholar, let alone a creative writer. For instance, the pioneering work by Jacob Bernays, *Die Grundzüge der verlorenen Abhandlung des Aristoteles über Wirkung der Tragödie*, Breslau, 1858, gave rise to more than seventy articles and books alone. Cf. *Jacob Bernays. Ein Lebensbild, in Briefen*, ed. Michael Fränkel, Breslau, 1932, p. 11.

24. On Aristotle cf. Humphry House, *Aristotle's Poetics*, London, 1958, for a most sensible account of this problem.

25. *Anmerkungen zur Oper 'Aufstieg und Fall der Stadt Mahagonny'*, B, xvii, p. 1004–8.

26. Cf. for instance *Kurze Beschreibung einer neuen Technik der Schauspielkunst, die einen Verfremdungseffekt hervorbringt*; B, xv, pp. 346 f.; cf. also *Der Messingkauf* ('Zweiter Nachtrag zur Theorie des Messingkaufs'); B, xvi, p. 653.

27. [*Über die Operette*]; B, xv, p. 73.

28. Cf. for instance the remarks recorded in *Bertolt Brecht-Archiv*, Mappe 40, 3, quoted by Käthe Rülicke-Weiler, *Die Dramaturgie Brechts. Theater als Veränderung*, Berlin, 1968, p. 8, who discusses this aspect.

29. *Geburt der Tragödie*; N, i, p. 75.

30. *Kleines Organon für das Theater*; B, xvi, p. 662. Cf. also Postscript to *Aufstieg und Fall der Stadt Mahagonny*; B, xv, p. 262.

31. For instance cf. *Der Messingkauf*; B, xvi, p. 350; B, vi, p. 679.

32. Postscript to *Kleines Organon für das Theater*; B, xvi, p. 701.

33. Marx/Engels, *Werke*, ii, Berlin 1962, p. 353. Brecht unmistakably alludes to this sentence in *Vergnügungstheater order Lehrtheater?* B, xv, p. 262; cf. also 'Episches Theater', *Katzgraben-Notate* (1953), B, xvi, p. 815. Cf. also Albercht Schöne, 'Bertolt Brecht, Theater theorie und dramatische Dichtung', *Euphorion*, lii, 1958, pp. 273 f., who makes the same point.

34. Cf. *Kleines Privatissimum für meinen Freund Max Gorelik*; B, xv, p. 469.
35. [*Shakespeare Studien*]; B, xvi, p. 334.
36. Cf. Mayer, pp. 110f. Mayer writes 'Brecht never liked them – those beautiful stories with their happy endings' (p. 111).
37. *Die Dialektik auf dem Theater*, B, xvi, pp. 867–941; *Notizen über die Dialektik auf dem Theater*, B, xvi, pp. 919–23; *Episches und dialektisches Theater*, B, xvi, pp. 923–6.
38. *Über gestische Musik*, B, xv, pp. 482–5 (approx. 1938); *Kleines Organon für das Theater*, B, xvi, p. 753.
39. Cf. Sokel; Arnold (cf. Chapter 2, note 4); and also Walter E. Riedel, *Der neue Mensch. Mythos und Wirklichkkeit*, Bonn, 1970, all of whom explore this question.
40. *Fünf Schwierigkeiten beim Schreiben der Wahrheit*; B, xviii, p. 222.
41. Aristotle, 'On the Art of Poetry' [*Poetics*], trs. T. S. Dorsch, *Classical Literary Criticism* (Penguin edition), ed. T. S. Dorsch, Harmondsworth, Middlesex, 1965, pp. 38 f.
42. Cf. Humphry House for comments on this subject.
43. Cf. for instance 'Der V-Effekt', B, xv, pp. 361 f., *Der Messingkauf*, B, xvi, p. 611 ff. *Entfremdung* is best translated with 'distancing'. The usual translation, 'alienation', is in fact misleading since it carries the Hegelian and Marxian meaning to which the word only alludes, but which it does not signify.
44. Cf. Helmut Flashar, 'Aristoteles und Brecht', *Poetica*, vi, 1974, who makes this point. The term appears in Aristotle, περὶ ποιητικῆς, ii, p. 1458*b* Dorsch translates ξενικόν by 'unfamiliar usage' (p. 63).
45. *Das epische Theater; Vergnügungstheater oder Lehrtheater?* B, xv, pp. 262–73.
46. Preface to *Kleines Organon für das Theater*, B, xvi, p. 662.
47. Cf. note 37.
48. This aspect is emphasised by Schöne, p. 277.
49. Cf. Schrimpf, p. 24.
50. *Der Messingkauf*; B, xvi, p. 637.
51. The following plays are generally ranked in that category: *Der Flug der Lindberghs* [*The Flight of the Lindberghs*] (1928/9), *Das Badener Lehrstück vom Einverständnis* [*The Didactic Play of Baden on Consent*] (1928/9), *Der Jasager* [*He who says 'Yes'*] (1929/30), *Der Neinsager* [*He who says 'No'*] (1930), *Die Maßnahme* [*The (disciplinary) Measure*] (1930), *Die Ausnahme und die Regel* [*The Exception and the Rule*] (1930), *Die Rundköpfe und die Spitzköpfe* [*The Roundheads and the Peakheads*] (1932–42), *Die Mutter* [*The Mother*] 1930/32) and *Die Horatier und die Curatier* [*The Horatians and Curatians*] (1934).
52. Cf. Anders, p. 10 (cf. note 3).
53. Cf. Anders, p. 12.
54. Preface to *Kleines Organon für das Theater*, B, xvi, p. 662.
55. Diary of 1 September 1948, B-A, ii, p. 837.
56. Cf. Schrimpf, p. 9.
57. Cf. Schrimpf, p. 13.
58. This point is made by Martin Esslin, *Brecht. A Choice of Evils. A Critical Study of the Man, his Work and his Opinions*, London, 1959, an excellent book to which I am much indebted. Cf. particularly pp. 201–36.
59. Cf. Esslin *passim*, who makes this observation; cf. also Schöne, who speaks of Brecht the creative artist overcoming Brecht the propagandist.

60. Cf. Schmidt (cf. note 10).
61. Cf. Julius Petersen, *Das Deutsche Nationaltheater*, Leipzig, 1919; Hans Kindermann, *Theatergeschichte der Goethezeit*, Vienna, 1948; W. H. Bruford, *Theatre, Drama, Audience in Goethe's Germany*, London, 1949; Willi Fleming, *Goethes Gestaltung des klassischen Theaters*, Cologne, 1949, for accounts of this important part of German cultural history.
62. Lessing, *Werke*, ed. Kurt Wölfel, II, Frankfurt/Main, 1967, p. 525.
63. *Dankgedicht an Marie Hold zum 5 Oktober 1934*; B, IX, p. 528.
64. ON READING HORACE

Even the Flood/did not last for ever./Eventually, the black waters /ebbed away; of course, how few things/lasted longer. (B, x, p. 1014.)
65. On listening to verses/by Benn who is addicted to death/I saw an expression on workers' faces/which had nothing to do with the verse form but was more precious/than the smile of the Mona Lisa.(B, x, p. 1018.)
66. I have argued this matter somewhat more fully in my article 'Problems of Demarcation in the Study of Literature, Some Reflections', *Dt. Vjs.*, XLVI, 1972.

CHAPTER 9 CONCLUSION

1. Cf. MacRae, *Max Weber* who stresses that this conception is at the centre of Weber's thought.
2. This idea is most powerfully expressed by Schiller in his poem *Die Götter Griechenlands* [*The Gods of Greece*] (1788), *Werke*, ed. Bellermann, I, Leipzig and Vienna, n.d., pp. 68–72.
3. Musil's ideas are most interesting cf. the very informative study by Marie-Louise Roth, *Robert Musil: Ethik und Ästhetik: Zum theoretischen Werk des Dichters*, Munich, 1972, particularly pp. 151–260.
4. Musil was, by training, a physicist and engineer, Broch a textile engineer, and Benn a physician who practised dermatology.
5. This view is particularly emphasised by Musil.
6. Cf. Peter Gay, 'The Hunger for Wholeness. Trials of Modernity', *Weimar Culture*, (Penguin edition), Harmondsworth, Middlesex, 1974, pp. 73–100 for an analysis of the widespread desire for 'wholeness'.
7. This aspect is emphasised by Wolfdietrich Rasch in an important essay 'Aspekte der deutschen Literatur um 1900', *Zur deutschen Literatur seit der Jahrhundertwende*. He writes that *Leben* is the basic word of the epoch, its central concept (p. 17).
8. T. J. Reed, 'Nietzsche's Animals. Image, Idea and Influence'.
9. Cf. Pascal, whose chapter on 'The Image of the Bourgeoisie' (pp. 16–41) is excellent. Cf. also Werner Sombart, *Der Bourgeois. Zur Geistesgeschichte des modernen Wirtschaftsmenschen*, Munich, 1913, a pioneering work.
10. Hermann Hesse, *An einen Staatsminister*, (1917), *Werke*, (*Werkausgabe*), 12 vols, Frankfurt/Main, 1970, x, p. 420.
11. Cf. Reed, *Thomas Mann*, p. 314, who makes this point and quotes a passage from Br. TM-H, p. 210, an address on the occasion of Heinrich Mann's 70th birthday (2 May 1941).
12. Hesse, x, p. 512.

13. Hesse, *Versuch einer Rechtfertigung*, (to Max Brod, 25 May 1948), x, p. 558 ff.
14. Hesse, *Versuch einer Rechtfertigung*, (to Max Brod, 25 May 1948), x, p. 560.
15. Hesse, x, p. 518 (c. 1932/33)
16. Cf. Caroline Cohn, *Karl Kraus*, Stuttgart, 1966, p. 73.
17. Cf. Hesse, *Sprache*, xi, p. 191, who describes the dual nature of language very persuasively.
18. Cf. A. Janik and S. E. Toulmin, *Wittgenstein's Vienna*, London, 1973
19. Cf. Thomas Mann, *Geist und Kunst*, Scherrer and Wysling, p. 174.
20. Cf. Roger Bauer, *Der Idealismus und seine Gegner in Österreich*, Heidelberg, 1966, who makes this important observation.
21. Cf. R. Hinton Thomas 'German and British Intellectuals', *Upheaval and Continuity, A Century of German History*, ed. Klaus Schulz, London, 1973, who discusses this aspect fully.
22. *Wilhelm Meisters Lehrjahre*, v, 6; W. A., I, 22, p. 173.
23. Cf. to Harriet Moore, 9 November 1914; *Letters of Ezra Pound 1907–1941*, London, 1951, p. 88; to William Carlos Williams, 18 March 1922, ibid., p. 238.
24. T. S. Eliot, *The Use of Poetry and the Use of Criticism*, London, 1933, p. 150.
25. Eliot, p. 154.
26. Eliot, p. 135.
27. Eliot, p. 154.
28. Eliot, p. 154.
29. Eliot, p. 154.
30. T. S. Eliot, *The Idea of a Christian Society*, London, 1939, p. 8.
31. D. H. Lawrence, 'Sex versus Loveliness', *Sex, Literature and Censorship*, essays ed. Harry T. Moore, London, 1955, p. 122.
32. Lawrence, 'The State of Funk', ibid., p. 137.
33. Lawrence, 'Introduction to his Paintings', ibid., p. 178.
34. Stéphane Mallarmé, *Sur l'Evolution Littéraire (Réponse à Jules Huser)*, Oeuvres *Complètes*, (Bibliothèque de la Pléiade), Paris, 1965, p. 872.
35. The reference is to George Santayana, *Egotism in German Philosophy*, London and Toronto, 1916.
36. Einstein's undated letter (probably of September 1945) is printed in Hermann Broch, *Gesammelte Werke: Briefe 1949–1951*, Zurich, 1952, p. 227.

Select Bibliography

PRIMARY SOURCES

FRIEDRICH NIETZSCHE

Kritische Gesamtausgabe, ed. Giorgio Colli and Mazzino Montinari (7 vols to date) Berlin, 1967– .
Werke, 3 vols, ed. Karl Schlechta, 2nd ed., Munich, 1960.
Werke (Großoktavausgabe), 20 vols, 2nd ed., Leipzig, 1901–26.
Historisch-Kritische Gesamtausgabe der Werke und Briefe. Abteilung Briefe, 4 vols to date, Munich, 1933– .
Gesammelte Briefe, 2nd ed., 4 vols, Leipzig, 1903– .
Der Streit um Nietzsches Geburt der Tragödie, ed. Karfried Gründer, Hildesheim, 1969.

STEFAN GEORGE

Werke (ed. Robert Böhringer), 2 vols, Munich/Düsseldorf, 1958.
Blätter für die Kunst, founded by Stefan George and ed. Carl August Klein, I-XII, Berlin, 1892—1919.
Blätter für die Kunst. Eine Auslese aus den Jahren 1892–8, 1898–1904, 1904–09, 3 vols, Berlin, 1899–1909 (Reprint, Berlin, 1929).
Briefwechsel zwischen Stefan George und Hofmannsthal, ed. Robert Böhringer, 2nd ed., Munich and Düsseldorf, 1953.
Briefwechsel Stefan George – Friedrich Gundolf, ed. Robert Böhringer and G. P. Landmann, Munich and Düsseldorf, 1962.

HUGO VON HOFMANNSTHAL

Sämtliche Werke, ed. H. O. Burger *et al.* (3 vols to date) Frankfurt/Main, 1975– .
Gesammelte Werke in Einzelausgaben, ed. H. Steiner, 15 vols, Stockholm/later Frankfurt/Main, 1945–59.
Hugo von Hofmannsthal – Leopold von Andrian. Briefwechsel, 1898–1929, ed. Hilde Burger, Frankfurt/Main, 1968.
Hugo von Hofmannsthal – Edgar Karg von Bebenburg. Briefwechsel, ed. Mary E. Gilbert, Frankfurt/Main, 1966.
Hugo von Hofmannsthal – Richard Beer-Hofmann. Briefwechsel, ed. Eugene Weber, Frankfurt/Main, 1972.
Hugo von Hofmannsthal – Eberhard von Bodenhausen. Briefe der Freundschaft, ed. Dora von Bodenhausen, Düsseldorf, 1953.
Hugo von Hofmannsthal – Rudolf Borchardt. Briefwechsel, ed. Marie Luise Borchardt and Herbert Steiner, Frankfurt/Main, 1954.

Hugo von Hofmannsthal – Carl J. Burckhardt. Briefwechsel, ed. Carl J. Burckhardt, Frankfurt/Main, 1958.

'Hugo von Hofmannsthal – Rudolf Borchardt. Unbekannte Briefe', ed. Werner Volke, *JDSG*, VIII, 1961, pp. 19–32.

'Hugo von Hofmannsthal – Hans Carossa. Briefwechsel 1907–1929', *Neue Rundschau*, LXXI, 1960, pp. 357–409 and 573–584.

Hugo von Hofmannsthal – Ottonie Gräfin Degenfeld. Briefwechsel, Frankfurt/Main, 1974.

'Hugo von Hofmannsthal. Unbekannte Briefe an Irene und Paul Hellmann', ed. Werner Volke, *JDSG*, XI, 1967, pp. 170–224.

Hugo von Hofmannsthal – Harry Graf Kessler. Briefwechsel. 1898–1929, ed. Hilde Burger, Frankfurt/Main, 1971.

Hugo von Hofmannsthal – Helene von Nostitz. Briefwechsel, ed. Oswalt von Nostitz, Frankfurt/Main, 1965.

Hugo von Hofmannsthal – Joseph Redlich. Briefwechsel, ed. Helga Fußgänger, Frankfurt/Main, 1972.

Hugo von Hofmannsthal – Arthur Schnitzler. Briefwechsel, ed. Therese Nickl and Heinrich Schnitzler, Frankfurt/Main, 1964.

Richard Strauss – Hugo von Hofmannsthal. Briefwechsel. Gesamtausgabe, ed. Willi Schuh, Zurich, 1964.

Der Briefwechsel Hofmannsthal – Wildgans, ed. Joseph A. von Bradish, Zurich, Munich and Paris, 1935.

RAINER MARIA RILKE

Sämtliche Werke, 6 vols, ed. Ernst Zinn, Wiesbaden, 1955–66.

Collected Letters and Diaries, all ed. Ruth Sieber-Rilke and Carl Sieber:

Briefe und Tagebücher 1899–1902, Leipzig, 1931.

Briefe 1902–1906, Leipzig, 1930.

Briefe 1906–1907, Leipzig, 1930.

Briefe 1907–1914, Leipzig, 1933.

Briefe 1914–1921, Leipzig, 1937.

Briefe aus Muzot 1921–1926, Leipzig, 1935.

Gesammelte Briefe 1892–1926, 5 vols, Leipzig, 1939–40.

Tagebücher aus der Frühzeit, Leipzig, 1942 (Reprint, Frankfurt/Main, 1973).

Gesammelte Briefe 1892–1926, 5 vols, ed. Ruth-Sieber Rilke and Carl Sieber, Leipzig, 1939–40.

Briefe, ed. Karl Altheim, 2 vols, Wiesbaden, 1950.

Rainer Maria Rilke und Lou Andreas-Salomé. Briefwechsel, ed. Erich Pfeiffer, Zurich, 1952.

Rainer Maria Rilke und Benvenuta [Magda von Graedener-Hattingberg], ed. Kurt Leonhard, Eßlingen, 1954.

Briefe an einen jungen Dichter [Frank Xaver Kappus], Leipzig, 1929.

Briefe an das Ehepaar S. Fischer, ed. Hedwig Fischer, Zurich, 1947.

Briefe an eine junge Frau [Lisa Heise], ed. Carl Sieber, Leipzig, 1930.

Briefe an eine Freundin [Claire Studer-Goll], New York, 1944.

Rainer Maria Rilke – André Gide. Correspondance 1909–1926, ed. Renée Lang, Paris, 1952.

Rainer Maria Rilke – André Gide – Emil Verhaeren. Correspondance inédite. ed. C. Bronne, Paris, 1955.

Briefe [*an R. R. Junghans und Rudolf Zimmermann*], *1919–1925*, Olten, 1945.
Rainer Maria Rilke und Katharina Kippenberg. Briefwechsel, ed. B. von Bomhard, Wiesbaden, 1954.
Rainer Maria Rilke et Merline [*Baladine Klossowska*] *Correspondance 1920–1926*, ed. Dieter Bassermann, Zurich, 1954.
Die Briefe an Frau Gudi Nölke, ed. P. Obermüller, Wiesbaden, 1953.
Briefe an eine Reisegefährtin. [Lotte Tronier-Funder]. *Eine Begegnung mit Rainer Maria Rilke*, Vienna, 1947.
Briefe an Auguste Rodin, Leipzig, 1928.
Rainer Maria Rilke und Marie v. Thurn und Taxis. Briefwechsel, ed. Ernst Zinn, Wiesbaden, 1951.
Briefe an seinen Verleger [*Anton Kippenberg*] *1906–1926*, 2 vols, 2nd ed., Wiesbaden, 1949.
Freundschaft mit R. M. Rilke [Nevar (? Raven), Elya], Berne, 1946.
Lettres à une amie [Mina Romanelli], Milan, 1941.
Aus Rainer Maria Rilkes Nachlaß, Wiesbaden, 1950 includes:
    Aus dem Nachlaß des Grafen C. W. Ein Gedicht-Kreis.
    Briefwechsel in Gedichten mit Erika Mitterer, 1924–26.
    Aus Taschen-Büchern und Merk-Blättern – in zufälliger Folge, 1925.
    Die Briefe an Gräfin Sizzo 1921 – 1926.
Lettres milanaises 1921–1926 [to Aurelia Galaratti-Scotti], ed. Renée Lang, Paris, 1956.

THOMAS MANN

Gesammelte Werke, 2nd ed., 13 vols, Frankfurt/Main, 1974.
Briefe, 3 vols: I, *1889–1936*; II, *1937–47*; III, *1948–55 und Nachlese*, ed. Erika Mann, Frankfurt/Main, 1961–5.
Geist und Kunst (notes for a projected essay), printed in Scherrer and Wysling, pp. 123–253.
Thomas Mann – Heinrich Mann, Briefwechsel 1900–1949, ed. Hans Wysling, Frankfurt/Main, 1968.
Briefe an Paul Ammann 1915–1952, ed Herbert Wegener, Lübeck, 1959.
Thomas Mann an Ernst Bertram. Briefe aus den Jahren 1910–1955, ed. Inge Jens, Pfullingen, 1960.
Thomas Mann – Karl Kerényi, Gespräch in Briefen, ed. Karl Kerényi, Zurich, 1960.
Hermann Hesse – Thomas Mann. Briefwechsel, ed. Anni Carlsson, Frankfurt/Main, 1968.
Thomas Mann – Robert Faesi, Briefwechsel, ed. Robert Faesi, Zurich, 1962.
Thomas Mann, Briefwechsel mit seinem Verleger Bermann Fischer 1932–1955, ed. Peter de Mendelssohn, Frankfurt/Main, 1973.
Briefe an Otto Grauhoff 1894–1928 und Ida Boyd-Ed 1903–1928, ed. Peter de Mendelsohn, Frankfurt/Main, 1975.
Smaller sets of letters are found in the *Blätter der Thomas-Mann-Gesellschaft*, for instance to Emil Preetorius (1963), Otto Basler (1965), Max Rychner (1967), Hans Reisiger (1968), Bruno Walter (1969), Erich von Kahler (1970), Kuno Fiedler (1971 and 1972).
For Thomas Mann's correspondence with Hugo von Hofmannsthal cf. *Fischer-Almanach 82* (1968).

'Der Briefwechsel [Benedetto] Croce/Mann', ed. Ottavio Besomi and Hans
Wysling; *Germanisch-Romanische Monatsschrift, Neue Folge*, xxv, 1975, pp.
129–50.

FRANZ KAFKA

Gesammelte Werke, 2nd ed., New York and Frankfurt/Main, ed. Max Brod except
where otherwise stated.
  Der Prozeß, 1950.
  Das Schloß, 1951.
  Tagebücher 1910–1923, 1951.
  Briefe an Milena, ed. W. Haas, 1952.
  Erzählungen, 1952.
  Amerika, 1953.
  Hochzeitsvorbereitungen auf dem Lande und andere Prosa aus dem Nachlass, 1953.
  Beschreibung eines Kampfes, Novellen, Skizzen, Aphorismen aus dem Nachlass, 1954.
  Briefe 1902–1924, 1958.
  Briefe an Felice, ed. E. Heller and J. Born, 1967.
  Briefe an Ottla und die Familie, ed. Hartmut Binder and Klaus Wagenbach,
    1974.
Gespräche mit Kafka, ed. Gustav Janouch, Frankfurt/Main, 1951.

BERTOLT BRECHT

Werke (Werkausgabe), 20 vols, Frankfurt/Main, 1967.
Arbeitsjournal 1938–55, 3 vols, ed. Werner Hecht, Frankfurt/Main, 1973.
Tagebücher 1920–1922. Autobiographische Aufzeichnungen 1920–1954, ed. Herta Ran-
    thun, Frankfurt/Main, 1975.
Brecht im Gespräch. Dokumente. Dialoge, Interviews, ed. Werner Hecht, Frankfurt/
    Main, 1975.

OTHERS

Benn, Gottfried, *Gesammelte Werke (DTV Taschenbuchausgabe)*, ed. Dieter Wellers-
    hof, Munich, 1973.
Broch, Hermann, *Gesammelte Werke*, 10 vols, ed. Erich Kahler *et al.*, Zurich,
    1953–61.
Kraus, Karl, *Werke*, 14 vols, ed. Heinrich Fischer, Munich, 1952–67; *Die Fackel
    1899–1936*, 39 vols (reprint), ed. Heinrich Fischer, Munich, 1968–73.
Hesse, Hermann, *Gesammelte Werke (Werkausgabe)*, Frankfurt/Main, 1970.
Musil, Robert, *Gesammelte Werke in Einzelausgaben*, 3 vols, ed. A. Frisé, Hamburg,
    1952–7.

SECONDARY SOURCES

I *Bibliographies*

FRIEDRICH NIETZSCHE

Reichert, Herbert W., and Schlechta, Karl, *International Nietzsche Bibliography*, Chapel Hill, N.C., 1960.

STEFAN GEORGE

Landmann, George Peter, *Stefan George und Sein Kreis. Eine Bibliographie*, Hamburg, 1960.

HUGO VON HOFMANNSTHAL

Weber, Horst, *Hugo von Hofmannsthal. Bibliographie des Schrifttums 1892–1963*, Berlin, 1968.
Hugo von Hofmannsthal Bibliographie. Werke, Briefe, Gespräche, Übersetzungen, Vertonungen, Berlin, 1972.

RAINER MARIA RILKE

Ritzer, Walter, *Rainer Maria Rilke Bibliographie*, Vienna, 1951.

THOMAS MANN

Bürgin, Hans, *Das Werk Thomas Manns*, Frankfurt/Main, 1959.
Matter, Harry, *Die Literatur über Thomas Mann 1898–1969*, 2 vols, Berlin and Weimar, 1972.
Jonas, Klaus W., *Die Thomas Mann Literatur. Bibliographie der Kritik 1896–1955*, I, Berlin, 1972, Vol. II (*1955–1975*) is due to appear in Berlin in 1977.

FRANZ KAFKA

Hemmerle, Rudolf (ed.), *Franz Kafka. Eine Bibliographie*, Munich, 1958.
Järv, Harry, *Die Kafka-Literatur*, Mälmo/Lund, 1961.
Flores, Angel, *A Kafka Bibliography 1908–1976*, New York, 1976.

BERTOLT BRECHT

Petersen, Klaus-Dietrich, *Bertolt Brecht Bibliographie*, Bad Homburg von der Höhe/Zurich, 1969.
Seidel, Gerhart, *Bibliographie Bertolt Brecht. Titelverzeichnis*, I (*Veröffentlichungen aus den Jahren 1913–1972. Werke von Brecht-Sammlungen Dramatik*), Berlin/Weimar, 1975.

II *Critical Writings*

FRIEDRICH NIETZSCHE

Andler, Charles, *Nietzsche. Sa vie et sa pensée*, 6 vols, Paris, 1920–31.
Bindschedler, Maria, *Nietzsche und die poetische Lüge*, Basle, 1966.
Frenzel, Ivo, *Nietzsche in Selbstzeugnissen und Bilddokumenten* (with a most useful bibliography), Reinbek bei Hamburg, 1961.
Howald, Ernst, *Nietzsche und die klassische Philologie*, Gotha, 1920.
Hultberg, Helge, *Die Kunstauffassung Nietzsches*, Bergen and Oslo, 1962.
Jaspers, Karl, *Nietzsche. Einführung in das Verständnis seines Philosphierens*, 3rd ed., Berlin, 1950.
Kaufmann, Walter A., *Nietzsche. Philosopher. Psychologist. Antichrist*, Princeton, N.J., 1950.
Lloyd-Jones, Hugh, 'Nietzsche and the Study of the Ancient World', *Studies on Nietzsche and the Classical Tradition*, ed. James C. O'Flaherty *et al.*, Chapel Hill, N.C., 1976.
Pütz, Peter, *Friedrich Nietzsche*, Stuttgart, 1967 [a survey of Nietzsche's scholarship].
Kunst und Künstlerexistenz bei Nietzsche und Thomas Mann, Bonn, 1963.
Reed, T.J., 'Nietzsche's Animals. Image, Idea and Influence', *The Impact of Nietzsche*, ed. Malcolm Pasley (to be published in London, 1977).
Reyburn, H.A. *et al.*, *Nietzsche. The Story of a Human Philosopher*, London, 1949.
Vogel, Martin, *Apollinisch-Dionysisch. Geschichte eines genialen Irrtums*, Regensburg, 1966.
For essays and a bibliography on the *Geburt der Tragödie* cf. *The Malahat Review*, 24, 1972 (published by the University of Victoria, B.C.).

STEFAN GEORGE

Bennett, E.K., *Stefan George*, Cambridge, 1954.
Böhringer, Robert, *Mein Bild von Stefan George*, Munich, 1951.
David, Claude, *Stefan George. Son oeuvre poétique*, Lyon and Paris, 1952. (German ed.: *Stefan George. Sein dichterisches Werk*, trs. A. Remmen and K. Thiemer, Munich, 1967.)
Durzak, Manfred, *Der junge Stefan George, Kunsttheorie und Dichtung*, Munich, 1968.
——*Stefan George. Zwischen Symbolismus und Expressionismus*, Stuttgart, Berlin, Cologne and Mayence, 1974.
Goldsmith, Ulrich K., *Stefan George: A Study of his Early Work*, Boulder, Colorado, 1959.
Klussman, Paul Gerhard, *Stefan George. Zum Selbstverständnis der Kunst und des Dichters der Moderne*, Bonn, 1961.
Metzger, Michael and Metzger, Erika A., *Stefan George*, New York, 1972.
Schonauer, Franz, *Stefan George in Selbstzeugnissen und Bilddokumenten* (with a most useful bibliography), Reinbek bei Hamburg, 1961.
Winkler, Michael, *Stefan George*, Stuttgart, 1970 (a survey of George scholarship)
——*George-Kreis*, Stuttgart, 1972 (a survey of the 'George-Kreis' scholarship).

HUGO VON HOFMANNSTHAL

Alewyn, Richard, *Hugo von Hofmannsthal*, Göttingen, 1963.
Broch, Hermann, *Hofmannsthal und seine Zeit. Eine Studie*, Munich, 1964. (Also in Broch, *Gesammelte Werke*, VI, *Essays*, I, Zurich, 1955, pp. 43–181.)
Coghlan, Brian, *Hofmannsthal's Festival Dramas*, Cambridge and Melbourne, 1964.
Jens, Walter, *Hofmannsthal und die Griechen*, Tübingen, 1955.
Norman, F. (ed.), *Hofmannsthal: Studies in Commemoration*, London, 1963.
Pulver, Elsbet, *Hofmannsthals Schriften zur Literatur*, Berne, 1956.
Tarot, Rolf, *Hugo von Hofmannsthal. Daseinsformen und dichterische Struktur*, Tübingen, 1970.
Volke, Werner, *Hugo von Hofmannsthal in Selbstzeugnissen und Bilddokumenten* (with a most useful bibliography), Reinbek bei Hamburg, 1967.
Wunberg, Gotthart, *Der frühe Hofmannsthal. Schizophrenie als dichterische Struktur*, Stuttgart, 1965 (contains a comprehensive bibliography).

RAINER MARIA RILKE

Butler, E.M., *Rainer Maria Rilke*, Cambridge, 1942.
Casey, T. J., *Rainer Maria Rilke. A Centenary Essay*, London, 1976.
Hamburger, Käte (ed.), *Rilke in neuer Sicht*, Stuttgart, Berlin, Cologne and Mayence, 1971.
Holthusen, Hans Egon, *Rainer Maria Rilke in Selbstzeugnissen und Bilddokumenten* (with a most useful bibliography), Reinbek bei Hamburg, 1958.
Mason, Eudo C., *Lebenshaltung und Symbolik bei R. M. Rilke*, Weimar , 1939.
——*Rilke*, Edinburgh, 1963.
——*Rainer Maria Rilke. Sein Leben und Werk*, Göttingen, 1964.
Rose, William, and Craig-Houston, Gertrude (eds.), *Rainer Maria Rilke. Aspects of his Mind and Thought*, London, 1938.
Ryan, Judith, *Umschlag und Verwandlung. Poetische Struktur und Dichtungstheorie in R. M. Rilkes Lyrik der Mittleren Periode* (1907–14), Munich, 1972.
Steiner, Jacob, *Rilkes Duineser Elegien*, Berne and Munich, 1962.
Stephens, Anthony R., *Rainer Maria Rilkes 'Gedichte an die Nacht': An Essay in Interpretation*, Cambridge, 1972.
Wood, Frank, *R. M. Rilke. The Ring of Forms*, Minneapolis, 1958.

THOMAS MANN

Heller, Erich, *The Ironic German*, London, 1957.
Koopmann, Helmut, *Thomas Mann. Konstanten seines literarischen Werkes*, Göttingen, 1975.
Lehnert, Herbert, *Thomas Mann, Fiktion. Mythos. Religion*, Stuttgart, 1965.
Maitre, Hans Joachim, *Thomas Mann. Aspekte der Kulturkritik in seiner Essayistik*, Bonn, 1970.
Mendelsohn, Peter de, *Der Zauberer. Das Leben des deutschen Schriftstellers Thomas Mann*, I (1875–1918), Frankfurt/Main, 1975.
Mommsen, Katharina, *Gesellschaftskritik bei Fontane und Thomas Mann*, Heidelberg, 1973.

Nündel, Ernst, *Thomas Manns Kunsttheorie*, Bonn, 1972.
Pütz, Peter (ed.), *Thomas Mann und die Tradition*, Frankfurt/Main, 1972.
Reed, T.J.,*Thomas Mann. The Uses of Tradition*, Oxford, 1974.
Scherrer, Paul, and Wysling, Hans, *Quellenkritische Studien zum Werk Thomas Manns*, *Thomas Mann Studien*, 1 Berne and Munich, 1967.
Schröter, Klaus, *Thomas Mann in Selbstzeugnissen und Bilddokumenten* (with a most useful bibliography), Reinbek bei Hamburg, 1964.
——(ed.) *Thomas Mann in Urteil seiner Zeit. Dokumente 1891 - 1955*, Hamburg, 1969.
Wysling, Hans, *Thomas Mann Heute*, Berne and Munich, 1976.
——*Dokumente und Untersuchungen. Beiträge zur Thomas Mann Forschung*, Thomas Mann Studien, III Berne and Munich, 1974.
——*et al.* (ed.), *Thomas Mann. Dichter Über Dichtungen*, (1881 - 1971) I, Munich, n.d. [1975] (vols II and III to appear 1977).

FRANZ KAFKA

Beicken, Peter, *Franz Kafka. Eine kritische Einführung in die Forschung*, Frankfurt/Main, 1974.
Hibberd, John, *Franz Kafka*, London, 1974.
Politzer, Heinz, *Franz Kafka. Parable and Paradox*, Ithaca, N. Y., 1962.(German ed. *Franz Kafka. Der Künstler*, Frankfurt/Main, 1965.)
Sokel, Walter M., *Franz Kafka. Tragik und Ironie*, Munich, 1964.
Thorlby, Anthony, *A Student's Guide to Kafka*, London, 1972.
Wagenbach, Kurt, *Franz Kafka in Selbstzeugnissen und Bilddokumenten* (with a most useful bibliography), Reinbek bei Hamburg, 1964.
Wagenbach, Kurt (ed.), *Kafka Symposium*, Berlin, 1965.

BERTOLT BRECHT

Demetz, Peter (ed.), *Brecht: A collection of Critical Essays*, Englewood Cliffs, N. J., 1962.
Esslin, Martin, *Brecht. A Choice of Evils. A Critical Study of the Man, his Work and his Opinions*, London, 1959.
Grimm, Reinhold, *Bertolt Brecht. Die Struktur seines Werkes*, 4th ed., Nuremberg, 1965.
——*Bertolt Brecht*, 3rd ed., Stuttgart, 1971 (a survey of Brecht scholarship).
Hinck, Walter, *Die Dramaturgie des späten Brecht*, Göttingen, 1960.
Hultberg, Helge, *Die ästhetischen Anschauungen Bertolt Brechts*, Copenhagen, 1962.
Kesting, Marianne, *Bertolt Brecht in Selbstzeugnissen und Bilddokumenten* (with a most useful bibliography), Hamburg, 1959.
Knopf, Jan, *Bertolt Brecht. Ein kritischer Forschungsbericht. Fragwürdiges in der Brecht-Forschung*, Frankfurt/Main, 1974.
Mayer, Hans, *Brecht und die Tradition*, Pfullinger, 1961.
Rüllicke-Weiler, Käthe, *Die Dramaturgie Brechts. Theater als Mittel der Veränderung*, Berlin, 1968.
Schrimpf, Hans Joachim, *Brecht und Lessing. Von der Aufklärung auf dem Theater*, Pfullingen, 1965.
Schuhmacher, Ernst, *Drama und Geschichte. Bertolt Brechts Leben des Galilei und andere Stücke*, Berlin, 1965.

Willett, John, *The Theatre of Bertolt Brecht. A Study from Eight Aspects*, London, 1959.

GENERAL

Bruford, W. H., *The German Idea of Self-Cultivation. From Goethe to Thomas Mann*, Cambridge, 1975.

Closs, August (ed.), *Introduction to German Literature*, IV, *Twentieth-Century German Literature*, London, 1969.

Gay, Peter, *Weimar Culture*, Penguin, Harmondsworth, Middlesex, 1974.

Just, K. G., *Von der Gründerzeit bis zur Gegenwart. Geschichte der deutschen Literatur seit 1871* Berne and Munich, 1973.

Kluckhohn, Paul, *Dichterberuf und bürgerliche Existenz*, Tübingen and Stuttgart, n.d. [1949].

Pascal, Roy, *From Naturalism to Expressionism. German Literature and Society 1880–1918*, London, 1973 (contains an excellent bibliography).

Rasch, Wolfdietrich, *Zur deutschen Literatur seit der Jahrhundertwende, Gesammelte Aufsätze*, Stuttgart, 1967.

Rohner, Ludwig, *Der Deutsche Essay. Materialien und Ästhetik einer literarischen Gattung*, Neuried and Berlin, 1967.

Rosenhaupt, H. W., *Der deutsche Dichter um die Jahrhundertwende und seine Abgelöstheit von der Gesellschaft*, Berne and Leipzig, 1939.

Rothe, Wolfgang, *Der Schriftsteller und die totalitäre Welt*, Berne and Munich, 1966.

Soergel, Albert, and Hohoff, Curt, *Dichtung und Dichter der Zeit*, 2 vols. Düsseldorf, 1964.

Sokel, Walter H., *The Writer in Extremis, Expressionism in Twentieth-Century German Literature*, Stanford, California, 1959. (Revised German ed.: *Der literarische Expressionismus*, Munich, 1970.)

Ziolkowski, Theodore, *Dimensions of the Modern Novel, German Texts and European Contexts*, Princeton, N. J., 1969.

Index

PERSONS (mentioned in text)

WORKS (of authors discussed in text)

220

INDEX